INTRINSIC

INTRINSIC

Using LEAPS to Retire Early

MIKE YUEN

PEW PEW PRESS

Carlsbad, California

Library of Congress Control Number: 2020923969

ISBN: 978-0-578-81416-2 (pbk)

Printed in the United States of America.

Donna, hang on cc. The journey continues. Thank you for allowing me to fly.
Jake, fail as many times as you need to succeed. Scientia potentia est.

You cannot swim for new horizons until you have courage to lose sight of the shore.

—William Faulkner

CONTENTS

PREFACE

*Enjoy the little things in life, for one day you may look back
and realize they were the big things.*

— *Robert Brault*

W HEN I GRADUATED from college and started working full
time, one of my goals was to retire by 50. I missed, but only by
two years. On a partially cloudy day on December 15, 2016, I
walked to the company cafeteria, bought a salad for lunch, returned to my
office, took a sip from a can of A&W Root Beer, and at 12:13 p.m. I clicked the
send button on an email that I had written the night before.

After 15 years with Qualcomm including several at the QCV-backed startup Zeebo,
I've decided to retire. My last day will be January 13, 2017. I have enjoyed working
for the company and appreciate the opportunities and support provided to me over
the years.

The highlight of my time at Qualcomm was helping to create the BREW developer
ecosystem which paid out billions of dollars to content providers. It was especially
fun being one of the early pioneers of mobile gaming in North America.

Another highlight was co-founding and later becoming CEO of Zeebo which
launched a 3G set top box in the Brazilian and Mexican consumer retail markets.
We never launched in China and India and sometimes you learn as much in
failure as you do in success.

PREFACE

When I joined Qualcomm, the phone I used was the camera-less monochrome Kyocera QCP-3035e and today it's the Google Nexus 5X. It's amazing how much and how fast mobile technology changes — much of it due to Qualcomm.

While I look forward to enjoying my retirement and spending more time with my family while my son is still young, I will miss working for Qualcomm and I wish everyone and the company continued success.

One last thing. If you haven't seen Steve Jobs' 2005 Stanford Commencement Address, I encourage you to check it out:

http://news.stanford.edu/2005/06/14/jobs-061505/

I've always found it to be a very inspiring speech — "If today were the last day of my life, would I want to do what I am about to do today?"

Happy holidays and enjoy the ride!

When I sent the email above, I was doing business development work for Qualcomm in San Diego. I was touched by the numerous responses I received from domestic and international co-workers, my first boss who hired me, and even a former CEO who was one of the first to reply to my email. In the days and weeks that ensued, a recurring question started to be asked, "How did you do it?" In other words, financially be able to retire early. Don't get me wrong, Qualcomm was a great place to earn a living; but for me, it wasn't great enough from a financial standpoint to enable me to retire early. Trading options is what enabled me to do that.

Perhaps you may be disappointed to hear that I didn't use some magical combination of straddles, strangles, spreads, and/or collars. And while I did try some of these more advanced options strategies, I concluded that the easiest and most efficient way for me to make money in the stock market was being long and leveraged. I used LEAPS (Long-term Equity Anticipation Securities). This unsophisticated and rather simple approach to options trading, more often than not, provided me with awesome returns and ultimately enabled me to reach my retirement number much faster than if I had only invested in tech stocks, which is primarily what I had been doing thus far.

The main reason I wanted to retire early was not to ride off into the sunset, although that is for sure on my future to-do list, but to maximize the time with my family; and in particular, with my son, while he was still relatively young

(he was in the 6th grade when I retired from Qualcomm). The clock is ticking for all of us. There are only 24 hours or 1,440 minutes available in a day—life's common denominator shared by all humans. Retiring early literally enabled me to gain more time. Kids grow fast. Time flies. One day they're in diapers. The next day they're leaving for college. Then, in a blink of an eye, they're graduating and heading off into the world. Months before his untimely passing, NFL Hall of Fame Chicago Bears running back Walter Payton said,

The best things in life are free, like my son's hand-drawn artwork.

"Tomorrow is promised to no one." Today my days are filled with what matters the most to me. The time I've been able to spend with my wife and son since retiring has been priceless.

In 2017, only 2.17% of Americans between the ages of 50-54 were retired, just 0.29% of those aged 45-49 were retired, and a mere 0.13% of those aged 40-44. How awesome would it be if you could become a member of one of these rather exclusive clubs? That is what this book is all about. I will tell you how I achieved my financial independence early. Then, you can decide if it's something that you can benefit from by following in my footsteps or not.

Everyone wants to beat the market (i.e., the S&P 500 (Standard & Poor's 500)); however, the reality is it's difficult to do consistently over time. Over the past 15 years (from January 1, 2005, to December 31, 2019), 90% of active large-cap and 93% of active large-cap growth fund managers underperformed the S&P 500, and 89% of active small-cap and 93% of active small-cap growth fund managers could not beat the S&P 500. The last time the majority (57%) of domestic equity funds outperformed the S&P 1500 was in 2013, and this has happened only 6 times in the last 19 years between 2001-2019. The compounded average growth rate (CAGR) for the S&P 500 for the 3.75 years (January 3, 2017, to September 30, 2020) since I retired was 11.2%. For the Dow Jones Industrial Average (DJIA), it was 9.1%, for the Nasdaq, it was 21.2%, and for the Nasdaq 100, it was 27.8%. Over this same time frame, the CAGR or annual return (AR) for my portfolio was 39.2%, and this was after withdrawing the cash required each year to cover taxes and living expenses.

Over the years, I've been diligently scribbling notes and observations into an indigo blue 5¼" x 8¼" Moleskine Cahier Journal. The main reason why I

My original Moleskin Journal.

wrote this book was to compile the information contained in this journal and then pass this knowledge onto my son with the hope that someday he too would be financially independent of work, retire early, and be able to spend more time with who and on what mattered most to him in his life. My gift to my son is now perhaps also a gift to you. And if you do find value in this book, don't delay. Someday is today. Henry Ford's words are quite apropos, "If you think you can, or you think you can't, you're probably right." The market waits for no one. I wish you good health, happiness, and a safe and prosperous journey in life.

Mike Yuen
Carlsbad, California
October 2020

INTRODUCTION

Acknowledging what you don't know is the dawning of wisdom.

—*Charlie Munger*

W HEN I WROTE this book, I only had two goals as an author: 1) make it simple, 2) make it actionable. Simple to me means easy to read. I didn't want to write something that read like a college textbook and bogged the reader down in theory. Simple also means, although there are complex mathematical models like Black-Scholes behind how options are priced, there's no need to understand how these complex models work, nor is there a need to use advanced options strategies such as calendar spreads, short straddles, or iron butterflies. I've been successful trading options using nothing more than calls and puts. If you're interested in the theory behind options, by all means, you should read up on it to satisfy your curiosity. However, from a real-world practical options trading perspective, it's not required. Actionable to me ultimately means making money, and if how I trade options works for me, then maybe it'll work for you too. The secret is being able to identify which options to buy. I'll explain the process I go through when making these decisions, and you might be surprised to discover that what I do isn't that complicated. Do I always have winning trades? No. But fortunately, I've had more wins than losses, and if you're right more often than you're wrong, you come out ahead. Since I have a more intuitive feel for picking stocks that are going up rather than down, the vast majority of my option trades are calls, not puts. After making over 90 options trades in the 3.75 years since retiring, my winning (i.e., profitable) call options trade percentage is 89%.

This book is organized into five parts. In Part One, I'll explain what got me interested in the stock market—a Nissan 300ZX Z31 Turbo played a key role in this. I'll also share with you my own financial journey from buying my first tech stocks (Advanced Micro Devices (AMD) and Silicon Graphics (SGI)) in 1993 to retiring early from Qualcomm 24 years later in 2017. In Part Two, I'll discuss why I like stocks, and technology in particular, over any other type of investment, including real estate. I'll also share with you a San Diego condo tale about something awesome that could have happened but didn't. In Part Three, I'll provide a brief review of options and the Greeks, and why I really don't pay any attention to them even though delta is pretty cool. Most importantly, I'll discuss why I especially like LEAPS. Part Four is where the rubber meets the road. I suspect this is the section of the book you're probably most interested in. I'll discuss how I decide which LEAPS to buy and also provide actual examples of some trades that I've made so you can see what kind of ROI (return on investment) I've achieved thus far since purchasing these options. Please note, I will not reveal the exact number of option contracts I've bought and sold or the actual dollar amounts I've paid in premiums because I think these aspects of the trades should remain private. I'll close out this section by discussing what I think about some additional financial topics such as 401(k) plans, 529 plans, portfolio diversification, and emergency funds. Fair warning. My thoughts may be controversial versus what a financial advisor will tell you; hence, your actual mileage may vary based on your specific individual situation. Finally, in Part Five, I'll provide a recap of the book and wrap it all up with what I hope are a few words of departing wisdom and inspiration.

As you progress through the book, I've also included three interim checkpoints to briefly review key takeaways covered thus far to ensure you're capturing the main points. Checkpoint One occurs after Chapters 1-3, Checkpoint Two occurs after Chapters 5-7, and Checkpoint Three occurs after Chapters 9-10.

INTRODUCTION

I'm making three important assumptions. 1) you have some knowledge of the stock market and how it works. 2) you know how to buy and sell stocks. 3) you have a basic understanding of what options are and know how to buy and sell simple calls and puts. While I consider this book to be beginner level in terms of content, if you don't know what options are and how they work, I would strongly recommend that you first obtain this knowledge. This is so you don't get scared away or unnecessarily confused by commonly-used options jargon. Many introductory books have been written about options, and I strongly encourage you to read one. Books can be very subjective in terms of what one reader finds valuable versus another. Personally, for me, I really liked *Understanding Options* by Michael Sincere. It was the first book I read on options, and as a complete rookie at the time, it provided me with an excellent easy-to-understand introduction. On the other hand, if you're looking for a complete reference-oriented type book (1,000+ pages), you might like *Options as a Strategic Investment* by Lawrence McMillan. Finally, you can also find lots of free information about options on the Internet via Google Search and by watching YouTube videos.

The person that will benefit the most from reading this book will have a profile as follows. 1) someone aged 35-50 who wants to retire early (note, this book is certainly applicable to those younger than 35 or older than 50). 2) someone who likes technology and is not afraid of investing in growth stocks such as FAANGM (Facebook (FB), Amazon (AMZN), Apple (AAPL), Netflix (NFLX), Google (i.e., Alphabet) (GOOG), Microsoft (MSFT)) or even high fliers like Shopify (SHOP), The Trade Desk (TTD), Tesla (TSLA), Nvidia (NVDA), Roku (ROKU), MercadoLibre (MELI). 3) someone who has traded options before but hasn't had a lot of success yet. 4) someone who doesn't panic and has the right temperament to ride the inevitable rollercoaster of market ups and downs, which for sure will be amplified due to the use of options. 5) someone who has non-taxable (e.g., ROTH IRA (individual retirement account)), tax-deferred (e.g., traditional IRA, SEP (simplified employee pension) IRA, 401(k) with employee matching), and taxable accounts. Lastly, as you read this book, you'll immediately notice that I'll use a stock ticker symbol instead of the company's name. This is so that you become acquainted with the tickers for tech stocks if you're not already familiar with them.

As you read the pages of this book, you may think to yourself, "Hmmm, why has he done some of the things he has done and he continues to do?" The answer is quite simple. It's because it has worked for me. Like anything you read, you'll need to decide for yourself what you will or will not do with the information you acquire. Whether you take away a little or a lot, if I can help you reach your retirement number faster so that you can retire sooner than you had planned, then mission accomplished. However, I acknowledge that what I've done is probably not for everyone because I'm not everyone. Everyone is different, and you have to be comfortable with the investment and trading decisions you make so that you can sleep at night. Are you still intrigued? Then read on!

Part One

THE CLOCK IS TICKING

Your time is limited, so don't waste it living someone else's life.

—Steve Jobs

1

HOW DID HE DO THAT?!

An investment in knowledge pays the best interest.
—*Benjamin Franklin*

IN ELEMENTARY SCHOOL, I can distinctly remember sitting at the dining table staring at row after row and page after page of short combinations of letters and numbers with lots of fractions in the local newspaper and wondering what it all meant. Ten years later, when I was in high school, my dad told me one day that the new black 2-door Nissan 300ZX Z31 Turbo in the driveway in front of our house was paid for entirely by money he made in the stock market. My first thought was, "How did he do that?!" My second thought was, "I need to learn what he did so that I can do the same thing!"

Blue Horseshoe Loves Bluestar Airlines

In 1988, during my senior year in college at UC San Diego, I watched the movie *Wall Street*. There's one particular scene that I absolutely love. While it involves insider trading, anyone who has ever felt the adrenaline rush of stock suddenly spiking and then selling to lock in the gain knows the feeling.

Bud Fox:	I want to make it up to you. Bluestar. Put all your clients in it.
Marv:	Ok Buddy Buddy. We are back in business on Bluestar.
Bud Fox:	Bluestar Mr. Mannheim. Put all your clients in it. It's gonna move.

Lou Mannheim:	I don't know where you get your information son, but I don't like it. The main thing about money Bud, it makes you do things you don't want to do.
Bud Fox:	Marty, I need a favor. It's a quick scalp for you.
Marty:	Go.
Bud Fox:	Two hundred thousand shares Bluestar at 19½. Can you position it in one of your equity funds?
Office Admin:	The Chronicle's on 7.
Bud Fox:	Hold Marty. Listen, Blue Horseshoe loves Bluestar Airlines, got it?
The Chronicle:	Got it.
Bud Fox:	Right. Marty, you still there?
Marty:	Yeah.
The Chronicle:	Bluestar's in play. Let's check it out.
Marv:	Oh, I love it. I do love it so.
Bud Fox:	Yeah Gordon, I see it at 21 and 5/8 and don't know what to make of it.
Gordon Gekko:	The word is out pal. Your union buddies are talking. You get me in at a forty-five-degree angle. I mean all the way in. You slash and burn. You buy everything inside of 22. Then call me. When I get hold of the son of a b*tch who leaked this I'm gonna tear his eyeballs out. I'm gonna suck his f*cking skull.
Marv:	Stock's going to Pluto man.
Bud Fox:	Start unloading.
Marv:	What? Sell?
Bud Fox:	Dump it now! Dump it all! Where's Lou?
Marv:	He's right over there.
Marv:	Ken, yeah Ken, Marvin, Jackson Steinem. We gotta dump this baby. You gotta take the money and run on BST ok. We're getting out now.

After seeing *Wall Street*, I was hooked. While I majored in computer science due to my childhood fascination with the movie *TRON* and video game arcades, I caught a serious case of the stock market bug in college, which I still have today. In fact, I've always wondered what would have happened if I had majored in finance or economics and worked on Wall Street after college.

Four Figures

In 1986, when I was 21, my dad helped me open my first brokerage account at Prudential-Bache Securities. The first stock I owned in this account was Frigitronics. My dad purchased 32 shares a few years earlier and transferred

Type	Settlement Date	Entry	Quantity	Description	Price or Explanation	Amount Charged To Your Account	Amount Credited To Your Account
1	1231	DELIVERED	32-	FRIGITRONICS INC EXM CASH MERGER CUSIP NUMBER: 358640100	EXCHANGED		110400

A four-figure Prudential-Bache Securities account.

4

them to my account once it was opened to help me get started in the stock market. My portfolio was worth $1,104 (a four-figure account).

When I graduated from UC San Diego in June 1988, I worked as a software programmer for NCR in Rancho Bernardo, California. My portfolio had increased to $3,000 in my taxable account and $4,000 in my tax-deferred traditional IRA account. As a rookie investor, I initially followed my dad's lead when it came to picking stocks. I owned shares in companies such as Biomerica (BMRA), Citicorp (C), Ford (F), Sears (SHLD), Summa Medical (SMDL), and Telesphere Communications. It wasn't until five years later, when I was 28, that I started picking stocks myself, and that's when I began buying tech companies. By this time, the stocks that I had originally owned were no longer in my portfolio.

My First Tech Stocks

On July 16, 1993, I purchased my first tech stocks. I bought AMD and SGI on the same day. Why AMD? Because I was about to start a new job there, and this was my own little way of betting on myself. And why SGI? Because of the T-Rex, Raptors, and other dinosaurs brought to life by Industrial Light & Magic using SGI workstations in the 1993 blockbuster movie *Jurassic Park*.

Back in these days, you had to call your broker to make a trade. It cost me $85.03 in commissions to buy 100 shares of AMD and $106.53 to buy 100 shares of SGI. That's a total of $191.56 to buy 200 shares of stock—a far cry from the commission-free trades and online brokerages of today. To commemorate

AMD and SGI stock trade tickets.

the AMD and SGI trades, the original paper confirmations for these first two trades are now framed in a plaque sitting on a bookshelf in my home office.

All Tech All the Time

I've always found technology fascinating, and I've never been afraid to invest in tech growth stocks, even ones with soaring P/E (price to earnings) ratios, P/S (price to sales) ratios, or lofty revenue multiples that scare away some investors. I also never dismiss a stock's current or potential future price action if there's an opportunity to make money because valuations and metrics don't make sense. For me, it doesn't always have to make sense—if I can make money, I make money.

For example, if you look at the P/E for TSLA, you would probably conclude TSLA is insanely overvalued, and you would be crazy to buy the stock. TSLA's P/E on September 1, 2020, was 1,237.11x TTM EPS (trailing 12 months earnings per share). Compare that with the P/E for the S&P 500 on September 1, 2020, which was 33.92x TTM EPS, or the historical S&P 500 P/E, which was 16.92x TTM EPS from 1925-2020. TSLA has gone from $47.73/share on September 1, 2015, with negative EPS, to $475.05/share on September 1, 2020, for an ROI of 895.3%. In other words, if you had invested in TSLA five years ago, your original investment would have increased by nearly 10x (a 10-bagger). Here's another example. SHOP was $26.60/share on September 1, 2015, with negative EPS, and $1,134.32/share on September 1, 2020, for an ROI of 4,164.4%. An investment five years ago in SHOP would have increased by about 42.6x. SHOP's performance over five years was even more impressive than TSLA.

Apart from occasional educated speculative trades in non-tech stocks such as Moderna (MRNA), Beyond Meat (BYND), UnitedHealth (UNH), Ulta Beauty (ULTA), Chipotle (CMG), Weight Watchers (WW), and a few others, I only focus on tech stocks. More broadly, stocks are the only asset class that I've had a serious interest in. Other asset classes such as fixed income (bonds, CDs (certificate of deposit)), cash and cash equivalents (money market, US Treasury bills, commercial paper, short-term government bonds), futures, real estate (property, REIT (real estate investment trust), vacation/rental), or commodities (oil, gas, gold, precious metals) don't appeal to me the way stocks do. When I was younger, I invested in some popular Fidelity stock mutual funds such as Magellan (FMAGX), Contrafund (FCNTX), and Equity-Income (FEQIX). However, I later stopped and primarily focused only on buying and selling individual tech stocks. FYI, I went back through 30-plus years of brokerage account statements and compiled a list of every single tech company that I've ever bought and sold stock in and listed them below.

There's a total of 42. Most are still around today, some have been acquired, while others no longer exist. Note, I consider video game companies (e.g., Activision (ATVI)) and TSLA (an automobile manufacturer) to be tech stocks.

Acclaim Entertainment (----)	JDS Uniphase (VIAV/LITE)
Activision (ATVI)	LinkedIn (MSFT)
Advanced Micro Devices (AMD)	Macromedia (ADBE)
Alphabet (Google)(GOOG)	MercadoLibre (MELI)
Amazon (AMZN)	Microsoft (MSFT)
America Online (VZ)	Netflix (NFLX)
Apple (AAPL)	Nokia (NOK)
Broderbund Software (HMHC)	Nvidia (NVDA)
Cisco Systems (CSCO)	OpenTable (OPEN)
Cloudflare (NET)	Priceline (BKNG)
CMGI (STCN)	Qualcomm (QCOM)
Dell Computer (DELL)	Roku (ROKU)
DocuSign (DOCU)	Shopify (SHOP)
Electronic Arts (EA)	Silicon Graphics (RACK/SGI)
EMC (DELL)	Sun Microsystems (ORCL)
Engage (----)	Sycamore Networks (----)
Exodus Communications (----)	Tesla (TSLA)
Facebook (FB)	The Trade Desk (TTD)
Intel (INTC)	The Learning Company (HMHC)
Intuit (INTU)	Xilinx (XLNX)
Iomega (DELL)	Yandex (YNDX)

The table below shows which tech industries I've invested in over the past 30-plus years. Nearly 1 in 3 (31%) were in software, over half (57%) were in software or hardware, and just over one-fourth (26%) were in services.

Industry	# of companies	% of total
Software	13	31
Hardware	11	26
Services	11	26
Semiconductors	5	12
Other	2	5

Behold the Power of Buy and Hold, But Only If You Hold

I've been lucky to have owned shares in several tech stocks when they were relatively cheap. Adjusted for splits, I owned AMZN at $35.05/share, INTU at $6.77/share, and NFLX at $3.33/share. It's always fun to play the what if I had bought and held game, especially with stocks because you usually always come out way ahead. So, what if I had bought and held shares in the three stocks I just mentioned? If I had invested $10,000 each in AMZN, INTU, and NFLX, then as of market close February 11, 2020 (about a week before the market decline began due to the Coronavirus COVID-19 pandemic), these stocks would be worth $622,996, $438,551, and $1,122,191 respectively. Hence, a combined $30,000 investment in these three stocks would have turned into $2,183,738 for an ROI of 7,179%. Now assume that I panicked and sold these three stocks on March 23, 2020 (the low point thus far of the S&P 500 due to the on-going COVID-19 pandemic). I wouldn't have done this, but just for the sake of argument, let's see what would have happened if I did. In this case, AMZN, INTU, and NFLX would have been sold for $524,307, $287,601, and $1,081,891, respectively. In other words, $30,000 would have turned into $1,893,799 for an ROI of 6,213%. Panic selling would have resulted in an additional loss of $289,939. However, despite this added loss, the ROI on the original investment still would have been amazing. The market later recovered from the COVID-19 pandemic crash, and tech started to climb again throughout the summer of 2020. As of the close of the market on September 1, 2020, if I were still holding AMZN, INTU, and NFLX, the $30,000 would be worth $3,181,354 for an ROI of 10,505%. These ROIs highlight the remarkable results that are possible with a long-term buy and hold investing strategy if you're lucky enough to identify winners early and buy, hold, and not sell—always easier said than done.

$1.34 Per Share

After I got my MBA from UC Davis in June 1993, I joined AMD in Sunnyvale, California. During my product marketing training program rotation in San Jose, the director of sales I was assigned to shadow repeatedly mentioned a company that he thought would soon take off. Unfortunately, I waited five years before I bought shares in this company. If I had purchased shares when I first heard about it at AMD, I could have picked shares up for just $1.34 each. That company was CSCO, and a $10,000 investment sold before the dot-com bubble burst would have turned into $596,960. My guess is similar results would have been possible with other companies on the list of 42 tech stocks above if I had, again, only bought and held for the long run—but I didn't. Not for AMZN, INTU, NFLX, CSCO, or any of the others. C'est la vie.

22,400 Shares

One final truly mind-boggling buy and hold example. On September 16, 1985, Steve Jobs resigned as chairman of AAPL after losing a bitter boardroom battle for control of the company, with then CEO John Sculley. The stock opened for trading the next day at $12.05/share (adjusted for splits, this would be $0.0538/share today). What happens next is improbable at best, but just for fun, play along with me. Let's assume you thought Jobs wasn't good for the company, and you were happy to see him get the boot. So, you decided to buy 100 shares on September 17, 1985, when the market opened the day after Jobs resigned. You would have spent $1,205 less any fees to buy AAPL at $12.05/share. On October 4, 1985, AAPL hit a low for the year of $11.87/share (adjusted for splits, this would be $0.053/share today); however, over the next eight months, AAPL climbed to $30.76/share (adjusted for splits, this would be $0.1373/share today) by June 5, 1986. This would have been an ROI of 159.06%, and your $1,205 would have grown to $3,075.52. Your original assumption that Jobs wasn't good for the company is looking clairvoyant. Now, what if you did nothing for the next 35 years and held those 100 shares to today? Adjusted for splits, your 100 shares would have become 22,400 shares (not including any dividend reinvestments to buy additional shares). As of September 1, 2020, when AAPL was $134.18/share, your AAPL shares, which you initially spent $1,205 less any fees buying, would be worth $3,005,632 (ROI 249,305%). Those are not typos. Now the fun part. If you had instead purchased 1,000 shares for $12,050, today they would be worth $30,056,320. Behold the power of buying and holding tech stocks.

Five, Six, and Seven Figures

In 1994, when I was 30, my portfolio had increased to $78,000 (a five-figure account), and I had no debt. Not bad, but it still seemed light years away from having enough money to retire comfortably by the age of 50. And I only had 20 years left to reach this goal. Nevertheless, I was proud of the fact that I was actively investing in the stock market, making some money, and learning what worked for me and what didn't.

Three years later, in 1997, I left Accolade, a video game company based in San Jose, California, and took a huge pay cut to work at my first startup in Encinitas, California, earning barely enough ($35,000/year) to cover my rent and bills and invest what little I had left. I was also trying to save for a wedding. By 1999 when I was 35, my portfolio value had increased to $500,000 (a six-figure account). Ten years later, in 2009, when I was 45 and working at my second startup in San Diego, California, my portfolio finally surpassed $1 million (a seven-figure account). One million dollars seemed like a lot of money, but for someone who had a goal of retiring by the age of 50, now only five years away, it didn't provide a large enough safety net for me to hit the work eject button because I was planning for 50 years of retirement. And to be conservative in my planning, I didn't include Social Security when calculating my retirement number. I needed to be sure because my son was only five years old, and neither my wife nor I planned to ever go back to work again in any material way.

Special Purpose Vehicles

In 2011, when I was 47, I bought my first shares in pre-IPO (initial public offering) tech companies via the secondary market. I acquired what is known as units (i.e., shares) in FB and LinkedIn (LNKD) as limited partners (LP) in single-asset special purpose vehicles (SPV), the contractual structure most commonly used for these types of private investments. After these companies went public (LNKD in May 2011 for $45/share and FB in May 2012 for $38/share) and their lock-up periods expired, I later sold my shares, which I acquired below their IPO share prices, in both companies for a profit. Note, while I didn't do this, I could have also just sat on the shares and let them appreciate. On June 10, 2016, LNKD was selling for $131.08/share (2.91x its IPO price). On June 13, 2016, MSFT announced that they were acquiring LNKD for $196/share (4.36x its IPO price) in an all-cash deal valuing LNKD at $26.2 billion. As of the close of the market on August 7, 2020, FB was selling for $268.44/share (7.06x its IPO price).

Currently, I'm holding units in SPVs for two private tech companies that I'm patiently waiting to go public. Both are up about 3x from my original investment. Founded in 2010 and often dubbed the Amazon of South Korea, the first is Coupang, which hopefully IPOs in the next 2-3 years. Founded in 2002, the second is Space Exploration Technologies Corp. (aka SpaceX), which isn't likely to IPO until they send a crewed mission to Mars in 2026.

Secondary markets and direct private company investments are additional strategies that can generate potentially higher ROIs; however, these investments are not for everyone. 1) they require you to invest a minimum amount of capital (usually $100,000). 2) you'll be charged very high transaction fees to purchase units in an SPV (although you can negotiate lower fees). 3) you can't withdraw your money from SPVs until there's a liquidity event (an IPO or possibly an acquisition by a publicly-traded company). 4) you're subject to lock-up periods (usually 90-180 days or longer) like employees and shareholders of the company holding pre-IPO shares.

All Options All the Time and Surpassing My Retirement Number

By 2014, I was almost exclusively trading options. What attracted me to options is the ability to potentially amplify my ROI multiple times over what I could achieve from just investing in tech stocks. The trades that helped accelerate me towards achieving my retirement number were calls in AAPL, AMZN, FB, MSFT, NFLX, and NVDA. The specific trade that ultimately pushed me over the top was AAPL calls, which expired on April 17, 2015. I was 50 at the time, and I can still recall looking at my laptop—my total portfolio value was greater than my retirement number. I continued to work for another 1½ years. In hindsight, I really should have hung it up sooner. I thought it would be interesting to see what tech stocks I've traded options in since retiring and then see how it overlaps with the list of 42 tech stocks mentioned above.

Activision (ATVI)	Blue Apron (APRN)
Advanced Micro Devices (AMD)	Box (BOX)
Alibaba (BABA)	Broadcom (AVGO)
Amazon (AMZN)	Cloudflare (NET)
Apple (AAPL)	Coupa Software (COUP)

DocuSign (DOCU)
Electronic Arts (EA)
Facebook (FB)
MercadoLibre (MELI)
Microsoft (MSFT)
Nvidia (NVDA)
NXP Semiconductors (NXPI)
Qualcomm (QCOM)

Riot Blockchain (RIOT)
Roku (ROKU)
Shopify (SHOP)
Snap (SNAP)
Tesla (TSLA)
The Trade Desk (TTD)
Universal Display Corp (OLED)
Yelp (YELP)

There are 26 stocks that I've traded options in since I retired (mostly calls, but also some puts), and 16 (61.5%) also appear on the list of 42 tech stocks. Many are well known, such as AMZN, AAPL, FB, MSFT, and NVDA; some are lesser-known, like COUP, DOCU, MELI, NET, SHOP, SNAP, and TTD; and finally, there are some outliers (Blue Apron (APRN), Box (BOX), Riot Blockchain (RIOT)) where I was making educated speculative option trades. The table below summarizes industries I've traded options in since retiring.

Industry	# of companies	% of total
Software	10	38
Other	6	23
Semiconductors	5	19
Services	3	12
Hardware	2	8

The chart below compares industries that I have invested in stocks versus which ones I traded options in the past few years since retiring.

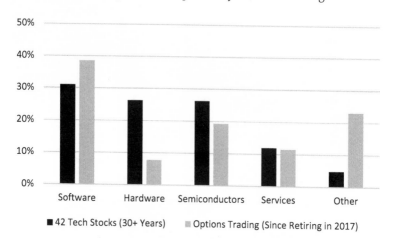

■ 42 Tech Stocks (30+ Years)   ▧ Options Trading (Since Retiring in 2017)

Retirement Account Balances

According to Federal Reserve, FDIC (Federal Deposit Insurance Corporation), and MagnifyMoney (Lending Tree) estimates, as of June 2019, among all US households, including those with no retirement accounts, the average American household had $149,790 in one or more retirement savings accounts including IRAs, 401(k)s, etc. Furthermore, according to a 2016 survey by the Federal Reserve, 52% of US households had a retirement account, and the total average balance was $287,736. Among the different generations, millennials had saved an average of $34,570, generation Xers had saved an average of $168,480, and baby boomers and those born before 1946 had saved an average of $386,110 in retirement accounts.

Retirement Confidence in America

According to the *2019 Retirement Confidence Survey* by EBRI (Employee Benefit Research Institute) and Greenwald & Associates, when US workers were asked if they agree or disagree with the statement, "You dream of retiring." 71% agreed, and of that 71%, 33% strongly agreed, and 38% somewhat agreed.

The two charts below show workers and retirees' responses to the question, "Overall, how confident are you that you (and your spouse) will have enough money to live comfortably throughout your retirement years." In 2007, the subprime mortgage housing bubble burst, wiping out almost $8

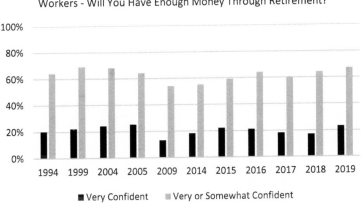

Workers - Will You Have Enough Money Through Retirement?

■ Very Confident   ▨ Very or Somewhat Confident

Source: EBRI *2019 Retirement Confidence Survey*, Greenwald & Associates.

trillion in stock market wealth and $6 trillion in home value over the next few years. This is probably why confidence levels of both existing workers and retirees, who were very or somewhat confident, dropped to their lowest levels ever reported in the past 25 years in 2009.

Retirees - Will You Have Enough Money Through Retirement?

Source: EBRI *2019 Retirement Confidence Survey*, Greenwald & Associates.

Retiring Early

The table below shows the percentage of people retired for different age groups based on survey data from the 2017 Federal Reserve *Survey of Household Economics and Decisionmaking*. Each respondent was classified as working (as a paid employee or self-employed), not working (looking for work, disabled, other, or on temporary layoff), or not working (retired). Only 2.17% of Americans between the ages of 50-54 were retired. Even rarer, just 0.29% of those aged 45-49 were retired, 0.13% of those aged 40-44, and 0.29% of those aged 17-39. All pretty exclusive clubs to be a member of.

Age group	% retired	Age group	% retired	Age group	% retired
17-39	0.29	45-49	0.29	55	0.76
40-44	0.13	50-54	2.17	56-61	10.45

Source: Federal Reserve.

Part Two

ALMOST FRICTIONLESS

One of the funny things about the stock market is that every time one person buys, another sells, and both think they are astute.

—William Feather

2

STOCKS

If you don't find a way to make money while you sleep, you will work until you die.

—*Warren Buffet*

I N APRIL 2020, Gallup's annual *Economy and Personal Finance Survey* reported that just under half (45%) of all Americans do not own a single stock. This is based on a question asking survey respondents about any individual stocks they own, including stocks held in mutual funds, 401(k)s, or IRAs. Over the past five years (2016-2020), US adult stock ownership averaged 54%, over the past 10 years (2011-2020), it has also averaged 54%, and over the past 23 years (the number of years Gallup has asked this question), it averaged 61%. Since Gallup has been asking this question, 67% was the highest reported figure in June 2002. From 1998-2020 stock ownership by Americans has never fallen below 52%. Survey respondents were also asked, "If you had a thousand dollars to spend, do you think investing it in the stock market would be a good or bad idea?" Americans were evenly divided on the answer, with 48% saying yes and 49% saying no. If you average the yes and no responses dating back to February 1990 when Gallup first started asking this question, the answer remains split among US adults, with roughly 49% saying yes and 49% saying no. In January 2000, about two months before the dot-com bubble burst, Americans reported the highest yes response at 67%. The highest no response was 68% in February 1990, the first year Gallup asked this question in a poll to US adults.

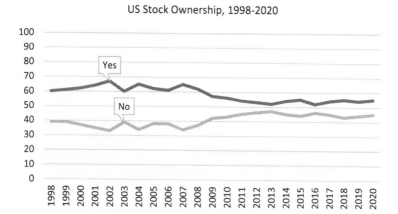

US Stock Ownership, 1998-2020

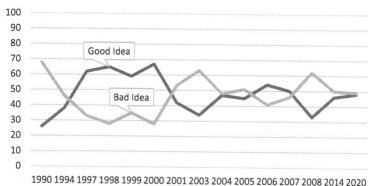

Is Investing In the Stock Market a Good or Bad Idea

Source: Gallup.

Among millennials, comprised of about 87 million people in the US, stock ownership is lower. A survey by LendEDU in 2019 found that only 30% invested outside of a 401(k) or IRA in a brokerage or investment account. Furthermore, a 2019 BlackRock Global *Investor Pulse Survey* found that 70% of adults ages 25-36 invested only in cash assets such as savings accounts, money market accounts, and CDs. More recently, however, with the impact of the 2020 COVID-19 pandemic stay-at-home restrictions and the rapid rise in popularity of mobile trading app Robinhood, stock investing among millennials has been experiencing an uptick.

Americans Like Real Estate

In the April 2020 survey, Gallup also asked, "Which of the following do you think is the best long-term investment (bonds, real estate, savings accounts or CDs, stocks or mutual funds, or gold)?" The chart below shows the results over the past 10 years.

Americans' Views on the Best Long-Term Investment

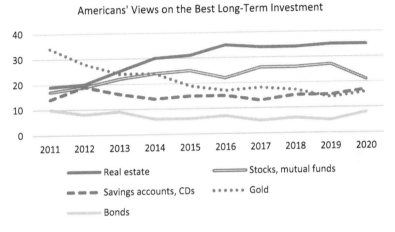

Source: Gallup.

In 2020, 1 in 3 (35%) picked real estate and 1 in 5 (21%) chose stocks. Real estate has climbed steadily over the past decade, rising from 19% in 2011 to 35% in 2016 and averaging 34-35% for the past five years from 2016-2020. Due to the economic fallout of the 2020 COVID-19 pandemic and the end of the longest bull market in US history, the appeal of stocks dropped six percentage points from 2019 and is at the lowest level recorded since 2012 while savings accounts, CDs, gold, and bonds, all moved up a few percentage points from 2019. Over the past decade, bonds have consistently been chosen by Americans as the worst of the five investment choices averaging just 7%.

Three other data points of note from prior Gallup surveys. 1) in 2002, as housing prices were rising rapidly and after the dot-com bubble burst, 50% of US adults said real estate was the best long-term investment (this is the highest percentage recorded by Gallup for any investment type in a single year). 2) between 2008-2010, when home and stock values plummeted due to the ongoing fallout from the subprime mortgage housing crash, US adults were just as likely to pick savings accounts including CDs as the best long-term investment as real estate or stocks. 3) gold (34%) was selected as the best long-term investment in 2011, 2012 (28%), and was essentially tied for first in 2013 (24%) with real estate (25%).

In May 2020, COVID-19 caused Americans to hoard more money than ever before as widespread fear, unemployment, stay-at-home orders and lockdowns, and social unrest curbed consumer spending. Per the US Bureau of Economic Analysis, the personal savings rate (savings as a percentage of disposable income) hit a historic high of 33% in April 2020, the highest level ever seen since the department started tracking this statistic beginning in the 1960s. According to FactSet, the previous record was 17% in May 1975.

Gallup's findings also suggest that US investors inflate homeownership value beyond its inherent underlying financial return as an investment because of the additional value homeowners derive out of it as a place to live and as a place they call home. This is why Americans continue to select real estate as the best long-term investment even though past performance doesn't support this belief (i.e., historically, stocks have outperformed real estate and other types of investments in the long run). A 2018 Wells Fargo/Gallup survey asked Americans: what is the best long-term investment. However, in this case, respondents were US investors with $10,000 or more in investments. The results: 54% picked mutual funds, 19% picked real estate, and 11% picked individual stocks. Note, respondents were asked to exclude their primary home when considering real estate as an investment; hence, these findings suggest that many stock owners see a primary home as a solid long-term investment on par with stocks. However, they don't consider a second home or other real estate investments as having the same value as a primary home.

Despite more Americans choosing real estate over stocks as the best long-term investment, I would personally pick stocks based on my experience. However, I've also never seriously pursued real estate as an investor. A professional who has flipped almost 200 houses said in an August 2019 *Forbes* article titled "Can You Make $1 Million A Year Flipping Houses?" that his average profit is about $25,000. A 2019 ATTOM Data Solutions year-end report found that the average profit made on flipping a house was between $20,000-$30,000, and it took an average of 178 days to complete. In 2018, *CNBC* reported that in the best states (e.g., Tennessee, Pennsylvania, New Jersey) for fixing and flipping houses, it takes on average 180 days to flip while in the worst states (e.g., Mississippi, Montana, Hawaii), the average is 203 days. The *Forbes* article and the AATOM Data Solutions report did not mention how much initial capital was required to make $20,000-30,000 in profit. Having this additional piece of data would then allow an ROI to be calculated. In general, however, from a pure dollar perspective, waiting on average 6-7 months to make $20,000-30,000 is not appealing to me as an investor versus what I think I could earn in the stock market over the same time period.

Starting A Small Business

Starting a small business to help build wealth and reach your retirement number more quickly is another strategy that some people will also pursue. According to the September 2019 US SBA (Small Business Administration) Office of Advocacy FAQ: 1) in 2016, there were 30.7 million small businesses (i.e., independent businesses with fewer than 500 employees) and 81% (24.8 million) had no employees and 19% (5.9 million) had paid employees, 2) in 2016, there were about 433,192 new business startups (i.e., companies less than 1-year old) and 399,923 business closures, 3) nearly 4 out of 5 (79%) businesses that started in 2017 survived until 2018, which is in line with the average 1-year survival rate from 2008-2018 of 79%, 4) half (50%) of all businesses survive five years or longer, and in the past decade, this ranged from a low of 45% for businesses started in 2016, to a high of 51% for those starting in 2010, 5) one-third (33%) of businesses survive at least 10 years. If you're working a full-time 40 hours/week job, starting a small business will be a lot of work. Furthermore, if just half of all small businesses survive five years or longer and only 1 in 3 survive at least 10 years, again, at least for me, I think my odds of succeeding are much greater investing in stocks or trading options than in starting a small business.

Ultimately, investing in real estate, stocks, and/or a small business to build wealth is a personal decision on what you're most comfortable doing. Real estate investors like real estate because it's a tangible asset that they can exert direct control over. However, as an investor, although I own shares or options in a company, I don't control the company. I view having control as my ability to decide if and when I buy and sell stocks or options.

A San Diego Condo Tale

My first real estate experience, albeit indirect and as an observer, was in 1987. That year my parents paid $150,000 all cash to buy a new condo in San Diego as an investment property. In 2005, the condo was sold for $555,000. The

A San Diego condo.

condo was a rental unit for 10 of the 18 years and generated about $144,000 in income, and roughly $63,450 was paid in property taxes. Hence, the profit was $485,550 (AR 8.4%, ROI 324%). Now consider the scenario where my parents had invested $150,000 into the market instead. I.e., what if they bought shares in an S&P 500 index fund in 1987 and

then sold those shares in 2005? Despite the 2000 dot-com crash, $150,000 still would have grown to $638,335 for a profit of $488,335 (AR 8.4%, ROI 326%), which is effectively the same results as buying and selling the condo without all of the hassles of property and rental ownership. However, what if my parents had purchased shares in well-known tech stocks instead of an S&P 500 index fund? If they had purchased an equal amount ($37,500) in Hewlett Packard (HPQ), International Business Machines (IBM), INTC, and MSFT, then $150,000 would have become $3,891,163 (AR 19.8%, ROI 2,494.11%). Note, my dad has owned stock in HPQ, IBM, INTC, and MSFT, so it's not impossible that this scenario could have occurred. Now, what if they had bought only one tech stock like INTC or MSFT? In these cases, $150,000 would have become $4,380,668 (AR 20.6%, ROI 2,820.45%) or $10,376,913 (AR 26.5%, ROI 6,817.94%) respectively.

The table below shows the results of investing $150,000 in several different options. 1) real estate (condo). 2) $37,500 each in HPQ, IBM, INTC, MSFT. 3) some tech stocks that were publicly trading in 1987 (note, there weren't as many as there are today and AMZN, CSCO, DELL, NVDA, YHOO had not gone public yet). 4) FMAGX, a well-known Fidelity mutual fund. To simplify, taxes, costs for property repairs/upkeep and management (the condo wasn't located in the same city where my parents lived), dividend payments and DRIPs, and bank interest earned on rental income deposits are not included in the calculations. Hence, AR and ROI are not exact, but close enough for comparisons to be made.

1987 investment	2005 value $	Total gain $	AR %	ROI %
Advanced Micro Devices (AMD)	291,854	141,854	3.77	94.57
International Business Machines (IBM)	304,473	154,473	4.01	102.98
Fidelity Magellan Fund (FMAGX)	306,633	156,633	4.05	104.42
Hewlett Packard (HPQ)	495,200	345,200	6.86	230.13
Condo (my parents purchased)	635,550	485,550	8.35	323.70
S&P 500 Index Fund	638,335	488,335	8.38	325.56
Apple (AAPL)	752,154	602,154	9.37	401.44
HPQ/IBM/INTC/MSFT	3,891,163	3,741,163	19.83	2,494.11
Intel (INTC)	4,380,668	4,230,668	20.62	2,820.45
Microsoft (MSFT)	10,376,913	10,226,913	26.54	6,817.94
Oracle (ORCL)	11,964,693	11,814,693	27.54	7,876.46

Between 1987-2005, two key events occurred: 1) the October 19, 1987, Black Monday crash (on a single day, the DJIA declined 22.6% and the S&P 500 fell 18%), 2) the 2000 dot-com crash, which resulted in the Nasdaq falling 77% from 5,048.62 on March 2000 to 1,139.90 by October 2002 (the market also entered a 30-month bear market after the dot-com bubble burst). Investing $150,000 into AAPL, INTC, MSFT, or ORCL would have returned 5x, 29.2x, 69.2x, or 79.8x the original investment, and this was despite absorbing the negative effects of both the Black Monday crash and the dot-com crash.

Brain Versus Gut

My second real estate experience is from 2017. After New Year's, my wife and I had to make a financial decision about what to do with our primary home mortgage. My brain was conservatively saying, "Mike, since you're retiring, pay off the $450,000 mortgage and be 100% debt free." My gut was more aggressively saying, "Dude, don't do it, invest the money and you'll come out ahead because you'll be able to pay off the mortgage a few years later with the money you make in the market." My brain ended up winning, and on January 6, 2017, we paid off the mortgage. I admit, there was satisfaction in paying off the mortgage early and being 100% debt free; however, in hindsight, I should have gone with my intuition, which has always served me well when it comes to the market.

Let's do a similar exercise that I did with the San Diego condo and see what would have happened if I had invested $450,000 into the stock market instead of paying off the mortgage. FYI, I would have most likely used the money to trade options, but to be conservative, let's assume I just bought and held stock. Let's also assume there was a 3-year time frame (January 2017 to January 2020) for this investment, which in this specific situation is what I would have done. The four stock investment choices that I would have seriously considered making at this time include 1) 100% in AAPL, 2) 100% in MSFT, 3) 50% each in AAPL and MSFT, and 4) 25% each in the FANG stocks (FB, AMZN, NFLX, GOOG). Most likely, I would have invested 50% each in AAPL and MSFT. Also, one thing I know for sure is that I wouldn't have put the money into an S&P 500 ETF (exchange-traded fund) like Vanguard's VOO, but for the sake of argument, I'll also include this as a fifth choice.

The table below shows the results of investing $450,000 in the investment scenarios mentioned above. To simplify, taxes, dividend payments, and/or DRIPs (if applicable) are not included. Hence, the AR and ROI are not exact, but close enough for comparisons to be made.

2017 investment	2020 value $	Total gain $	AR %	ROI %
Pay off mortgage ($450,000)	0	0	0	0
S&P 500 ETF (VOO)	639,517	189,517	12.43	42.11
FANG	943,922	493,922	28.01	109.76
Microsoft (MSFT)	1,138,814	688,814	36.27	153.07
AAPL/MSFT	1,141,346	691,346	36.38	153.63
Apple (AAPL)	1,144,037	694,037	36.48	154.23

After three years, all five investment scenarios generated positive gains, ARs, and ROIs. If I had followed my gut instead of my brain, not only would I have been able to pay off the entire $450,000 mortgage, but I would have also ended up with "free" money that could have been reinvested back into the market for more gains. Furthermore, if I had gone with the investment scenario I most likely would have selected, I would have ended up with $691,346 in extra money after paying off the mortgage (less either 15% or 20% long-term capital gains, the net would have been $587,644 or $553,077 respectively). Also, note, since both AAPL and MSFT stocks were up, if I had traded options instead, the total gain would have been well over $1 million and a multiple of what the stocks returned. I should have followed my intuition but didn't.

Now let's run through one last scenario. What if I didn't sell any stock in January 2020 and instead panicked and sold on March 23, 2020, which was the low point of the S&P 500 in March due to the COVID-19 pandemic. The longest bull market run in US history ended March 11, 2020, and the S&P 500 fell 31.3% from 3,257.85 on January 6, 2020, to 2,237.40 by March 23, 2020. I wouldn't have panicked and sold, but let's see what would have happened anyway. The results are shown in the table below.

2017 investment	2020 value $	Total gain $	AR %	ROI %
Pay off mortgage ($450,000)	0	0	0	0
S&P 500 ETF (VOO)	440,768	-9,232	-0.69	-2.05
Apple (AAPL)	856,196	406,196	23.91	90.27
FANG	859,200	409,200	24.06	90.93
AAPL/MSFT	914,906	464,906	26.68	103.31
Microsoft (MSFT)	973,753	523,753	29.34	116.39

Investing in VOO would have resulted in a loss of $9,232 and a -0.7% AR and -2.1% ROI. All four other investment scenarios would still have resulted in positive gains, ARs, and ROIs despite the S&P 500 losing nearly a third of its value. If I had gone with the investment I most likely would have picked (50% each in AAPL and MSFT), I would have ended up with $464,906 in extra money after paying off the mortgage (less 15% or 20% long-term capital gains, the net would have been $395,170 or $371,925 respectively).

In my case, since I wouldn't have invested in VOO, based on the other investment choices described above and regardless of whether or not I sold stock in January 2020 or on March 23, 2020, I shouldn't have paid off the mortgage. In general, if you can earn a better ROI than the mortgage rate you pay, then you shouldn't pay off your mortgage. For example, if you earn 9.8% per year on your investments and you pay 3.125% interest on a 30-year fixed-rate mortgage, you're better off letting your portfolio grow.

Rental Property Versus S&P 500

If you had $200,000 to invest, would you rather make a down payment to buy an income-generating rental property or buy shares in an S&P 500 ETF? Let's perform some calculations to determine which is the better investment choice.

Scenario One

Assume a $200,000 down payment was paid to buy a house for $1 million. A 30-year 3% fixed-rate loan is taken out for the $800,000 balance. Property taxes are 1% and the value of the house increases 4% on average per year. The market rent for a property is dependent on a lot of different factors, but ultimately it comes down to supply and demand. To simplify, I found 33 houses in Zillow valued around $1 million (as of September 2020) and that were within 1.5 miles of my primary home in California. The average Zillow rent estimates for these 33 properties is $3,738/month. Assume you can collect $4,000/month for 360 consecutive months. After 30 years the house would be worth $3,243,398 (ROI 224.3%) and you would have collected $1,440,000 in rental income for a combined 368.3% ROI. If the house is sold, the net gain (less $200,000 down payment, $1,214,249 total mortgage cost, and $593,283 in property taxes) would be $2,675,866 (ROI 267.6%) not including capital gains taxes, unearned income taxes, and any benefits from mortgage interest tax deductions. To simplify the calculation, costs such as insurance, maintenance, renovation, update, and selling costs are not included.

Scenario Two

Assume the $200,000 down payment was invested into an S&P 500 ETF for 30 years with a 9.8% AR. Past performance is never a guarantee of future results; however, the AR for the stock market (i.e., the S&P 500) over the past 90 years is 9.8%. After 30 years the investment would be worth $3,304,458 (ROI 1,552%). If the investment were sold, the net gain would be $3,104,458 (ROI 1,452%) not including capital gains taxes. The net gain for Scenario Two is $428,592 more than the net gain in Scenario One despite propping up the Scenario One gain by not including costs such as insurance, maintenance, renovation, and property selling costs as well as assuming the property is 100% occupied for 360 consecutive months (i.e., 30 years). Contrast this with the zero-commission cost of buying and selling S&P 500 ETF shares. Even if the monthly rental income were increased to $5,000/month, despite generating an additional $360,000 over 30 years, the net gain of Scenario Two would still be $68,592 more than Scenario One. Lastly, both scenarios assume that when you sell either the investment rental property or S&P 500 ETF shares, you're not selling in a down housing or stock market (i.e., if either was down, you would delay selling until the market recovered).

Obviously, the calculations above are not exact, but it's still clear that after 30 years, investing in the S&P 500 results in ROI that beats rental property. In this case, investing in the S&P 500 produces an extra $428,592 and was practically frictionless apart from maintaining a brokerage account whereas owning rental property would require more effort, time, and costs. Furthermore, if the $200,000 was invested in the Nasdaq, Nasdaq 100, or individual tech stocks like AAPL or MSFT over 30 years, the ROI would have been much higher than the return of the S&P 500. Admittedly, my experience with real estate as an investment is minimal; however, based on my limited sample size, I remain firmly convinced that stocks are a superior investment vehicle for a retail investor over real estate.

The Powder Monkey

As just mentioned, stock trading is almost frictionless, and you can trade from just about anywhere in the world. That's what I find so appealing about the stock market from a transactional and efficiency standpoint over other investments. As long as you have an Internet connection and a laptop or PC, you can initiate buy and sell trade orders. Worst case scenario, you can trade from a computer at a public library or even a smartphone on a cellular network. Recall in the 2015 movie *The Big Short* where Brad Pitt plays Ben Rickert, a character based on former Deutsche Bank derivatives trader Ben Hockett. In August 2007, Hockett was on vacation and sitting in a pub called The Powder Monkey in Exmouth (England). Over the course of the next four days, with nothing more than his cell phone and a laptop, Hockett sold $205 million worth of credit default swaps (CDS) and made $80 million for his hedge fund Cornwall Capital. What made The Powder Monkey so special that Hockett decided to sit in this pub for days on end trading? The answer is that The Powder Monkey had the town's only reliable public wi-fi Internet connection.

$1 Million Hedge Fund Challenge

In 2007, storied investor Warren Buffet issued a challenge to the hedge fund industry. His assertion: "Over a 10-year period commencing on January 1, 2008, and ending on December 31, 2017, the S&P 500 will outperform a portfolio of funds of hedge funds, when performance is measured on a basis net of fees, costs, and expenses." This challenge also shined a spotlight on two fundamentally different investing philosophies. Active versus passive investing. Out of thousands of hedge funds, only Protege Partners accepted the challenge, and a $1 million bet was made via Long Bets. The participants agreed that the winnings would be donated to the winner's charity of choice.

Buffet won the bet when Protege conceded defeat seven months before the challenge end date of December 31, 2017. Buffet selected the Vanguard S&P 500 Admiral Fund (VFIAX), which produced an AR of 7.1%. Protege picked a basket of five hedge funds, which returned an AR of just 2.2% after fees. Buffet estimated that over 9 years this accounted for roughly 60% of all gains. This means that $1 million invested with Protege would have returned $220,000. In comparison, if you followed Buffet's advice and invested the $1 million into VFIAX, you would have made $854,000. Per Buffet's agreement with Protege, the names of the funds of funds have never been publicly disclosed. Buffet was, however, allowed to see their annual audits. The table below summarizes the results of the challenge.

Year	Fund of Funds A %	Fund of Funds B %	Fund of Funds C %	Fund of Funds D %	Fund of Funds E %	VFIAX Return %
2008	-16.5	-22.3	-21.3	-29.3	-30.1	-37.0
2009	11.3	14.5	21.4	16.5	16.8	26.6
2010	5.9	6.8	13.3	4.9	11.9	15.1
2011	-6.3	-1.3	5.9	-6.3	-2.8	2.1
2012	3.4	9.6	5.7	6.2	9.1	16.0
2013	10.5	15.2	8.8	14.2	14.4	32.3
2014	4.7	4.0	18.9	0.7	-2.1	13.6
2015	1.6	2.5	5.4	1.4	-5.0	1.4
2016	-2.9	1.7	-1.4	2.5	4.4	11.9
Gain to date	8.7	28.3	62.8	2.9	7.5	85.4

Source: 2016 annual letter to Berkshire Hathaway shareholders.

Active Versus Passive Investing

In his 2016 annual letter to Berkshire Hathaway shareholders, Buffet discussed some of the assertions he made in his original 2007 hedge fund challenge of why he believed active investing wouldn't beat passive investing.

From Page 23

"Costs skyrocket when large annual fees, large performance fees, and active trading costs are all added to the active investor's equation. Funds of hedge funds accentuate this cost problem because their fees are superimposed on the large fees charged by the hedge funds in which the funds of funds are invested.

A number of smart people are involved in running hedge funds. But to a great extent their efforts are self-neutralizing, and their IQ will not overcome the costs they impose on investors."

From Page 24

"There are, of course, some skilled individuals who are highly likely to out-perform the S&P over long stretches. In my lifetime, though, I've identified – early on – only ten or so professionals that I expected would accomplish this feat.

There are no doubt many hundreds of people – perhaps thousands – whom I have never met and whose abilities would equal those of the people I've identified. The job, after all, is not impossible. The problem simply is that the great majority of managers who attempt to over-perform will fail."

"The bottom line: When trillions of dollars are managed by Wall Streeters charging high fees, it will usually be the managers who reap outsized profits, not the clients. Both large and small investors should stick with low-cost index funds."

The key takeaway is that, at a minimum, the average retail investor should invest in the stock market by buying shares in a low-cost, passive S&P 500 ETF. Note, I prefer an ETF over an index fund because ETFs trade intra-day like stocks versus index funds trade like mutual funds. In other words, the price you buy or sell an index fund is not a price. It's the NAV (net asset value), which gets set at the end of a trading day. Also, ETFs are more liquid than index funds because they're priced and traded like stocks, and you can also short ETFs. FYI, the first S&P 500 index fund was launched by mutual fund legend John Bogle in December 1975 and was called the First Index Investment Trust. Today, it's known as the Vanguard 500 Index Fund (VFINX). First listed in January 1993, the SPDR S&P 500 ETF (SPY) was the first ETF. Not only is SPY the largest ETF by AUM (assets under management), but it's also the most widely traded and most widely held ETF by individual investors.

The average retail investor should not try to time the market, and instead, should invest for the long term by buying and holding and cost averaging over time. Investors get in trouble when they let their emotions get the best of them, and they either buy low and sell lower or buy high and sell low. Note, fractional shares can be purchased in individual stocks like AAPL or MSFT and S&P 500 ETFs like Vanguard's VOO. Robinhood's minimum investment for fractional shares is $1 and allows partial investments into 7,000 stocks and ETFs. Charles Schwab's minimum fractional shares investment is $5 and allows partial investments into any S&P 500 stock. Fidelity allows fractional investments into any NYSE (New York Stock Exchange) or Nasdaq exchange-listed stock or ETF as long as it comprises at least one one-hundredth (0.001) of a share of stock. For example, if a stock costs $10/share, Fidelity's minimum investment required is one penny ($0.01). Hence, if all you can invest is $10 or whatever amount you can afford, you can still participate in market growth. Saying that you don't have enough money to invest in the market is an excuse. No one is preventing you from investing other than yourself.

It's Not How You Sell 'em, It's How You Tell 'em

In his 2016 annual letter to Berkshire Hathaway shareholders, Buffet also discussed wealthy investor psychology and the intellectual pride of desiring to be smarter than others. His comments are insightful and repeated below.

From Page 24

"Over the years, I've often been asked for investment advice, and in the process of answering I've learned a good deal about human behavior. My regular recommendation has been a low-cost S&P 500 index fund. To their credit, my friends who possess only modest means have usually followed my suggestion."

From Page 25

"I believe, however, that none of the mega-rich individuals, institutions or pension funds has followed that same advice when I've given it to them. Instead, these investors politely thank me for my thoughts and depart to listen to the siren song of a high-fee manager or, in the case of many institutions, to seek out another breed of hyper-helper called a consultant.

That professional, however, faces a problem. Can you imagine an investment consultant telling clients, year after year, to keep adding to an index fund replicating the S&P 500? That would be career suicide. Large fees flow to these hyper-helpers, however, if they recommend small managerial shifts every year or so. That advice is often delivered in esoteric gibberish that explains why fashionable investment 'styles' or current economic trends make the shift appropriate.

The wealthy are accustomed to feeling that it is their lot in life to get the best food, schooling, entertainment, housing, plastic surgery, sports ticket, you name it. Their money, they feel, should buy them something superior compared to what the masses receive.

In many aspects of life, indeed, wealth does command top-grade products or services. For that reason, the financial 'elites' – wealthy individuals, pension funds, college endowments and the like – have great trouble meekly signing up for a financial product or service that is available as well to people investing only a few thousand dollars. This reluctance of the rich normally prevails even though the product at issue is – on an expectancy basis – clearly the best choice. My calculation, admittedly very rough, is that the search by the elite for superior investment advice has caused it, in aggregate, to waste more than $100 billion over the past decade."

"Human behavior won't change. Wealthy individuals, pension funds, endowments and the like will continue to feel they deserve something "extra" in investment advice. Those advisors who cleverly play to this expectation will get very rich. This year the magic potion may be hedge funds, next year something else. The likely result from this parade of promises is predicted in an adage: 'When a person with money meets a person with experience, the one with experience ends up with the money and the one with money leaves with experience.'

Long ago, a brother-in-law of mine, Homer Rogers, was a commission agent working in the Omaha stockyards. I asked him how he induced a farmer or rancher to hire him to handle the sale of their hogs or cattle to the buyers from the big four packers (Swift, Cudahy, Wilson and Armour). After all, hogs were hogs and the buyers were experts who knew to the penny how much any animal was worth. How then, I asked Homer, could any sales agent get a better result than any other?

Homer gave me a pitying look and said: 'Warren, it's not how you sell 'em, it's how you tell 'em.' What worked in the stockyards continues to work in Wall Street."

I believe hedge funds didn't take Buffet up on his challenge because they couldn't afford to lose. There was no upside to losing so they didn't take the bet. If they win, it's because they're supposed to win. If, however, they lose, their reputation will be tarnished, and their ability to raise more assets for a new fund in the future will be strained. This translates into a loss of large future fees, which they would no longer be able to collect. I.e., if they can't beat the S&P 500, why would a wealthy investor want to pay 2 and 20 fees (2% management and 20% performance fees) to invest their money with them when investing in an S&P 500 ETF like VOO would cost them nothing. Note, however, there are at least two hedge funds and likely many more that would have beaten Buffet. The first is Ray Dalio's Bridgewater Associates and the second is Jim Simon's Renaissance Technologies. Bridgewater's flagship Pure Alpha Fund has generated a 12% AR after fees from 1991-2018 while Renaissance's flagship Medallion Fund (closed to outside investors in 1993 and only available to current and past Renaissance employees and their families) has averaged a staggering 39% annually from 1988-2018 after hefty 5 and 44 fees, which dwarfs the industry standard of 2 and 20. There's no publicly available performance information for these two hedge funds between January 1, 2008, and December 31, 2017, so I don't know for sure that they would have beaten the S&P 500's performance during this time period (the same time frame as Buffet's $1 million hedge fund challenge), but my guess is both funds did. These two hedge funds have done very well over prolonged periods of time and in the ultra-competitive world of Wall Street, there's nothing for these secretive hedge funds to gain by revealing what they're doing to an astute investor like Buffet. The AR for BRK.A (as of the time Buffet wrote the 2016 annual shareholder letter) was 20.8% and this was over a period of 51 years from 1965-2016 versus the S&P 500 was 9.7%. Recall, Buffet was allowed to review the annual audits for the funds of hedge funds that accepted his $1 million challenge, which would likely disclose more information than what is shown in a Form 13F filing that hedge funds are required to submit to the SEC (Securities and Exchange Commission) up to 45 days after the end of each quarter.

Savings Accounts, Money Market Accounts, and CDs

From June 2009 to June 2019, according to the FDIC and NCUA (National Credit Union Administration), since the subprime mortgage housing crisis and recession, total savings in US commercial banks grew by nearly $4 trillion to $9.75 trillion, and in US credit unions, by about $400 million to $990 billion. In banks, customers held the most in money market accounts, followed by savings accounts, and then CDs. In credit unions, customers held the most money in savings accounts, followed by roughly an even split between money market accounts and CDs.

Per Federal Reserve, FDIC, and MagnifyMoney (Lending Tree) estimates, as of June 2019, among all US households including those with no account, the average US household savings account balance was $17,750, the average US household had $9,430 in money market accounts, and the average US household had $6,220 in CDs. For US households that own a particular account, 51% had a savings account with a $34,730 average balance, 18% had a money market account with a $74,970 average balance, and 7% had CDs with an average total value of $95,600.

Online banks tend to offer the best rates compared to traditional brick-and-mortar banks and credit unions. FYI, a money market account is not the same thing as a money market fund. The former is a federally insured account that earns interest, whereas the latter is an investment in short-term debt, which is considered low risk but does not provide a guaranteed rate-of-return. While your money is protected from loss (note, for FDIC member firms, savings/money market accounts are insured up to $250,000), earning 0.26% APY is simply not going to build wealth in the long run. For example, if you put $10,000 into an FDIC-insured money market account and assume it paid 1.00% APY, after 10 years, you would have $11,046 (ROI 10.46%). In comparison, $10,000 invested in the S&P 500 earning its historical 9.8% AR would become $25,470 (ROI 154.7%). It would take 94 years for $10,000 to grow to $25,481 (approximately the same amount $10,000 invested in the S&P 500 would have become in 10 years) at an APY of 1.00%. After 94 years, $10,000 invested in the S&P 500 with a 9.8% AR would become $65,557,136 (ROI 655,471%). The numbers speak for themselves, and it is not even close. Robert G. Allen once stated, "How many millionaires do you know who have become wealthy by investing in savings accounts? I rest my case."

Per NCUA data from June 2019, the chart below shows the APY for savings accounts, money market accounts, a 1-year CD, and a 3-year CD for commercial banks and credit unions. Again, compared to the 9.8% historical AR of the S&P 500, all of these rates are low, and frankly, I think a complete waste of time if you're using them to increase your wealth over time. Based on Bankrate.com, BLS, FactSet, the Federal Reserve System, and J.P. Morgan

Average APY For Savings/Money Market Accounts and CDs

Source: NCUA, June 2019.

Asset Management, income earned today on $100,000 based on the national average APY on money market accounts from 2010 onward is $220, which is $1,522 less than the income required to beat inflation (2020). The yield is so low that it doesn't even keep up with the cost of living. CDs are considered another safe investment for risk-averse investors. To lock in the rate, you have to commit to the term of the CD. Investors typically structure CD investments using ladders (i.e., allocating the same amount of money across different CDs with different maturities). According to FDIC estimates, as of June 2019, about $1.86 trillion was held in CDs by customers in US commercial banks, which was less than the $2.24 trillion held in CDs in June 2009. Online banks usually offer the best rates. CDs are time-based deposits, and the longer the money is held on deposit, the higher the interest rate paid. A CD with a 1.95% APY will turn $10,000 into $10,596.53 (ROI 5.96%) after three years. In comparison, after three years, $10,000 invested in the S&P 500, earning its historical AR of 9.8%, would have become $13,237.53 (ROI 32.38%).

US Treasury Savings Bonds

Backed by the full faith and credit of the US government, US Treasury savings bonds can be purchased from the US Treasury Department and are one of the safest investments. Series EE bonds are guaranteed to double in value over the purchase price when they mature 20 years from issuance, which is an effective rate of about 3.5%. The bond, however, will continue to earn interest for a total of 30 years. Interest accrues monthly and is compounded semiannually. Series I bonds have a variable yield based on inflation, and the interest rate consists of two components: 1) a fixed rate, which remains constant over the life of the bond, 2) a variable rate adjusted every six months from the time the bond is purchased based on the current inflation rate. Series I savings bonds currently yield 1.06%. Note, bonds held less than five years are subject to a 3-month interest penalty. An individual can buy a maximum of $10,000 worth of savings bonds of each series per calendar year or a total of $20,000. Like savings accounts, money market accounts, and CDs, US Treasury savings bonds don't come close to the ROI of the S&P 500.

The Market (aka S&P 500)

According to the S&P Dow Jones Indices *2019 S&P Indices Versus Active (SPIVA) Scorecard* year-end report, over the past 15 years (January 1, 2005, to December 31, 2019), 90% of active large-cap and 93% of active large-cap growth fund managers underperformed the S&P 500, 89% of active small-cap and 93% of active small-cap growth fund managers underperformed the S&P 500, and 89% of all US domestic fund managers (including real estate, multi-cap, large-cap, mid-cap, small-cap, growth, value, and core) underperformed the S&P 500. SPIVA also reported that outside of the US, over 90% of active foreign fund managers have failed to beat the S&P 500 International 700 Index since the start of 2005. The S&P 500 AR fluctuates yearly. In 2003 the S&P 500 returned 29%. In 2008 it returned -37%. Historically over the past 90 years, the S&P 500 has returned 9.8%. Assuming you're investing for the long run, putting money in a passively-managed S&P 500 ETF like Vanguard's VOO is far superior to putting money into savings accounts, money market accounts, CDs, or US Treasury savings bonds.

Stocks Versus Other Asset Classes (2019)

In 2019, per *Visual Capitalist*, crude oil was the best-performing asset class followed by stocks and then real estate. Note, the total returns of all indices (S&P 500, Russell 2000, etc.) shown below are with dividends reinvested.

Asset class	Total return %
US Dollar (US Dollar Index)	0.3
US Bonds (US Aggregate Bond)	8.7
US Corporate Bonds (Bloomberg Barclays Corporate Bonds)	14.5
Gold	17.4
Commodities (S&P GSCI)	17.6
Emerging Market Stocks (MSCI EEM)	18.0
Canadian Stocks (S&P/TSX Composite)	21.0
Europe, Australia, Far East Stocks (MSCI EAFE)	22.0
US Small Caps (Russell 2000)	25.5
US Real Estate (Dow Jones Real Estate Index)	28.9
US Stocks (S&P 500)	31.5
Crude Oil (WTI Oil)	34.1

Source: *Visual Capitalist*.

In Gallup's April 2020 *Economy and Personal Finance Survey*, 1 in 6 (16%) Americans thought gold, savings accounts, or CDs were the best long-term investments. How does gold compare to the long-term return of the S&P 500? In the table below, the AR and ROI for gold (based on price per ounce) is shown for 10 years (January 2010-2020), 20 years (January 2000-2020), 30 years (January 1990-2020), 40 years (January 1980-2020), and 50 years (January 1970-2020). Gold beats savings and money market accounts, CDs, and US Treasury savings bonds but doesn't beat the S&P 500 historical AR of 9.8%.

# of years gold held	AR %	ROI %
10 years	3.12	35.93
20 years	8.81	441.56
30 years	4.57	282.08
40 years	2.54	172.48
50 years	7.84	4,245.78

Source: SD Bullion.

S&P 500 Sector Performance (2019)

The S&P 500 finished 2019 with an AR of 28.3%, its best since 2013. Per *Visual Capitalist*, the information technology sector beat all other S&P 500 sectors in 2019 with a 50.3% AR. The second best-performing sector was communication services with a 32.7% AR. Note, this sector includes tech companies like GOOG, FB, and NFLX. One third (33.6%) of the S&P 500 weighting in 2019 was made up of the information technology and communication services sectors. Despite rising oil prices, energy stocks were not able to lift the energy sector, and it was the worst-performing sector in 2019.

S&P 500 sector	S&P 500 weighting %	Total return %
Energy	4.3	11.8
Health Care	14.2	20.8
Materials	2.7	24.6
Utilities	3.3	26.4
Consumer Staples	7.2	27.6
Consumer Discretionary	9.8	27.9
Real Estate	2.9	29.0
Industrials	9.1	29.4
Financials	13	32.1

Communication Services	10.4	32.7
Information Technology	23.2	50.3

Source: *Visual Capitalist.*

Best-Performing Stocks (2009-2019)

After an 11-year run, which began on March 9, 2009, the US stock market ended the longest bull run in history on March 11, 2020. Per *CNBC*/FactSet, the ROIs of the best-performing tech stocks of 2019 with a market cap over $5 billion: 1) ROKU (355%), 2) SHOP (195%), 3) SNAP (191%), 4) AMD (150%), 5) COUP (140%). One-third of the top 10 best-performing stocks (based on total return with reinvested dividends) from December 31, 2009, to December 5, 2019, were tech: NFLX #1, AVGO #5, AMZN #10. NFLX produced a 44.1% AR, which means $100 invested in NFLX would have become $3,867. In comparison, $100 invested in the S&P 500 would have become $344 over the same time period for a 13% AR. The final values shown in the table below represent the final value of a $100 investment in each of the top 10 best-performing stocks after 10 years.

Rank	Company	Final value $	AR %
1	Netflix (NFLX)	3,867	44.12
2	MarketAxess Holdings (MKTX)	3,282	41.78
3	Abiomed (ABMD)	2,221	36.35
4	TransDigm Group (TDG)	2,165	36.00
5	Broadcom (AVGO)	2,019	35.06
6	Align Technology (ALGN)	1,558	31.60
7	United Rentals (URI)	1,534	31.40
8	Regeneron Pharmaceuticals (REGN)	1,530	31.36
9	Ulta Beauty (ULTA)	1,333	29.53
10	Amazon (AMZN)	1,309	29.33

Source: *MarketWatch.*

Top 10 Highest-Paid Hedge Fund Managers (2019)

In 2019, according to *Institutional Investors*, the 25 highest-earning hedge fund managers made a combined $20.2 billion, the most since 2013. If you're one of the highest-paid managers, you also earned the carry, an incentive-based performance fee paid out when the manager beats a predefined performance benchmark. To make the top 25, you would have had to earn a minimum of $230 million. Eight fund managers made more than $1 billion each. Together, the top 10 earned $12.6 billion in 2019. Jim Simons is the only person that has made the top 10 all 19 years *Institutional Investors* has published the list. Ken Griffin and Izzy Englander have each made the top 10 list 18 times.

Rank	Fund manager	Hedge fund	Earnings $ million
1	Chris Hohn	TCI Fund Management	1,800
	Jim Simons	Renaissance Technologies	1,800
3	Ken Griffin	Citadel	1,500
	Izzy Englander	Millennium Management	1,500
5	Chase Coleman	Tiger Global Management	1,400
6	Steve Cohen	Point72	1,300
	David Tepper	Appaloosa Management	1,300
8	Ray Dalio	Bridgewater Associates	1,100
9	Stephen Mandel Jr.	Lone Pine Capital	850
10	Nelson Peltz	Trian Partners	835

Source: *Institutional Investors.*

Hedge Fund Performance (2019)

Despite their mystique, hedge funds don't always beat the market. According to 2019 Eurekahedge data, after fees, hedge funds returned a disappointing 7% on average in 2019. In contrast, the S&P 500 returned 29%, the DJIA 22%, and the Nasdaq 35%. Furthermore, globally, investors pulled $131.8 billion ($59 billion in North America alone) from hedge funds in 2019. Some of the better performing funds and their 2019 ROIs included: Melvin Capital (46%), TCI (41%), Renaissance Medallion Fund (39%), Lone Cascade (37%), Lone Cypress (36%), Tiger Global Investments (33%), Trian (30%), and Tiger Global Long Opportunities (30%).

Top 10 Stocks Owned by Hedge Funds (Q1 2020)

According to Insider Monkey, if you focused on the top 10 most commonly held stocks by hedge funds, they returned 185% since the end of 2014 and outperformed the S&P 500 by more than 109 percentage points. Listed below are the top 10 most commonly held stocks by hedge funds as of Q1 2020.

Rank	Stock	# of hedge funds	Total dollar long hedge fund positions $ billion	% of hedge funds with long positions
1	Amazon (AMZN)	251	32.9	30.8
2	Microsoft (MSFT)	235	31.4	28.8
3	Facebook (FB)	213	19.6	26.1
4	Alibaba (BABA)	167	19.4	20.5
5	Alphabet (GOOGL)	167	11.1	20.5
6	Visa (V)	157	14.4	19.1
7	Alphabet (GOOG)	147	15.3	17.9
8	Mastercard (MA)	139	11.9	16.9
9	Bristol-Myers Squibb (BMY)	126	6.9	15.3
10	Apple (AAPL)	123	74.8	15.0

Source: Insider Monkey.

30.8% held AMZN. 7 of 10 (70%) were tech stocks (#1 AMZN, #2 MSFT, #3 FB, #4 BABA, #5 GOOGL, #7 GOOG, #10 AAPL) representing a combined total dollar amount of long positions of $204.5 billion (86%). The top five stocks by total dollar amount were: 1) AAPL $74.8 billion, 2) AMZN $32.9 billion, 3) MSFT $31.4 billion, 4) FB $19.6 billion, 5) BABA $19.4 billion.

SEC Form 13F Filings

Since the top funds have practically unlimited access to resources to perform proprietary research and analysis (e.g., Coatue Management with $25 billion AUM reported in a 2015 shareholder letter that its investment research budget was $70 million), many investors are interested in what stocks smart money held. One way to do this is to review SEC Form 13F filings. These forms must be filed quarterly by all institutional managers (e.g., mutual funds, hedge funds, trust companies, pension funds, insurance companies, registered investment advisors) with a minimum of $100 million in AUM.

When looking at 13F filings, there are some important points to note. 1) they're filed up to 45 days after the end of a quarter (most fund managers often file as late as possible for competitive reasons), which means when you look at a 13F, you may be looking at positions that might have been in place up to 4½ months before the filing. 2) filings may contain errors (the SEC has acknowledged that the data may be unreliable because they don't verify the accuracy and completeness of the filings). 3) behavioral herd bias among professional investors can lead to overcrowded trades and overvalued stocks (e.g., no one will probably get fired for buying AAPL or MSFT). 4) funds are only required to report long positions, long call and put options, ADRs (American depositary receipts), and convertible notes on their filings (futures, currencies, and short positions are not disclosed, so it's unclear if listed long positions are true long positions or hedges to short positions).

Despite the time lag and potential shortcomings of 13F filings, I still like to look at them, especially for hedge funds with successful track records of outperforming the market. I also like to look at the 13F filings for any hedge funds that are tech-centric. At a minimum, I can compare their long positions and long call/put options (if any) to positions I held in my portfolio up to 4½ months ago. 13F filings for hedge funds that favor short-term trading or are very broad and diversified are less valuable because they don't align with my general investing and trading strategy. In practice, however, I've never made drastic changes to my portfolio based on 13F filings.

Hedge Fund Holdings

According to BarclayHedge, as of Q4 2019, the total hedge fund industry AUM was $3.2 trillion. *Institutional Investors'* top 10 highest-paid hedge fund managers managed a combined $546.4 billion representing 17.1% of the entire hedge industry. Hedge funds employ all types of trading strategies from activist-long-only to long-short to long-only to risk-parity to multi-strategy to quantitative and more. The table below shows the number of holdings in each of the top 10 highest-paid hedge fund managers' funds along with the total value of each fund's holdings. Again, remember this is not the fund's total AUM since they're not required by the SEC to report their short positions in their quarterly 13F filings. It's important to keep in mind that the number of holdings nor the total value of a fund's holdings is necessarily a reflection of how successful a fund is. The number of holdings is more often a reflection of the fund's strategy. The table below contains data from 13F filings filed by hedge funds with the SEC on February 13-14, 2020. This means you could be looking at positions held by these ten hedge funds as far back as October 2019, and they may not necessarily be still holding them as of the 13F filing dates.

Hedge fund	# holdings	Value of holdings $ 000s
Citadel	8,843	230,470,163
Renaissance Technologies	3,469	130,130,783
Millennium Management	4,140	79,928,100
TCI Fund Management	17	22,602,340
Point72	917	19,018,144
Lone Pine Capital	43	18,860,782
Tiger Global Management	73	18,121,848
Bridgewater Associates	471	9,794,186
Trian Partners	8	9,484,455
Appaloosa Management	23	3,980,548

Source: February 13-14, 2020 SEC 13F filings.

Citadel held 8,843 positions, while Trian only held 8. Citadel was also the largest in terms of the total value of its holdings ($230.5 billion), which is nearly 58x larger than Appaloosa ($3.98 billion).

The table below shows each hedge fund's #1 holding, the dollar value of that holding, and what percentage it represented of the fund's total holdings. Note, a high percentage suggests the holding is important to the success of the fund. For example, PG is an important position for Trian.

Hedge fund	#1 holding	#1 holding value $ 000s	#1 holding % of total holdings
Trian Partners	Procter & Gamble (PG)	4,016,113	42.34
Bridgewater Associates	SPDR S&P 500 ETF (SPY)	2,249,694	22.97
TCI Fund Management	Charter Communications (CHTR)	4,935,336	21.84
Appaloosa Management	Alphabet (Google)(GOOG)	588,289	14.78
Tiger Global Management	JD.com (JD)	1,861,918	10.03
Citadel	SPDR S&P 500 ETF (SPY) Put	18,359,602	7.97
Lone Pine Capital	Alibaba (BABA)	1,323,459	7.02
Millennium Management	SPDR S&P 500 ETF (SPY)	4,139,477	5.18
Renaissance Technologies	Bristol Myers Squibb (BMY)	3,864.922	2.97
Point72	SPDR S&P 500 ETF (SPY)	432,902	2.28

Source: February 13-14, 2020 SEC 13F filings.

4 of the 10 top holdings were not stocks, but an S&P 500 ETF (SPY), and in the case of Citadel, it was a SPY put. 3 of the top 10 were tech stocks (GOOG, JD, BABA), and two were Chinese (JD, BABA). In terms of dollar value, Citadel

had the largest holding (SPY put worth $18.4 billion), while Point72 had the smallest holding (also in SPY, worth $432.9 million). As far as percentage of total holdings, Trian had the largest, with $4 billion in PG (representing 42.3% of their total reported holdings), and Point72 had the smallest, with $432.9 million in SPY (representing 2.3% of their total reported holdings).

Billion Dollar Hedge Fund Positions

Let's look at each of the hedge funds listed above run by the top 10 highest-paid hedge fund managers and note how many billion-dollar holdings they held per their February 13-14, 2020, 13F filings. I think this is useful because it shows where the hedge fund was (or is), at one point in time, placing their largest long stock and long option bets. The 10 hedge funds held 55 positions (49 were unique), each individually valued at over $1 billion, and combined, they were worth $124.5 billion, representing almost one-fourth (24.2%) of the combined value of all 10 funds. Collectively, the 10 funds had billion-dollar positions in 10 individual tech stocks (AAPL, AMZN, BABA, FB, GOOG, JD, MSFT, Palo Alto Networks (PANW), TSLA, Verisign (VRSN)). Citadel also held calls and puts in seven tech stocks (AAPL, AMZN, BABA, FB, MSFT, NFLX, TSLA). Additionally, Citadel also held calls and puts in Invesco QQQ Trust ETF (QQQ), which mirrors the Nasdaq 100, a tech-heavy index made up of 100 of the largest non-financial companies listed on Nasdaq. Each hedge fund's specific interest in tech is obviously dependent on the fund manager's investment and trading strategy. Nevertheless, when I see funds that have billion-dollar long positions in the same tech companies that I'm in, at a minimum, it's an additional vote of confidence. Out of the 10 tech stocks held by hedge funds that were billion-dollar positions listed above, I'm currently in four of them (AAPL, AMZN, MSFT, TSLA) and have exited positions in one (FB). Again, keep in mind that when looking at each of the tables below, it represents a snapshot of positions held by each specific fund in the past that could be up to 4½ months before the SEC filing of each fund's 13F.

Hedge fund:	TCI Fund Management
Num of $ billion holdings:	8
Total value of $ billion holdings:	$19,570,279,000
Total value of holdings:	$22,602,340,000

Holding	Value $ 000s	% value of total holdings
Alphabet (GOOG)	4,171,085	18.45
Anthem (ANTM)	1,208,171	5.35
Canadian National Railway (CNI)	1,852,238	8.19
Canadian Pacific Railway (CP)	2,797,878	12.38
Charter Communications (CHTR)	4,935,336	21.84
Microsoft (MSFT)	1,684,194	7.45
Moody's (MCO)	1,429,900	6.33
Raytheon (RTN)	1,491,477	6.6

Source: February 2020 SEC 13F filing.

2 out of 8 (25%) were tech (GOOG, MSFT), which represented 25.9% of the total value of all holdings, and 29.9% of the total value of the fund's billion-dollar holdings. The largest position was CHTR, which represented 21.8% of the total value of all holdings, and 25.2% of the total value of the fund's billion-dollar holdings. Railroad companies represented 20.6% of the total value of all holdings and 23.8% of the total value of the fund's billion-dollar holdings. Billion-dollar holdings represented 86.6% of the total value of all positions in the fund. Obviously, billion-dollar positions in this fund are important. TCI's portfolio consists of just 17 holdings, so it's also clear TCI focuses its activities on just a few companies.

Hedge fund:	Renaissance Technologies
Num of $ billion holdings:	11
Total value of $ billion holdings:	$17,247,832,000
Total value of holdings:	$130,130,783,000

Holding	Value $ 000s	% value of total holdings
Abbvie (ABBV)	1,044,484	0.80
Bristol Myers Squibb (BMY)	3,864,922	2.97
Chipotle Mexican Grill (CMG)	1,476,279	1.13
Gilead Sciences (GILD)	1,102,252	0.85
Humana (HUM)	1,081,689	0.83
Novo-Nordisk A/S (NVO)	1,517,441	1.17
Palo Alto Networks (PANW)	1,309,442	1.01
Tesla (TSLA)	1,647,443	1.27
Verisign (VRSN)	1,593,597	1.22
Vertex Pharmaceuticals (VRTX)	1,549,418	1.19
Walmart (WMT)	1,060,865	0.82

Source: February 2020 SEC 13F filing.

3 out of 11 (27%) were tech (PANW, TSLA, VRSN), which represented 3.5% of the total value of all holdings, and 26.4% of the total value of the fund's billion-dollar holdings. The largest position was BMY, which represented 3% of the total value of all holdings, and 22.4% of the total value of the fund's billion-dollar holdings. Pharmaceutical companies represented 7.8% of the total value of all holdings and 58.9% of the total value of the fund's billion-dollar holdings. Billion-dollar holdings represented 13.3% of the total value of all positions in the fund. Given Renaissance's portfolio was comprised of 3,469 positions, quantitative algorithmic trading is probably being used.

Hedge fund: Citadel
Num of $ billion holdings: 21
Total value of $ billion holdings: $69,830,671,000
Total value of holdings: $230,470,163,000

Holding	Value $ 000s	% value of total holdings
Alibaba (BABA) Call	1,455,261	0.63
Alibaba (BABA) Put	5,521,900	2.4
Amazon (AMZN) Call	5,353,008	2.32
Amazon (AMZN) Put	7,199,000	3.12
Apple (AAPL) Call	3,661,698	1.59
Apple (AAPL) Put	2,885,170	1.25
Facebook (FB) Call	1,611,828	0.7
Facebook (FB) Put	1,340,159	0.58
Invesco QQQ Trust ETF (QQQ) Call	1,858,977	0.81
Invesco QQQ Trust ETF (QQQ) Put	3,003,648	1.3
iShares Trust Put	1,512,568	0.66
iShares Trust Put	1,233,490	0.54
Microsoft (MSFT) Call	1,046,434	0.45
Microsoft (MSFT) Put	1,073,475	0.47
Netflix (NFLX) Call	1,221,962	0.53
Netflix (NFLX) Put	1,129,453	0.49
SPDR S&P 500 ETF (SPY) Put	1,062,138	0.46
SPDR S&P 500 ETF (SPY) Call	5,739,311	2.49
SPDR S&P 500 ETF (SPY) Put	18,359,602	7.97
Tesla (TSLA) Call	1,593,597	0.69
Tesla (TSLA) Put	1,967,992	0.85

Source: February 2020 SEC 13F filing.

14 out of 21 (67%) were tech (BABA call/put, AMZN call/put, AAPL call/put, FB call/put, MSFT call/put, NFLX call/put, TSLA call/put), which represented

16.1% of the total value of all holdings, and 53.1% of the total value of the fund's billion-dollar holdings. The largest position was a SPY put, which represented 8% of the total value of all holdings, and 26% of the total value of the fund's billion-dollar holdings. ETFs made up 14.2% of the total value of all holdings and 46.9% of the total value of the fund's billion-dollar holdings. It's hard to know what Citadel was doing with the options, but interestingly, every stock position consisted of both calls/puts as did QQQ. iShares Trust were both puts and SPY had two puts to one call with one put being the largest position as mentioned. This could be hedging or a market decline bet. Billion-dollar holdings represented 30.3% of the total value of all positions in the fund. Like Renaissance, Citadel is probably using quantitative algorithmic trading to manage its 8,843 positions.

Hedge fund:	Millennium Management
Num of $ billion holdings:	2
Total value of $ billion holdings:	$5,174,828,000
Total value of holdings:	$79,928,100,000

Holding	Value $ 000s	% value of total holdings
Apple (AAPL)	1,035,351	1.3
SPDR S&P 500 ETF (SPY)	4,139,477	5.18

Source: February 2020 SEC 13F filing.

1 out of 2 (50%) was tech (AAPL), which represented 1.3% of the total value of all holdings, and 20% of the total value of the fund's billion-dollar holdings. The largest position was SPY, which represented 5.2% of the total value of all holdings, and 80% of the total value of the fund's billion-dollar holdings. Millennium was managing thousands of positions, and billion-dollar holdings only represented 6.5% of the total value of all positions in the fund. Quantitative algorithmic trading is probably being used due to the number of holdings (4,140).

Hedge fund:	Tiger Global Management
Num of $ billion holdings:	6
Total value of $ billion holdings:	$9,325,598,000
Total value of holdings:	$18,121,848,000

Holding	Value	% value of
	$ 000s	total holdings
Amazon (AMZN)	1,130,952	6.24
Apollo Global Management (APO)	1,796,926	9.92
Facebook (FB)	1,707,577	9.42
JD.com (JD)	1,816,918	10.03
Microsoft (MSFT)	1,716,265	9.47
TransDigm Group (TDG)	1,156,960	6.38

Source: February 2020 SEC 13F filing.

4 out of 6 (67%) were tech (AMZN, FB, JD, MSFT), which represented 35.2% of the total value of all holdings, and 68.3% of the total value of the fund's billion-dollar holdings. The largest position was JD, a Chinese company, which represented 10% of the total value of all holdings, and 19.5% of the total value of the fund's billion-dollar holdings. Billion-dollar holdings represented half (51.5%) of the total value of all positions in the funds, so they have a big influence on fund performance. This fund currently focuses a lot on tech.

Hedge fund:	Point72
Num of $ billion holdings:	0
Total value of holdings:	$19,018,144,000

Hedge fund:	Appaloosa Management
Num of $ billion holdings:	0
Total value of holdings:	$3,980,548,000

Source: February 2020 SEC 13F filing.

Out of 917 positions, Point72 had no positions worth $1 billion or more. Out of 23 positions, Appaloosa also had no positions worth $1 billion or more. Like TCI, Appaloosa also focuses on a smaller portfolio with just 23.

Hedge fund:	Bridgewater Associates
Num of $ billion holdings:	2
Total value of $ billion holdings:	$3,350,667,000
Total value of holdings:	$9,794,186,000

Holding	Value	% value of
	$ 000s	total holdings
SPDR S&P 500 ETF (SPY)	2,249,694	22.97
Vanguard Intl Equity Index	1,100,973	11.24

Source: February 2020 SEC 13F filing.

0 out of 2 (0%) were tech. The largest position was SPY, which represented 23% of the total value of all holdings, and 67.1% of the total value of the fund's billion-dollar holdings. Billion-dollar holdings represented a third (34.2%) of the total value of the 471 positions in the fund. This fund had a big bet on SPY.

Hedge fund:	Lone Pine Capital
Num of $ billion holdings:	2
Total value of $ billion holdings:	$2,570,832,000
Total value of holdings:	$18,860,782,000

Holding	Value $ 000s	% value of total holdings
Alibaba (BABA)	1,323,459	7.02
UnitedHealth Group (UNH)	1,247,373	6.61

Source: February 2020 SEC 13F filing.

1 out of 2 (50%) was tech (BABA), which represented 7% of the total value of all holdings and a little over half (51.5%) of the total value of the fund's billion-dollar holdings. The largest position was BABA. Billion-dollar holdings represented 13.6% of the total value of the 43 positions in the fund.

Hedge fund:	Trian Partners
Num of $ billion holdings:	3
Total value of $ billion holdings:	$7,078,436,000
Total value of holdings:	$9,484,455,000

Holding	Value $ 000s	% value of total holdings
Mondelez International (MDLZ)	1,037,066	10.93
Procter & Gamble (PG)	4,016,113	42.34
Sysco (SYY)	2,025,257	21.35

Source: February 2020 SEC 13F filing.

0 out of 3 (0%) were tech. The largest position was PG, which represented 42.3% of the total value of all holdings, and 56.7% of the total value of the fund's billion-dollar holdings. PG is obviously important to Trian. Billion-dollar holdings represented 74.6% of the total value of all positions in the fund and have a large impact on the fund. Trian also clearly focuses on a small number of companies since their portfolio only consisted of 8 positions.

A Final Note About Hedge Funds and Their Interest in Tech

Since I like tech stocks, let's see if the 10 hedge funds previously discussed had positions in FANG (FB, AMZN, NFLX, GOOG), AAPL, and/or MSFT. Note, I selected these large-cap tech stocks as a quick snapshot of each fund's activity in tech; however, these are far from the only tech companies these funds held. In fact, combined, the 10 hedge funds held positions in dozens of tech stocks.

Software
ADBE, GOOG, Autodesk (ADSK), COUP, Dropbox (DBX), eBay (EBAY), FB, INTU, MSFT, MongoDB (MDB), NFLX, ORCL, PayPal (PYPL), Salesforce (CRM), SHOP, SNAP, Spotify (SPOT), Take-Two (TTWO), TTD, Twilio (TWLO), VRSN, VMware (VMW), Zoom Video (ZM), etc.

Hardware
AAPL, CSCO, DELL, Seagate (STX), Western Digital (WDC), etc.

Semiconductors
AMD, Analog Devices (ADI), AVGO, INTC, Maxim Integrated (MXIM), Micron (MU), NVDA, NXPI Semiconductor (NXPI), Qorvo (QRVO), QCOM, XLNX, etc.

The FANG column in the table below indicates which FANG stocks the fund held positions in (e.g., Point72 had positions in AN (AMZN, NFLX)).

Hedge fund	FANG	AAPL	MSFT
TCI Fund Management	G	No	Yes
Renaissance Technologies	FANG	Yes	No
Citadel	FANG	Yes	Yes
Millennium Management	FANG	Yes	Yes
Tiger Global Management	FANG	No	Yes
Point72	AN	No	No
Appaloosa Management	FAG	No	No
Bridgewater Associates		No	No
Lone Pine Capital	FAN	No	Yes
Trian Partners		No	No

Source: February 2020 SEC 13F filings.

8 out of 10 (80%) had some position in FANG. 3 out of 10 (33%) had positions in FAANG. 2 out of 10 (20%) had positions in FAANGM. 7 out of 10 (70%) were in AMZN. 6 out of 10 (60%) were in FB, NFLX, or GOOG. 5 out of 10

(50%) were in MSFT. 3 out of 10 (30%) were in AAPL. 2 out of 10 (20%) were in FANG, AAPL, or MSFT. The most active in tech were Renaissance, Citadel, Millennium, and Tiger.

Over 90 Years the Market Has Always Gone Up

The chart below shows the S&P 500 from 1925-2020.

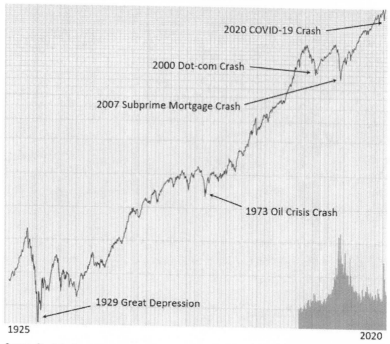

Source: Stockcharts.com.

Despite several big crashes over the years, including the 1929 Great Depression, the 1973 oil crisis, the 2000 tech-fueled dot-com bubble and crash, the 2007 subprime mortgage housing crash and recession, and most recently, the 2020 COVID-19 crash, the S&P 500 still generated a 9.8% AR over the past 90 years. On January 3, 1928, the S&P 500 closed at 17.76. Fifty years later, on January 3, 1978, the S&P 500 closed at 93.82 for an ROI of 428.27%. Fast forward to today, and the S&P 500 closed at 3,257.85 as of January 3, 2020, for an ROI of 3,372.45%.

Smart money also likes to trade the S&P 500. As just discussed, in 2019, of the top 10 highest-paid hedge fund managers, 4 out of 10 (40%) had their largest single holding in SPY. Despite having a slightly higher expense ratio than VOO, active institutional traders prefer SPY due to its higher trading volume. This allows them to buy and sell large amounts of SPY with minimal price impact. Based on their February 13-14, 2020, SEC 13F filings, Citadel was holding $18.4B in SPY puts (it's not clear if this put was a hedge or a market decline bet or both), Millennium was holding $4.14B in SPY, Bridgewater was holding $2.25B in SPY, and Point72 was holding $432.9M in SPY.

The two tables below are based on Pew Research Center 2020 analysis of the 2016 *Survey of Consumer Finances*. The first table shows the percentages of people with direct or indirect investments in the stock market by age. The second table shows the percentages of families with direct or indirect investments in the stock market based on family income. Not surprisingly, the older someone is, and the wealthier a family is, the higher the median holding value. In general, Pew Research Center found that the majority (52%) of families are invested in the stock market with a median holding of $40,000.

Age	% with investments in the stock market	Median holding $
Less than 35	41	7,700
35–44	56	22,000
45–54	57	51,000
55–64	58	80,000
65 and over	50	100,000

Family income	% of families with investments in the stock market	Median holding $
Less than $35,000	19	8,400
$35,000 – $52,999	44	12,000
$53,000 – $99,999	66	26,000
Over $100,000	88	138,700

Source: Pew Research Center, 2020.

Wealthy families invest in the stock market more frequently than lower-income families; however, despite this discrepancy, investing in a low-cost S&P 500 ETF like VOO enables retail investors to participate in the future growth of the market for as little money as they are comfortable investing because fractional shares can be purchased. Robinhood's minimum investment requirement for fractional shares is just $1. In other words, there's no excuse for not participating in the long-term growth of the market, which again, for the S&P 500, it has returned a 9.8% AR over the past 90 years. In the long run, stocks have outperformed other investments such as real estate, gold, savings accounts, money market accounts, CDs, and US Treasury savings bonds. Past performance is never a guarantee of future results; however, the market has thus far always gone up over time. Ultimately, the only thing that really matters to an investor is, beat the market (i.e., S&P 500). If you cannot do that, then you're better off parking your money in an S&P 500 ETF (VOO), a Nasdaq ETF (ONEQ), or Nasdaq 100 ETF (QQQ) and patiently waiting for the market to go up over time.

Up and To the Right

Let's look at three tech stocks that have been publicly traded for 30 years. Below is the stock chart for AAPL for the past 30 years from 1990-2020.

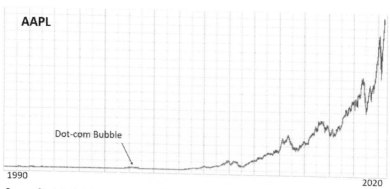

Source: Stockcharts.com.

From 1990-2004 AAPL was basically flat for nearly 15 years. Steve Jobs returned to AAPL in 1996 when the company purchased NeXT, a computer maker that Jobs founded in 1985. Note that in a 30-year chart, the dot-com bubble barely registers as a blip even though AAPL had lost about two-thirds of its value after the crash. AAPL was trading for less than $1 per share during this time. Then, beginning in 2004, the overall long-term trend line is up and to the right with the slope continuing to increase. Tim Cook was named CEO in 2011. Some key AAPL announcements over the past two decades include iPod (October 2001), MacBook Pro (January 2006), iPhone (January 2007), MacBook Air (January 2008), App Store (July 2008), iPad (January 2010), Apple Watch (April 2015), AirPods (December 2016).

Below is the stock chart for MSFT for the past 30 years from 1990-2020. As part of the Wintel juggernaut, with the launch of Windows 95, MSFT continued to grow rapidly from 1993-2000. After the 2000 dot-com crash, MSFT lost about half of its value, and it remained essentially flat for over a decade after the dot-com bubble burst. Then, beginning around 2013, the overall long-term trend line is up and to the right with the slope continuing to increase. In 2014, Satya Nadella was named the third CEO after Steve Ballmer and Bill Gates. Since taking over as CEO, Nadella has skillfully and successfully reinvigorated growth by transitioning MSFT from a software licensing-based business to a subscription, cloud, and SaaS (software-as-a-service) based company, and Wall Street has rewarded the stock price and company valuation accordingly.

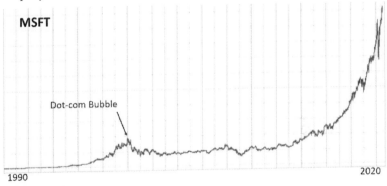

Source: Stockcharts.com.

Finally, below is the stock chart for ORCL for the past 30 years from 1990-2020. On the chart, you can see how spectacular tech stocks like ORCL shot up before the dot-com bubble burst in 2000-2001. Then in 2003, notice how the overall long-term trend line is up and to the right. In fact, if you erase the dot-com rise and fall in the stock price, ORCL would be sloping upwards from the single digits in the early 90s, to today where it is trading in the high 50s per share. Some important ORCL acquisitions over the past two decades: PeopleSoft December 2004, Siebel Systems September 2005, Sun Microsystems April 2009, NetSuite July 2016. In 2010, ORCL filed a multibillion-dollar lawsuit against GOOG. ORCL alleged that GOOG had illegally used portions of Java in its Android mobile phone operating system. In 2016, a jury found that GOOG had not violated ORCL's copyrights. Larry Ellison gave up the CEO role in 2014.

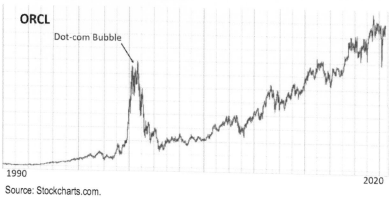

Source: Stockcharts.com.

A Great Equalizer

I think the stock market is a great equalizer that practically anyone can use to build wealth. The market doesn't care, nor does it know if you're rich or poor, young or old, male or female, or if you're on vacation sitting in a pub in Exmouth making tens of millions of dollars using a cell phone and a laptop. All the market ultimately cares about is, can buyer and seller be matched to complete a trade. Martin Schwarz, author of the book *Pit Bull: Lessons from Wall Street's Champion Day Trader*, said, "Trading is a psychological game. Most people think they are playing against the market, but the market doesn't care. You're really playing against yourself." The beauty about the market is that it's accessible by nearly anyone and something you can do all by yourself. If you need more education on the market, there are plenty of books you can buy or check out from your local public library as well as there's an abundance of free websites, blogs, discussion forums, and YouTube videos online. "It's never too late to learn," as Malcolm Forbes once said. Unlike owning a small business, there's also no need to hire and manage employees. Furthermore, unlike investing in real estate, there's no need to manage a rental property or secure financing to update a house to flip it. In contrast, the ability to trade stocks is virtually frictionless. With zero-commission trades, there's no cost to enter or exit stock positions, and you can place buy and sell trade orders from almost anywhere in the world. Furthermore, the ability to buy fractional shares enables retail investors to participate in the future growth of the market for as little money as they're comfortable investing. Fractional shares can be purchased in low-cost ETFs that mirror the performance of market indices such as the S&P 500 (VOO), Nasdaq (ONEQ), Nasdaq 100 (QQQ), and individual tech stocks like AAPL and MSFT. There is no reason why you shouldn't be invested in the market today and building wealth for tomorrow.

3

TECHNOLOGY

Any sufficiently advanced technology is indistinguishable from magic.
　　　　　　　　　　　　　　　　　　　　　　—*Arthur C. Clarke*

IN THE PREVIOUS chapter, I discussed the frictionless nature of stock trading and why it is the best vehicle for building wealth for the average investor. Open a brokerage account, deposit some money, and you can immediately be up and running and investing in the stock market. If you are comfortable investing in the market in individual stocks, this chapter will discuss why you should focus your time and attention on tech stocks. Corporate raider T. Boone Pickens said, "The older I get, the more I see a straight path where I want to go. If you're going to hunt elephants, don't get off the trail for a rabbit." Tech stocks have always been elephants for me.

The Influence of Tech on the S&P 500, Nasdaq 100, and Nasdaq
FAANGM (FB, AMZN, AAPL, NFLX, GOOG, MSFT) has heavy influence on the S&P 500. At the peak of the dot-com bubble, the information technology sector accounted for 33.6% of the total market cap and 28.2% of the total EPS (earnings per share) contribution of the S&P 500. Today, it's 28.2% and 23.7%, respectively. However, if you combine the information technology sector with the communications services sector, which includes notable tech companies such as GOOG, FB, and NFLX, among others, the combined weight of these two sectors on the market capitalization of the S&P 500 is 39%.

According to Dow Jones Market Data, the combined weighting of the S&P 500's five largest companies increased from 11.6% at the end of 2013 to 20.4% as of June 5, 2020. At the end of 2013, three of the five largest companies in the S&P 500 were tech companies with a combined total of 7.2%: 1) AAPL 3%, 2) Exxon Mobile (XOM) 2.7%, 3) GOOG 2.3%, 4) MSFT 1.9%, 5) BRK.A 1.8%. By June 5, 2020, the five largest companies in the S&P 500 were all tech companies with a combined total of 20.3%: 1) AAPL 5.1%, 2) MSFT 5%, 3) AMZN 4.4%, 4) GOOG 3.5%, 5) FB 2.3%. In Yardeni Research's April 30, 2020, *Stock Market Briefing: Market Capitalization* report, as of April 24, 2020, 22.8% of the S&P 500 market capitalization was represented by FAANGM, up from about 9% at the start of 2013. Since the S&P 500 is a market-cap weighted index, this means the performance of six tech stocks that make up FAANGM drives nearly one-quarter of the movement in the S&P 500 (note, the top 10 stocks represent 29.2% of the market cap of the S&P 500). This means FAANGM will also drive the performance of the multitude of S&P 500 index funds and ETFs that track to the performance of the S&P 500. Over the past 90 years, the historical AR of the S&P 500 has been 9.8%. In the past 10 years, the AR for the S&P 500 was 20.2%. FAANGM in particular, and tech in general, has definitely contributed to the above-average AR of the S&P 500 in the past decade.

On April 30, 2020, the total market cap of the S&P 500 was $24.14 trillion. On this day, there were three trillion-dollar market cap companies in the S&P 500. All were tech companies (AAPL ($1.273 trillion), AMZN ($1.234 trillion), MSFT ($1.359 trillion)). Also, of note, GOOG was worth $920.62 billion (GOOG surpassed the trillion-dollar mark for the first time on January 16, 2020, and was the fourth US company to do so), and FB was worth $583.24 billion. Combined, AAPL, AMZN, and MSFT were worth $3.866 trillion and represented 16% of the entire S&P 500 market capitalization. Add GOOG and FB into the mix, and the combined total climbs to $5.37 trillion, which would account for a little more than one fifth (22.24%) of the entire S&P 500.

In 1960, there were no tech companies in the top five most valuable companies in the S&P 500 (#1 AT&T (T), #2 General Motors (GM), #3 DuPont de Nemours (DD), #4 New Jersey Standard Oil, #5 General Electric (GE)). By 1980, the top five included one tech company occupying the top spot (#1 IBM,

#2 T, #3 XOM, #4 Indiana's Standard Oil, #5 Schlumberger (SLB)). Ten years later, in 1990, IBM was still number one (#1 IBM, #2 XOM, #3 GE, #4 Philip Morris (PM), #5 Royal Dutch Shell (RDS.B)). By 2000, IBM was no longer in the top five, but CSCO appeared at number five (#1 GE, #2 XOM, #3 Pfizer (PFE), #4 Citigroup (C), #5 CSCO). Ten years later, in 2010, there were two tech companies, AAPL and MSFT, in the top five (#1 XOM, #2 AAPL, #3 MSFT, #4 BRK.A, #5 GE). Most recently, as of April 30, 2020, the top five most valuable companies in the S&P 500 were now all tech companies (#1 MSFT, #2 AAPL, #3 AMZN, #4 GOOG, #5 FB). In the past, the US economy was powered by oil. Today, the engine that drives the US economy and the stock market is clearly technology, and the future shows no signs of being any different, not just in the US but also globally.

The Nasdaq 100 is a tech-heavy index made up of 100 of the largest, most actively traded nonfinancial US companies on Nasdaq. The index is re-ranked every December, and as of May 10, 2020, about half (54.4%) of the index were tech companies. As of July 2020, six tech companies (AAPL 12%, MSFT 11.3%, AMZN 11.2%, FB 4.2%, GOOG 3.8%, GOOGL 3.8%, TSLA 2.7%) made up about half (49%) of the total value of the Nasdaq 100. These six companies also made up 41% of the value of the Nasdaq index, which is comprised of more than 2,700 companies. Like the S&P 500, both the Nasdaq 100 and Nasdaq are also market-cap-weighted indices; hence, if these six tech stocks move higher or lower, then the Nasdaq 100 and Nasdaq are also likely to move higher or lower. Similar for any Nasdaq 100 and Nasdaq-based index funds and ETFs. Clearly, six tech stocks (AAPL, AMZN, FB, GOOG/GOOGL, MSFT, TSLA) exert incredible influence on the overall performance of the S&P 500, Nasdaq 100, and Nasdaq indices.

Tech Stock Performance in the Nasdaq 100

Let's take a look at tech stocks and their AR and ROI performance in the Nasdaq 100. The table below contains the tech companies in the Nasdaq 100 that have existed for at least 10 years and shows what would have happened if $10,000 was invested in each of these companies from January 4, 2010, through January 2, 2020 (note, dividends are not included). For comparison, the table also contains the 10-year performances for the same time period for the DJIA, S&P 500, Nasdaq, and QQQ (a widely-held ETF designed to mirror the performance of the Nasdaq 100). Some companies in the Nasdaq 100 are not included in the table below because they have not been publicly traded for more than 10 years. This includes companies such as CDW (CDW), FB, JD, NXPI, PYPL (acquired by eBay in 2002 and spun out in 2015), Splunk Technology (SPLK), TSLA, Workday (WDAY), and ZM. Note, some of the best-performing Nasdaq tech stocks (e.g., COUP, ROKU, TTD) of recent years are not included because they're not part of the Nasdaq 100. Finally, some tech stocks are listed on the NYSE but not listed in the Nasdaq like BABA, SHOP, SNAP, and Taiwan Semiconductor Manufacturing (TSM).

2010 investment	2020 value	Gain	AR	ROI
	$	$	%	%
Western Digital (WDC)	14,436	4,436	3.74	44.36
NetApp (NTAP)	18,329	8,329	6.25	83.29
Qualcomm (QCOM)	18,891	8,891	6.57	88.91
Cisco Systems (CSCO)	19,610	9,610	6.97	96.10
Expedia Group (EXPE)	21,419	11,419	7.91	114.19
Cognizant Technology Solutions (CTSH)	26,440	16,440	10.21	164.40
DJIA	27,276	17,276	10.55	172.76
S&P 500	28,754	18,754	11.14	187.54
Maxim Integrated Products (MXIM)	30,466	20,466	11.78	204.66
Citrix Systems (CTXS)	32,719	22,719	12.58	227.19
Check Point Software Technologies (CHKP)	32,892	22,892	12.64	228.92
Baidu (BIDU)	33,587	23,587	12.88	235.87
Cerner (CERN)	34,896	24,896	13.31	248.96
eBay (EBAY)	36,082	26,082	13.69	260.82
Microchip Technology (MCHP)	36,799	26,799	13.92	267.99
Analog Devices (ADI)	37,936	27,936	14.26	279.36
Nasdaq	39,387	29,387	14.69	293.87
Xilinx (XLNX)	40,050	30,050	14.88	300.50
Applied Materials (AMAT)	43,478	33,478	15.83	334.78
Alphabet (GOOG)	43,541	33,541	15.85	335.41
Automatic Data Processing (ADP)	45,135	35,135	16.27	351.35
Invesco QQQ Trust ETF (QQQ) Nasdaq 100	46,474	36,474	16.61	364.74
KLA (KLAC)	49,294	39,294	17.29	392.94
Texas Instruments (TXN)	49,755	39,755	17.40	397.55
Advanced Micro Devices (AMD)	31,670	21,670	12.22	216.70
Micron Technology (MU)	51,014	41,014	17.70	410.14
Activision (ATVI)	51,511	41,511	17.81	415.11

Microsoft (MSFT)	51,881	41,881	17.90	418.81
Ansys (ANSS)	58,148	48,148	19.25	481.48
Electronic Arts (EA)	59,037	49,037	19.43	490.37
Intel (INTC)	59,502	49,502	19.52	495.02
Synopsys (SNPS)	63,577	53,577	20.32	535.77
Autodesk (ADSK)	73,066	63,066	22.00	630.66
Lam Research (LRCX)	74,473	64,473	22.24	644.73
NetEase (NTES)	78,888	68,888	22.94	688.88
Verisign (VRSN)	79,479	69,479	23.03	694.79
Skyworks Solutions (SWKS)	82,006	72,006	23.42	720.06
Booking Holdings (BKNG)	85,058	75,058	23.87	750.58
Intuit (INTU)	86,236	76,236	24.04	762.36
ASML Holding (ASML)	87,215	77,215	24.18	772.15
Adobe (ADBE)	89,962	79,962	24.57	799.62
Fiserv (FISV)	93,456	83,456	25.04	834.56
Apple (AAPL)	98,214	88,214	25.67	882.14
Cadence Design Systems (CDNS)	116,662	106,662	27.85	1,066.62
Take-Two Interactive Software (TTWO)	117,319	107,319	27.92	1,073.19
MercadoLibre (MELI)	120,207	110,207	28.23	1,102.07
Nvidia (NVDA)	125,231	115,231	28.76	1,152.31
Amazon (AMZN)	140,453	130,453	30.24	1,304.53
Broadcom (AVGO)	170,867	160,867	32.82	1,608.67
Netflix (NFLX)	431,391	421,391	45.71	4,213.91

The best-performing stock was NFLX (AR 45.7%, ROI 4,214%), then AVGO (AR 32.8%, ROI 1,609%) and AMZN (AR 30.2%, ROI 1,305%). The worst-performing stocks were WDC (AR 3.7%, ROI 44.4%), NTAP (AR 6.3%, ROI 83.3%), and QCOM (AR 6.6%, ROI 88.9%), which all underperformed the indices (S&P 500, DJIA, Nasdaq, Nasdaq 100 (QQQ)). Some other highlights. 1) 40 out of 46 (87%) of the tech stocks in the Nasdaq 100 outperformed the DJIA (AR 10.6%) and S&P 500 (AR 11.1%). 2) 33 out of the 46 (71.7%) of the tech stocks in the Nasdaq 100 outperformed BRK.A (AR 14%). 3) 32 out of 46 (69.6%) of the tech stocks in the Nasdaq 100 outperformed Nasdaq (AR 14.7%). 4) 28 out of 46 (60.9%) of the tech stocks in the Nasdaq 100 outperformed QQQ (AR 16.6%). 5) 7 out of 46 (15.2%) of the tech stocks in the Nasdaq 100 had ROIs greater than 1,000% (10-baggers).

If you had bought any tech stock in the Nasdaq 100 except for six (WDC, NTAP, QCOM, CSCO, EXPE, CTSH), your AR and ROI for that investment would have beaten the performance of both the S&P 500 and the DJIA. In fact, 87% of individual tech stocks in the Nasdaq 100 outperformed the S&P 500, including every stock in FANG and FAANGM, except for FB, which is not included because it hasn't been publicly traded for at least 10 years.

Let's look at the Nasdaq 100 for 20 years, from January 3, 2000, through January 2, 2020. Note, the Nasdaq 100 didn't contain the same companies as it does today (as of May 2020) since it gets re-balanced every December; however, to maintain a consistent list of companies so that we can make comparisons over time, we'll use the same list of companies as today. Also, over the past 20 years, two significant events occurred in the market worth noting. The first event was the dot-com crash. The tech-heavy Nasdaq plunged 77% from a peak of 5,048.62 in March 2000 to 1,139.90 in October 2002. It wasn't until 15 years later, on April 23, 2015, that the Nasdaq finally re-claimed its dot-com high by closing at 5,056.06. After the dot-com crash, the market also entered into a 30-month bear market. The S&P 500 lost 49.1% during this period. The second event was the subprime mortgage housing crash. By 2008, Bear Stearns and Lehman Bros. were in the midst of collapse, and the market was in full panic mode due to the subprime mortgage crisis. During this downturn, the S&P 500 declined a staggering 56.4%.

2010 investment	2020 value $	Gain $	AR %	ROI %
Alphabet (GOOG)	---	---	---	---
Baidu (BIDU)	---	---	---	---
Expedia Group (EXPE)	---	---	---	---
Fiserv (FISV)	---	---	---	---
MercadoLibre (MELI)	---	---	---	---
NetEase (NTES)	---	---	---	---
Netflix (NFLX)	---	---	---	---
Verisign (VRSN)	---	---	---	---
Cisco Systems (CSCO)	8,958	-1,042	-0.55	-10.42
Qualcomm (QCOM)	9,845	-155	-0.08	-1.55
Maxim Integrated Products (MXIM)	12,673	2,673	1.19	26.73
Intel (INTC)	13,932	3,932	1.67	39.32
Micron Technology (MU)	14,568	4,568	1.90	45.68
NetApp (NTAP)	14,751	4,751	1.96	47.51
Skyworks Solutions (SWKS)	19,346	9,346	3.35	93.46
Applied Materials (AMAT)	19,655	9,655	3.44	96.55
Xilinx (XLNX)	21,651	11,651	3.94	116.51
Citrix Systems (CTXS)	21,887	11,887	3.99	118.87
Nasdaq	22,009	12,009	4.02	120.09

S&P 500	22,387	12,387	4.11	123.87
Invesco QQQ Trust ETF (QQQ) Nasdaq 100	22,697	12,697	4.18	126.97
Texas Instruments (TXN)	25,137	15,137	4.72	151.37
DJIA	25,418	15,418	4.77	154.18
Analog Devices (ADI)	26,613	16,613	5.02	166.13
Microsoft (MSFT)	27,466	17,466	5.18	174.66
Check Point Software Technologies (CHKP)	30,759	20,759	5.78	207.59
Advanced Micro Devices (AMD)	31,670	21,670	5.93	216.70
Cadence Design Systems (CDNS)	32,362	22,362	6.05	223.62
KLA (KLAC)	33,593	23,593	6.25	235.93
Broadcom (AVGO)	35,141	25,141	6.49	251.41
Automatic Data Processing (ADP)	41,217	31,217	7.34	312.17
Electronic Arts (EA)	42,399	32,399	7.49	323.99
eBay (EBAY)	48,824	38,824	8.25	388.24
Microchip Technology (MCHP)	53,370	43,370	8.73	433.70
ASML Holding (ASML)	77,827	77,827	10.80	678.27
Lam Research (LRCX)	79,239	79,239	10.90	692.39
Intuit (INTU)	88,099	78,099	11.49	780.99
Take-Two Interactive Software (TTWO)	133,678	123,678	13.84	1,236.78
Western Digital (WDC)	166,609	156,609	15.10	1,566.09
Synopsys (SNPS)	171,015	161,015	15.25	1,610.15
Adobe (ADBE)	204,002	194,002	16.27	1,940.02
Amazon (AMZN)	210,679	200,679	16.46	2,006.79
Autodesk (ADSK)	224,833	214,833	16.84	2,148.33
Cerner (CERN)	288,664	278,664	18.31	2,786.64
Cognizant Technology Solutions (CTSH)	309,600	299,600	18.72	2,996.00
Booking Holdings (BKNG)	404,543	394,543	20.32	3,945.43
Activision (ATVI)	428,068	418,068	20.66	4,180.68
Nvidia (NVDA)	613,450	603,450	22.85	6,034.50
Apple (AAPL)	750,875	740,875	24.10	7,408.75
Ansys (ANSS)	937,120	927,120	25.48	9,271.20

The best-performing stock was ANSS (AR 25.5%, ROI 9,271%), followed by AAPL (AR 24.1%, ROI 7,409%) and NVDA (AR22.9%, ROI 6,035%). The worst-performing stocks were CSCO (AR -0.55% ROI -10.42%), QCOM (AR - 0.1%, ROI -1.65%), and MXIM (AR 1.2%, ROI 26.7%), which all underperformed the indices (S&P 500, DJIA, Nasdaq, Nasdaq 100 (QQQ)). Two stocks (QCOM, CSCO) produced negative ARs and ROIs over 20 years meaning an investor in these companies would have lost money. Some other highlights. 1) 28 out of 38 (73.7%) of the tech stocks in the Nasdaq 100 outperformed the S&P 500 (AR 4.1%), Nasdaq (AR 4%), and QQQ (AR 4.2%). 2) 27 out of 38 (71.1%) of the tech stocks in the Nasdaq 100 outperformed the

DJIA (AR 4.8%). 3) 16 out of the 38 (42.1%) of the tech stocks in the Nasdaq 100 outperformed BRK.A (AR 10.7%). 4) 13 out of 38 (34.2%) of the tech stocks in the Nasdaq 100 had ROIs greater than 1,000% (10-baggers).

The results above show the impact on some tech stocks of the dot-com bubble bursting in 2000, followed by the stock market entering into a 30-month bear market. CSCO and QCOM returned negative ARs and ROIs. QCOM effectively went nowhere in 20 years after rising more than 2,280% and being the best-performing stock in 1999. However, despite the dot-com and subprime mortgage housing crashes, 73.7% of tech stocks in the Nasdaq 100 still outperformed the S&P 500. My guess is very few people would have picked ANSS as the #1 best-performing tech stock from 2000-2020, turning $10,000 into $937,120 (AR 25.5%, ROI 9,271%) while beating out more well-known tech names like AAPL (#2), NVDA (#3), AMZN (#9), and MSFT (#26). Similarly, most wouldn't have picked ATVI to come in at #4 (AR 20.7%, ROI 4,181%. That's good enough to turn $10,000 into $428,068.

Let's look at the Nasdaq 100 for 30 years from January 2, 1990, through January 2, 2020. Again, the Nasdaq 100 didn't contain the same companies as it does today (as of May 2020), but we'll use the same list of companies as today so that comparisons can be made. This 30-year period also includes the aforementioned dot-com and subprime mortgage housing crashes. For some tech stocks, you'll see the difference in AR and ROI when purchasing near the highs (January 2000) two months before the dot-com bubble began to burst versus when there's no turmoil in the market (e.g., January 1990).

2010 investment	2020 value $	Gain $	AR %	ROI %
Activision (ATVI)	---	---	---	---
Alphabet (GOOG)	---	---	---	---
Amazon (AMZN)	---	---	---	---
Ansys (ANSS)	---	---	---	---
ASML Holding (ASML)	---	---	---	---
Baidu (BIDU)	---	---	---	---
Booking Holdings (BKNG)	---	---	---	---
Broadcom (AVGO)	---	---	---	---
Check Point Software Technologies (CHKP)	---	---	---	---
Cisco Systems (CSCO)	---	---	---	---
Citrix Systems (CTXS)	---	---	---	---

Cognizant Technology Solutions (CTSH)	---	---	---	---
eBay (EBAY)	---	---	---	---
Expedia Group (EXPE)	---	---	---	---
Fiserv (FISV)	---	---	---	---
Intuit (INTU)	---	---	---	---
MercadoLibre (MELI)	---	---	---	---
Microchip Technology (MCHP)	---	---	---	---
NetApp (NTAP)	---	---	---	---
NetEase (NTES)	---	---	---	---
Netflix (NFLX)	---	---	---	---
Nvidia (NVDA)	---	---	---	---
Qualcomm (QCOM)	---	---	---	---
Invesco QQQ Trust ETF (QQQ) Nasdaq 100	---	---	---	---
Skyworks Solutions (SWKS)	---	---	---	---
Synopsys (SNPS)	---	---	---	---
Take-Two Interactive Software (TTWO)	---	---	---	---
Verisign (VRSN)	---	---	---	---
Xilinx (XLNX)	21,651	11,651	2.61	116.51
S&P 500	90,574	80,574	7.62	805.74
DJIA	102,730	92,730	8.07	927.30
Advanced Micro Devices (AMD)	118,871	108,871	8.60	1,088.71
Cadence Design Systems (CDNS)	146,023	136,023	9.35	1,360.23
Western Digital (WDC)	152,238	142,238	9.50	1,422.38
Nasdaq	197,956	187,956	10.46	1,879.56
Automatic Data Processing (ADP)	344,728	334,728	12.53	3,347.28
Autodesk (ADSK)	373,406	363,406	12.83	3,634.06
Intel (INTC)	538,373	528,373	14.21	5,283.73
Texas Instruments (TXN)	546,656	536,656	14.27	5,366.56
Micron Technology (MU)	553,900	543,900	14.32	5,439.00
Analog Devices (ADI)	752,625	742,625	15.49	7,426.25
KLA (KLAC)	811,341	801,341	15.78	8,013.41
Maxim Integrated Products (MXIM)	1,200,529	1,190,529	17.30	11,905.29
Applied Materials (AMAT)	1,352,166	1,342,166	17.77	13,421.66
Lam Research (LRCX)	1,383,120	1,373,120	17.86	13,731.20
Electronic Arts (EA)	1,951,549	1,941,549	19.22	19,415.49
Apple (AAPL)	2,258,031	2,248,031	19.80	22,480.31
Microsoft (MSFT)	2,590,640	2,580,640	20.35	25,806.40
Adobe (ADBE)	2,633,302	2,623,302	20.42	26,233.02
Cerner (CERN)	3,681,000	3,671,000	21.77	36,710.00

The best-performing stock was CERN (AR 21.8%, ROI 36,710%), then ADBE (AR 20.4%, ROI 26,233%) and MSFT (AR 20.4%, ROI 25,806%). The worst-performing stock was XLNX (AR 2.6%, ROI 116.5%), which underperformed all indices (S&P 500, DJIA, Nasdaq). Note, QQQ didn't launch until March

1999 and hasn't existed for 30 years. Some other highlights. 1) 18 out of 19 (94.7%) of the tech stocks in the Nasdaq 100 outperformed the DJIA (AR 8.1%) and S&P 500 (AR 7.6%). 2) 15 out of 19 (79%) of the tech stocks in the Nasdaq 100 outperformed Nasdaq (AR 10.5%). 3) 10 out of the 19 (52.6%) of the tech stocks in the Nasdaq 100 outperformed BRK.A (AR 15%). 4) 18 out of 19 (94.7%) of the tech stocks in the Nasdaq 100 had ROIs greater than 1,000% (10-baggers), 8 out of 19 (42.1%) had ROIs over 10,000% (100-baggers), 4 out of 19 (21%) had ROIs over 20,000% (200-baggers).

Over 30-years and despite the dot-com and subprime mortgage housing crashes, tech stocks showcased their AR and ROI performance dominance over the S&P 500, with only XLNX underperforming the broader market index. In other words, every stock in the Nasdaq 100 except XLNX would have beaten the S&P 500. Like ANSS over 20-years, I'm also fairly confident very few people would have picked CERN as the best-performing tech stock from 1990-2020, beating both AAPL and MSFT. An investor buying $10,000 worth of CERN stock on January 2, 1990, would have acquired 50,000 shares for just $0.20/share. Thirty years later, on January 2, 2020, CERN was selling for $73.62/share, and $10,000 would have turned into $3,681,000 for an AR of 21.8% and ROI of 36,710%. A $10,000 investment each ($80,000 total) in the eight best-performing tech stocks (CERN, ADBE, MSFT, AAPL, EA, LRCX, AMAT, MXIM) would have resulted in a total combined value on January 2, 2020, of $17,050,337 (AR 19.6%, ROI 21,213%). Finally, it's also worth pointing out that over 30-years, slightly over half (52.6%) of the tech stocks in the Nasdaq 100 outperformed BRK.A (AR 15%)—if you pick the correct tech stocks you can outperform one of the world's greatest investors not just in the short term, but also over the long term.

Tech Stock Rankings in the Nasdaq 100

The tables below rank the tech stocks in the Nasdaq 100 based on their past AR and ROI performance by averaging their decade rankings over 20 and 30 years. Again, the Nasdaq 100 didn't contain the same companies 20 and 30 years ago as it does today (as of May 2020), but we'll use the same list to ensure consistency and enable a comparison to be made. The table below ranks all tech stocks in the Nasdaq 100 that have existed for at least 20 years (as of January 2020) and also includes key market indices (S&P 500, DJIA, Nasdaq, Nasdaq 100 (QQQ)). The ranking for each stock or index is based on the average of each stock's or index's ranking at 10 and 20 years (e.g., if a company was ranked #1 after 10 years and #3 after 20 years, then it's 20-year average rank would be #2, which is just the average of the two rankings).

Company	10-yr rank	20-yr rank	20-yr avg
Nvidia (NVDA)	4	3	3.5
Apple (AAPL)	8	2	5
Amazon (AMZN)	3	9	6
Booking Holdings (BKNG)	13	5	9
Take-Two Interactive Software (TTWO)	6	13	9.5
Adobe (ADBE)	10	10	10
Ansys (ANSS)	22	1	11.5
Broadcom (AVGO)	2	21	11.5
Synopsys (SNPS)	19	4	11.5
ASML Holding (ASML)	11	15	13
Autodesk (ADSK)	18	8	13
Intuit (INTU)	12	14	13
Activision (ATVI)	24	4	14
Cadence Design Systems (CDNS)	7	23	15
Lam Research (LRCX)	17	16	16.5
Electronic Arts (EA)	21	19	20
Cerner (CERN)	38	7	22.5
Microsoft (MSFT)	23	26	24.5
Advanced Micro Devices (AMD)	26	24	25
Automatic Data Processing (ADP)	30	20	25
KLA (KLAC)	28	22	25
Skyworks Solutions (SWKS)	14	36	25
Cognizant Technology Solutions (CTSH)	45	6	25
Microchip Technology (MCHP)	36	17	26.5
eBay (EBAY)	37	18	27.5
Texas Instruments (TXN)	27	29	28
Intel (INTC)	20	39	29.5
Invesco QQQ Trust ETF (QQQ) Nasdaq 100	29	30	29.5
Analog Devices (ADI)	35	27	31
Western Digital (WDC)	50	12	31
Micron Technology (MU)	25	38	31.5
Check Point Software Technologies (CHKP)	40	25	32.5
Nasdaq	34	32	33
Applied Materials (AMAT)	32	35	33.5
Xilinx (XLNX)	33	34	33.5

DJIA	44	28	36
Citrix Systems (CTXS)	41	33	37
S&P 500	43	31	37
Maxim Integrated Products (MXIM)	42	40	41
NetApp (NTAP)	49	37	43
Cisco Systems (CSCO)	47	41	44
Qualcomm (QCOM)	48	42	45

The stock with the highest average ranking over 20 years was NVDA, with an average ranking of 3.5, followed by AAPL with an average ranking of 5, and AMZN with an average ranking of 6. The stock with the lowest average ranking over 20 years was QCOM, with an average ranking of 45, which ranked lower than all four benchmark indices (S&P 500, DJIA, Nasdaq, Nasdaq 100 (QQQ)). Three other stocks (MXIM, NTAP, CSCO) also ranked lower than all indices. Some other highlights. 1) 34 out of 38 (89.5%) of the tech stocks in the Nasdaq 100 had a higher average ranking over 20 years than the S&P 500. 2) 33 out of 38 (86.8%) of the tech stocks in the Nasdaq 100 had a higher average ranking over 20 years than the DJIA. 3) 31 out of 38 (81.6%) of the tech stocks in the Nasdaq 100 had a higher average ranking over 20 years than the Nasdaq. 4) 27 out of 38 (71.1%) of the tech stocks in the Nasdaq 100 had a higher average ranking over 20 years than the Nasdaq 100 (QQQ).

The table below ranks the top five tech stocks based on their average ranking over 20 years (i.e., for stocks that have existed for 20 years, this ranking is an average of their two rankings at 10 and 20 years), after 10 years (i.e., for stocks that have existed for 10 years), and after 20 years (i.e., for stocks that have existed for 20 years). Note, NFLX went public in 2002 and MELI in 2007; hence, they haven't been around for 20 years (as of January 2020).

Ranking avg of 10, 20 yrs	Ranking 10 yrs	Ranking 20 yrs
1. NVDA	1. NFLX	1. ANSS
2. AAPL	2. AVGO	2. AAPL
3. AMZN	3. AMZN	3. NVDA
4. BKNG	4. NVDA	4. ATVI
5. TTWO	5. MELI	5. BKNG

The table below ranks all tech stocks in the Nasdaq 100 that have existed for at least 30 years (as of January 2020). It also includes key indices (S&P 500,

DJIA, Nasdaq). The ranking for each stock or index is based on the average rank at 10, 20, and 30 years (e.g., if a company was ranked #1 after 10 years, #3 after 20 years, and #5 after 30 years, then it's 30-year average rank would be #3, which is just the average of the three rankings).

Company	10-yr rank	20-yr rank	30-yr rank	30-yr avg
Apple (AAPL)	8	2	4	4.67
Adobe (ADBE)	10	10	2	7.33
Lam Research (LRCX)	17	16	6	13
Autodesk (ADSK)	18	8	14	13.33
Electronic Arts (EA)	21	19	5	15
Cerner (CERN)	38	7	1	15.33
Cadence Design Systems (CDNS)	7	23	18	16
Microsoft (MSFT)	23	26	3	17.33
KLA (KLAC)	28	22	9	19.67
Automatic Data Processing (ADP)	30	20	15	21.67
Micron Technology (MU)	25	38	4	22.33
Texas Instruments (TXN)	27	29	12	22.67
Advanced Micro Devices (AMD)	26	24	19	23
Analog Devices (ADI)	35	27	10	24
Intel (INTC)	20	39	13	24
Applied Materials (AMAT)	32	35	7	24.67
Western Digital (WDC)	50	12	17	26.33
Nasdaq	34	32	16	27.33
Xilinx (XLNX)	33	34	22	29.67
Maxim Integrated Products (MXIM)	42	40	8	30
DJIA	44	28	20	30.67
S&P 500	43	31	21	31.67

The stock with the highest average ranking over 30 years was AAPL, with an average ranking of 4.7, followed by ADBE with an average ranking of 7.3, and LRCX with an average ranking of 13. The stock with the lowest average ranking over 30 years was MXIM, with an average ranking of 30, which ranked lower than Nasdaq along with XLNX, but above the DJIA and S&P 500. Some other highlights. 1) 19 out of 19 (100%) of the tech stocks in the Nasdaq 100 had a higher average ranking over 30 years than the DJIA and S&P 500. 2) 17 out of 19 (89.5%) of the tech stocks in the Nasdaq 100 had a higher average ranking over 30 years than the Nasdaq.

The table below ranks the top five tech stocks based on their average ranking over 30 years (i.e., for stocks that have existed for 30 years, this ranking is an average of their three rankings at 10, 20, and 30 years), after 10 years (i.e., for stocks that have existed for 10 years), after 20 years (i.e., for stocks that have existed for 20 years), and after 30 years (i.e., for stocks that have existed for 30 years). ANSS went public in 1996, NVDA 1999, ATVI 1993, BKNG 1999 (i.e., they haven't been around for 30 years (as of January 2020)).

Ranking avg of 10, 20, 30 yrs	Ranking 10 yrs	Ranking 20 yrs	Ranking 30 yrs
1. AAPL	1. NFLX	1. ANSS	1. CERN
2. ADBE	2. AVGO	2. AAPL	2. ADBE
3. LCRX	3. AMZN	3. NVDA	3. MSFT
4. ADSK	4. NVDA	4. ATVI	4. AAPL
5. EA	5. MELI	5. BKNG	5. EA

Over the past 30 years, compared to the S&P 500, DJIA, Nasdaq, and BRK.A, the data in the tables above clearly show how well individual tech stocks have performed over long periods of time if you just bought and held. And this is true if you focused only on well-known tech stocks (e.g., AAPL, MSFT) as well as software companies (e.g., ADBE) or just video game companies (e.g., EA).

Out of the 46 tech stocks listed in the Nasdaq 100 as of May 2020, I've invested in 18 (39.1%) and have traded options in 13 (28.3%). The 18 tech stocks I've bought and sold stock include AAPL, AMD, AMZN, ATVI, AVGO, BKNG, CSCO, EA, FB, GOOG, INTC, INTU, MELI, MSFT, NFLX, NVDA, QCOM, and XLNX. The 12 tech stocks I've traded options include AAPL, AMD, AMZN, ATVI, AVGO, EA, FB, MELI, MSFT, NVDA, NXPI, and QCOM. FYI, there are several stocks that I've been interested in and watching for some time, but didn't pull the trigger earlier when I should have, and may in the future if a good entry point presents itself. These include ADBE, ANSS, Etsy (ETSY), Okta (OKTA), PayPal Holdings (PYPL), Sea Limited (SE), SNPS, Square (SQ), TTWO.

Top 10 Most Valuable Global Public Companies (2000, 2010, 2020)

The table below lists the most valuable public companies based on market cap as of the end of March 31, 2000. 3 out of 10 (30%) were tech companies (#2 CSCO, #5 MSFT, #9 INTC), and all were from the US. CSCO was building out the Internet while MSFT and INTC continued their Wintel dominance.

Rank	Company	Country	Market cap $ billion
1	General Electric (GE)	US	477.406
2	Cisco Systems (CSCO)	US	304.699
3	Exxon Mobile (XOM)	US	286.367
4	Pfizer (PFE)	US	263.996
5	Microsoft (MSFT)	US	258.436
6	Walmart (WMT)	US	250.955
7	Citigroup (C)	US	250.143
8	Vodafone (VOD)	UK	227.175
9	Intel (INTC)	US	227.408
10	Royal Dutch Shell (RDS.B)	Netherlands	206.34

Source: *Wikipedia*.

The table below lists the top 10 most valuable global public companies based on market cap 10 years later as of the end of March 31, 2010. 2 out of 10 (20%) were tech companies (#3 MSFT, #5 AAPL), and both were from the US. In 2010, China made its appearance on the world stage with three companies (#1 PTR, #4 IDCBY, #10 CHL) making the top 10. Two oil companies made the top 10 in 2000 (#3 XOM, #10 RDS.B) and 2010 (#1 PTR, #2 XOM). The decline of GE is also clearly evident.

Rank	Company	Country	Market cap $ billion
1	PetroChina (PTR)	China	329.2597
2	Exxon Mobile (XOM)	US	316.2308
3	Microsoft (MSFT)	US	256.8647
4	ICBC (IDCBY)	China	246.4198
5	Apple (AAPL)	US	213.0967
6	BHP Billiton (BBL)	Australia, UK	209.9351
7	Walmart (WMT)	US	209.0007
8	Berkshire Hathaway (BRK.A)	US	200.6205
9	General Electric (GE)	US	192.2462
10	China Mobile (CHL)	China	192.9986

Source: *Wikipedia*.

The table below lists the 10 most valuable global public companies based on market cap 10 years later as of the end of July 1, 2020. Within 10 years, the ascendancy of tech is on full display. 7 out of 10 (70%) were tech companies. Five companies were from the US (#1 AAPL, #2 MSFT, #3 AMZN, #4 GOOG,

#5 FB) and two were Chinese (#6 TCEHY, #7 BABA). The top three (#1 AAPL, #2 MSFT, #3 AMZN) were all trillion-dollar companies. Per Siblis Research, the top five had a combined market cap of $6.2 trillion, which represented 17.5% of the entire US market cap of $35.5 trillion as of June 30, 2020. Combined, the top seven, which were all tech, had a market cap of $7.4 trillion, which represented 85.9% of the top 10. MSFT has been in the top 10 for over three decades and has successfully transitioned from packaged software to the Internet to cloud and services while continuing to climb in the rankings from #5 (2000) to #3 (2010) to #2 (2020).

Rank	Company	Country	Market cap $ billion
1	Apple (AAPL)	US	1,576
2	Microsoft (MSFT)	US	1,551
3	Amazon (AMZN)	US	1,433
4	Alphabet (Google)(GOOG)	US	979.7
5	Facebook (FB)	US	675.69
6	Tencent (TCEHY)	China	620.92
7	Alibaba (BABA)	China	579.74
8	Berkshire Hathaway (BRK.A)	US	432.74
9	Visa (V)	US	412.71
10	Johnson & Johnson (JNJ)	US	370.59

Source: *Wikipedia.*

Top 10 Most Valuable Global Brands (2010, 2020)

Per *Forbes*, the table below lists the top 10 most valuable global brands in 2010.

Rank	Company	Country	Brand value $ billion
1	Apple (AAPL)	US	57.4
2	Microsoft (MSFT)	US	56.6
3	Coca-Cola (KO)	US	55.4
4	IBM (IBM)	US	43.0
5	Alphabet/Google (GOOG)	US	39.7
6	McDonald's (MCD)	US	35.9
7	General Electric (GE)	US	33.7
8	Marlboro (MO)	US	29.1
9	Intel (INTC)	US	28.6
10	Nokia (NOK)	Finland	27.4

Source: *Forbes.*

6 out of 10 (60%) were tech companies (#1 AAPL, #2 MSFT, #4 IBM, #5 GOOG, #9 INTC, #10 NOK) and all were from the US except NOK (Finland). The table below lists the top 10 most valuable brands in the world a decade later in 2020.

Rank	Company	Country	Brand value $ billion
1	Apple (AAPL)	US	241.2
2	Alphabet/Google (GOOG)	US	207.5
3	Microsoft (MSFT)	US	162.9
4	Amazon (AMZN)	US	135.4
5	Facebook (FB)	US	70.3
6	Coca-Cola (KO)	US	64.4
7	Disney (DIS)	US	61.3
8	Samsung (KRX:005930)	South Korea	50.4
9	Louis Vuitton (LVMUY)	France	47.2
10	McDonald's (MCD)	US	46.1

Source: *Forbes*.

The top five most valuable brands in the world were tech (#1 AAPL, #2 GOOG, #3 MSFT, #4 AMZN, #5 FB), and 6 out of 10 (60%) were tech (#1 AAPL, #2 GOOG, #3 MSFT, #4 AMZN, #5 FB, #8 KRX:005930) and all were from the US except Samsung (South Korea). US tech companies had a total combined brand value of $817.3 billion, representing 75.2% of the total combined top 10 brand value of $1,086.7 billion. By 2020, tech ruled the top 10 most valuable global companies by market capitalization and brand value.

Platform Economics

AMZN, AAPL, FB, GOOG, and MSFT are examples of tech companies that have leveraged platform economics. They have successfully created ubiquitous platforms and enabled flourishing 3rd party ecosystems. By providing the tools and support to enable 3rd parties to build businesses on top of their platforms, these companies have extended their platforms well beyond their original capabilities. And once platform dominance is achieved, it becomes nearly impossible for other competitors to catch up. MSFT and AAPL created empires with applications and games on top of Windows and iOS, while GOOG and FB did the same with advertising on top of search and social media. In 2019, per Marketplace Pulse, AMZN had more than 2.5

million third parties actively selling in its marketplace. AMZN also reported that small and medium-sized businesses (SMBs) were selling, on average, over 4,000 items a minute. ScrapeHero reported that as of April 2019, AMZN offered a total of 119,928,851 products to its customers. Reid Hoffman, co-founder of LinkedIn, and currently a venture capital partner at Greylock Partners, said, "I believe the secret to massive scale is compressed in three words: 'Be a platform.'"

Network Effects

Platform economics creates a virtuous cycle. More users mean more third parties mean more users—the cycle repeats. Hence, successful platforms are also the main beneficiary of network effects—the phenomenon that the value of a platform to everyone on the platform increases as the number of users increases. FB is a great example of a tech company that clearly benefits from network effects. As the number of FB users grows, FB can charge higher advertising fees and advertisers are willing to pay more because they now have a larger potential target audience with more granular data for more targeted ads with increased efficacy. A larger installed base of FB users also means customers can utilize FB features (timeline, comments, notifications, photo/video sharing, messaging, etc.) to find and connect with more friends, families, and businesses faster and more efficiently. Note, the incremental cost for FB to add a new user onto its platform is much smaller than the overall value the new user brings to the platform. Network effects can work for platform companies of any size; however, it's magnified several times for large platform companies resulting in even stronger competitive moats. This makes it even more difficult for new upstarts to displace the incumbents.

The Law of Accelerating Returns

The law of accelerating returns proposes that while most things advance linearly, technological change does not. Coined by futurist Ray Kurzweil in his 1999 book *The Age of Spiritual Machines*, Kurzweil says the technological change in computers, genetics, nanotechnology, robotics, and AI (artificial intelligence) increases exponentially. In other words, it accelerates over time. Kurzweil believes humans are linear by nature, whereas technology is exponential. He further predicted in his 2005 book *The Singularity Is Near*, at some point, the singularity will occur, and machine intelligence will become infinitely more powerful than all human intelligence combined—sounds like Skynet! The wheel was not invented until around 3500 BC; however, according to David Anthony, professor of anthropology at Hartwick College, the stroke of genius and real technological breakthrough did not occur until after 4000 BC with the invention of the wheel-and-axle. It took 500 years for humans to comprehend what was possible with the wheel. Fast forward to the late 1990s, and contrast the time it took to invent the wheel-and-axle, with the roughly 30 years it took for humans to grasp the significance of computers and then later create the Internet. Or consider that on January 9, 2007, while the tech world was attending CES in Las Vegas, 400 miles away in San Francisco at MacWorld, Steve Jobs introduced the iPhone, a smartphone that replaced physical buttons with a touch screen as the primary user interface. Apple then launched the App Store with 500 apps and games on July 10, 2008. Nine years later, in June 2017, Apple reported that 180 billion apps had been downloaded from the app store. By November 1, 2018, Apple announced that cumulatively 2.2 billion iPhones had been sold worldwide. Today in 2020, just 13 years after the introduction of the iPhone, nearly everyone carries an iOS or Android smartphone that has more than 100,000x the processing power of the computer that landed American astronauts on the moon in 1969. In 1971, Intel launched the 4004, the world's first commercially-produced single-chip microprocessor. It took another 12 years before Motorola launched the DynaTAC 8000x in 1983. It was the world's first commercially available handheld cellular phone. The DynaTAC 8000x weighed two pounds and cost $3,995. Contemplate for just a moment the reaction a NASA engineer would have if given a 5G iPhone 12 Pro Max in 1969 to play around with. I think Kurzweil's law of accelerating returns is extremely relevant for tech stock investors. Companies that create innovative new products, services, and platforms advance the tech industry forward at rapid speeds and reap the benefits such as rising stock prices and startup valuations. If you can identify and invest in the right stocks at the start of these technological advancements, you have a fantastic opportunity to build your wealth.

Technology Is A Leading Indicator

Tech stocks are now a leading indicator and not just for the US economy, but also the stock market in general. Reed Hastings, a co-founder of NFLX, said, "Stone Age. Bronze Age. Iron Age. We define entire epics of humanity by the technology they use." Characterized by a shift from industrial production to one based on information as a commodity and computerization, the Information Age is still going strong today. The invention of every modern device in the Information Age has involved some form of technology, which has permeated nearly every aspect of modern society and life. Someday, the Information Age will be supplanted. What will be next? The AI Age, Genetics Age, Space Colonization Age? No matter what comes next, I think technology innovation will be leading the charge. Satya Nadella, CEO of MSFT, said, "Our industry does not respect tradition—it only respects innovation." Innovation will more than likely be commercialized and brought to market by existing publicly-traded tech companies or entirely new private startups yet to emerge. If you've committed to investing in the stock market and you're comfortable investing in individual stocks, tech companies offer some of the best—if not the best—ARs and ROIs. I think this is true not only today but will also be true for the foreseeable future.

4

CHECKPOINT ONE

The stock market is filled with individuals who know the
price of everything, but the value of nothing.

—*Philip Fisher*

THIS IS THE first of three checkpoints that review key takeaways as we progress through the book. While past performance is never a guarantee for future results, I think the almost frictionless nature of stock trading and the ROI that the market has returned over the years make stocks a great equalizer for building wealth. For the average investor, in the long run, I believe investing in the stock market is a superior investment choice over real estate and starting a small business.

Over the past 10 years, the AR for the S&P 500 was 11.1%, and for Nasdaq 100 it was 16.6%. Over the past 90 years, the S&P 500 has produced an AR of 9.8%. At a minimum, you should be invested in the market by buying fractional shares (if you can't afford full shares) of a low-cost S&P 500 ETF like Vanguard's VOO with whatever amount you feel comfortable investing. Doing nothing more than investing in a passively-managed ETF like VOO or a more tech-heavy Nasdaq 100 ETF like Invesco's QQQ, over the past 15 years, you would have beaten the vast majority of professional actively-managed large-cap, large-cap growth, small-cap, and small-cap growth fund managers.

As of Q1 2020, 7 of the top 10 most commonly held stocks by hedge funds were tech stocks (#1 AMZN, #2 MSFT, #3 FB, #4 BABA, #5 GOOGL, #7 GOOG,

#10 AAPL) representing an overall combined total dollar amount of long positions of $204.5 billion. The top five stocks based on total dollar amount were: #1 AAPL ($74.8 billion), #2 AMZN ($32.9 billion), #3 MSFT ($31.4 billion), #4 FB ($19.6 billion), #5 BABA $19.4 billion.

Technology has become ubiquitous and has permeated into nearly every aspect of modern society and life. Once upon a time, the US economy was powered by oil. Today, the engine that drives the broader economy and the stock market is technology. Innovation-driven tech companies dominate not only the top 10 most valuable global companies by market capitalization and brand. I also like technology because of platform economics, network effects, and the law of accelerating returns. The industry-leading dominance of tech companies such as AAPL, AMZN, FB, GOOG, and MSFT have all benefitted from these effects.

If you're comfortable buying and holding individual stocks for 10 or more years, I think it's tough to beat the AR and ROI of high-quality tech growth stocks. Being invested in the right companies for the long haul far outweighs sitting on the sidelines waiting to buy at precisely the best time.

Part Three

LONG AND LEVERAGED

The worst form of inequality is to try to make unequal things equal.

—Aristotle

5

OPTIONS REFRESHER

The first step is to establish that something is possible;
then probability will occur.

—*Elon Musk*

A S MENTIONED IN the Introduction, I assume you have a basic understanding of options and how to buy and sell simple calls and puts. If you don't know what options are and how to complete simple buy and sell orders, I recommend that you first learn the basics. It's not because this book is difficult to understand. It's because, without a basic understanding, options may seem more complicated than they really are. For example, if you know nothing about Brazilian Jiu-Jitsu and I said pull closed guard, hip bump sweep to mount, and finish with an Americana, you would probably have no idea what I'm talking about when what I just described is pretty basic that any white belt with a few months of training would understand. Jargon is what makes it confusing and foreign-sounding. It can be similar to options when you first read about them or hear others talk about them. Note, this chapter provides a short review of options and is not intended to be comprehensive.

Options Become More Mainstream

The CBOE (Chicago Board Options Exchange) first introduced options in the US in 1973. They are known as derivatives because their value is derived from another underlying asset. Options contracts can be written for all types of assets, from stocks to bonds to currencies to commodities to futures. For stock options, every option is tied to an underlying stock. In addition to individual stocks like AAPL and MSFT, you can also trade options for stock indices like the S&P 500 (e.g., VOO) and Russell 2000 (e.g., iShares Russell 2000 ETF (IWM)), and the CBOE VIX (volatility index). Unlike stocks where there's a limited number of shares available for each publicly-traded stock, there's no limitation for options. As long as an option buyer and seller can be matched, market makers will make a market (including taking the other side of a trade if required) and happily charge both sides commissions for the trade.

Options trading has become very popular within the past 20 years. While stock trading volume has doubled since 2000, according to the OCC (Options Clearing Corporation), stock options trading volume has grown more than 6x to around 4.4 billion options contracts in 2019. Furthermore, per estimates by investment bank Sandler O'Neill + Partners, at brokerages TD Ameritrade and E*TRADE, options have risen from less than 10% of daily trades 10 years ago to 30% or more in recent years. On September 11, 2020, in the *Wall Street Journal* article titled "Are You an Investor or a Gambler," Jason Goepfert of Sundial Capital Research estimated that in late August 2020, a record 62% (the long-term average is 34%) of option premiums initiating bets on rising stock prices came from people buying no more than 10 contracts. Goepfert stated that in one week alone ending September 4, 2020, small traders, those buying no more than 10 contracts, paid $11.5 billion in options premiums, an all-time high and 9x last year's average. To put this figure in perspective, consider that for the entire year of 2019, Americans spent $91 billion on lottery tickets per the North American Association of State and Provincial Lotteries.

In the age of commission-free trading for stocks and ETFs, in addition to selling their stock order flow, one lucrative area that brokerages can still make money from their customers is by charging commissions for every options contract traded. Hence, many brokerages have stepped up their stock options trading advertising and marketing targeted at the average retail investor offering free options trading seminars, online education, and increased support by telephone.

Options Trading Approval

To trade options, you need to be approved by your brokerage. By answering a few simple questions in an online questionnaire and waiting 1-2 business days for review by your brokerage, it's not very difficult to get approved for Level 1 or Level 2 options trading. While I don't use Robinhood for trading, I was curious how fast it would take to get approved via their mobile app. It was surprisingly quick. Robinhood approved me for Level 3 within minutes. You'll need to be approved for Level 2 to trade straight calls and puts.

You Can Make Money Trading Options

In a *Wall Street Journal* article dated January 6, 2020, and titled "Investors Play the Stock-Options Lottery," Henry Schwartz, president of TradeAlert, an options data provider, estimated that up to two-thirds of retail option accounts lose money. There's a common myth that 80-90% of options expire with no value. The truth is that the majority of options contracts are actually closed before expiration. According to 2015 OCC statistics: 7% of options are assigned (i.e., exercised), 21.7% of options expire with no value, and 71.3% of options positions are closed before expiration. There are risks involved with trading options, but if you don't know what you're doing, that's true with almost anything in life. However, if used properly, options are powerful financial instruments that can help you achieve your financial goals. After making over 90 options trades in the 3.75 years since retiring, my winning (i.e., profitable) call options trade percentage is 89%. Hence, I believe you can make money trading options, and you don't need to be a professional either.

Option Quote Break Down

Listed below is what your brokerage will typically display when you look at an actual option quote. Note, there is no standard format that all brokerages must follow, so what you see may vary slightly from what is shown below. In this case, we're interested in buying one AAPL Jun17'22 $180 strike call. Note, the data shown below is from the market close on April 30, 2020.

APPLE INC COM	JUN-22 $180.00 CALL	AAPL Jun 17 '22 $180 Call			
Last Price	Today's Change	Bid (Size)	Ask (Size)	Day's Range	Volume
119.84	+2.05 (+1.74%)	120.00 x1	124.10 x1	119.84 – 119.84	1

Open	119.84	Last Day of Trading	6/17/2022
Previous Close	117.79	Expiration Date	6/17/2022
Open Interest	370	Exercise Style	American
Intrinsic Value	113.80	Options Multiplier	100
Time Premium	8.25		

UNDERLYING QUOTE

| Symbol | Last Price | Today's Change | Bid (Size) | Ask (Size) |
| AAPL | 293.80 | +6.07 (+2.11%) | 286.10 x2,000 | 286.30 x800 |

| Day's Range | Volume |
| 288.35 – 294.53 | 45,765,968 |

OPTION ANALYSIS

| Days to Expiration | 778 |

Delta	0.8552	Gamma	0.0011	Theta	-0.0307
Vega	1.0728	Rho	2.4618		
Theoretical Value	135.76	Implied Volatility	32.23%*		

* Based on midpoint of bid/ask

Let's break down the above option quote into four parts.

Option Quote Break Down – Part 1

APPLE INC COM	JUN-22 $180.00 CALL		AAPL Jun 17 '22 $180 Call	
Last Price	Today's Change	Bid (Size)	Ask (Size)	Day's Range	Volume
119.84	+2.05 (+1.74%)	120.00 x1	124.10 x1	119.84 – 119.84	1

Underlying Stock: AAPL

The underlying stock is Apple, and its ticker symbol is AAPL.

Strike Price: $180

The strike price (aka exercise price) is the cost that an options contract can be purchased or sold when exercised. For call options, the strike price is the price at which the stock can be purchased by the owner of the options contract. For put options, the strike price is the price at which the owner of the options contract can sell the stock for.

Option Type: Call

There are two types of stock options. Calls and puts. A call gives the buyer the right, but not the obligation, to buy a stock at a certain price (known as the strike price) by a certain date (known as the expiration date). A put gives the buyer the right, but not the obligation, to sell stock at a certain price by a certain date. A call buyer thinks the stock price is going up, whereas a put buyer thinks it's going down. If you're an option seller, the premium is the amount you receive for selling the option. If you're an option buyer, the premium is the price you pay for the option. In this case, we're buying a call.

Last Price: $119.84

The last price is the price at which the most recent trade occurred for a specific option contract. In this case, the AAPL Jun17'22 $180 strike call last traded for $119.84/contract (i.e., $11,984 per contract).

Today's Change: +2.05 (+1.74%)

The amount the option price has increased or decreased. In this case, the AAPL Jun17'22 $180 strike call was up 2.05 points or 1.74%.

Bid (Size): $120.00 x1

The bid price is the highest-priced buy order that is currently available. It's the price a buyer is willing to buy the option contract for. In this case, a buyer has placed an order to buy 1 AAPL Jun17'22 $180 strike call option for $120/contract (i.e., $12,000 per contract).

Ask (Size): $124.10 x1

Ask price is the lowest priced sell order that is currently available. It's the price a seller is willing to sell the option contract for. In this case, a seller is willing to sell 1 AAPL Jun17'22 $180 strike call option for $124.10/contract (i.e., $12,410 per contract). The difference between the bid and ask ($4.10 in this case) is known as the spread. In general, the smaller the spread, the better the liquidity of the option. The difference between the bid and ask is the market makers' compensation for making a market for a particular option. In this case, it would be $410 per contract or about 3.3% of the ask if a buyer bought at the ask. Note, brokerages may display price quotes that are delayed by 15-20 minutes. If it's important to have real-time price quotes, you'll need to contact your brokerage to enable this feature in your trading platform. Alternatively, you can also get real-time quotes directly from the Nasdaq web site. Nasdaq provides three levels of quotes. 1) Level 1, which includes the highest bid and lowest ask prices. 2) Level 2, which shows all public quotes of market makers and recently executed orders. 3) Level 3, which is used by market makers for trade execution. Note, the three quote levels described above shouldn't be confused with being approved for different levels of options trading by your brokerage.

Day's Range: $119.84 – $119.84

The day's range represents the range of prices that the option contract has traded for during the day. In this case, the AAPL Jun17'22 $180 strike call sold no lower or higher than $119.84/contract (i.e., $11,984 per contract). Note, usually the lowest and highest prices are not equal, but for this call, only one contract was sold; hence, why they're the same price.

Volume: 1

Volume is the number of options contracts traded during the day. This figure starts at 0 at the start of each trading day and increases based on the number of options contracts being closed and opened throughout the day. In this case, this is the volume for the AAPL Jun17'22 $180 strike call. Note, only one contract was traded. This suggests there was very little interest in this particular option contract for this trading day. When the volume exceeds the open interest (OI) of an option on a given day, this often suggests that trading in that option was unusually high, and new money is likely being put to work.

Option Quote Break Down – Part 2

Open	119.84	Last Day of Trading	6/17/2022
Previous Close	117.79	Expiration Date	6/17/2022
Open Interest	370	Exercise Style	American
Intrinsic Value	113.80	Options Multiplier	100
Time Premium	8.25		

Open: $119.84

The price the options contract first trades at. In this case, the AAPL Jun17'22 $180 strike call opened at $119.84/contract (i.e., $11,984 per contract).

Previous Close: $117.79

The prior trading day's final price for the options contract. In this case, the AAPL Jun 17'22 $180 strike call previously closed at $117.79/contract (i.e., $11,779 per contract).

Open Interest: 370

OI is the number of options contracts available at the end of a trading day not closed, exercised, or expired. OI starts at 0 when the options contract first begins trading and increases with each opening transaction. OI decreases with each closing transaction up until expiration. Note, OI isn't updated during a trading day. It's updated the next morning, which means you have to wait until the next day to see if there was any impact on the OI from the previous day's activity. OI also doesn't tell you whether or not the options were bought or sold. In this case, there were 370 AAPL Jun17'22 $180 strike call option contracts available at the end of trading on April 30, 2020. When options have a large OI, that means there are a lot of buyers and sellers. Comparing OI day to day can highlight whether there's been an unusual spike in options activity. For example, if OI for an option expiring on Friday was 1,000 at the close of trading on Wednesday, and Thursday morning OI spiked to 10,000, this suggests traders are expecting the underlying stock to make a big move. Finally, as previously mentioned, when the volume is greater than the OI for a particular option, this means new money is likely being put to work in the option (i.e., new positions have been opened).

Intrinsic Value: $113.80

The current price of an option is the premium. An option buyer pays the premium to an option seller and receives the rights granted by the option. Time value is also known as extrinsic value.

Option Price or Premium = Intrinsic Value + Time Value

Option Price or Premium = Intrinsic Value + Extrinsic Value

Breakeven (BE) is the theoretical price the underlying stock needs to reach for you to breakeven on an options trade.

BE for Call Option = Call Option Strike Price + Premium

BE for Put Option = Put Option Strike Price – Premium

The value of an option if it were exercised today is known as intrinsic value. Intrinsic value is the amount by which the strike price of an option is in-the-money (ITM) compared to the underlying stock's current price. A call option is ITM if the underlying stock price is greater than the strike price. It is said to be ITM because the call owner has the right to buy the stock at a price (i.e., strike price) lower than if the stock were purchased in the market. A put option is ITM if the underlying stock price is less than the strike price. It is said to be ITM because the put owner has the right to sell the stock at a price (i.e., strike price) greater than if the stock were sold in the market.

Intrinsic Value for a call = Underlying Stock Price – Option Strike Price
Intrinsic Value for a put = Option Strike Price – Underlying Stock Price

In this case, the strike price is $180, and the underlying stock closed at $293.80 on April 30, 2020; hence, the intrinsic value for the AAPL Jun17'22 $180 strike call is $113.80 (293.80 – 180). For a call option owner, if the strike price is greater than the underlying stock price, then the option is not profitable and is out-of-the-money (OOTM). For a put option owner, if the underlying stock price is greater than the strike price, then the option is OOTM. When an option is deep OOTM, this means the strike price is several strikes away in the option chain from the underlying stock price. For calls and puts, if the strike price is equal to the underlying stock's price, then the option is at-the-money (ATM). ATM and OOTM options have 0 intrinsic value (i.e., a buyer would never exercise an option for a loss). Only ITM options have intrinsic value. Note, an option's intrinsic value doesn't lose any value due to the passage of time and is only affected by moves in the underlying stock.

Time Premium: $8.25

Time premium (aka time value or extrinsic value) is the amount by which an option price exceeds its intrinsic value.

Extrinsic Value = Option Price – Intrinsic Value

All options that have not expired have extrinsic value. ATM and OOTM options only have extrinsic value. As time passes, time premium will decay, and the option will lose value. This decay will accelerate dramatically in the last 30 days as expiration gets nearer, and on expiration, time premium will become 0 since there's no time left on the contract. Implied volatility (IV) will also affect extrinsic value. In this case, since the intrinsic value for the AAPL

Jun17'22 $180 strike call is $113.80 and the extrinsic value is $8.25, this suggests the contract price is $122.05 (113.80 + 8.25). Note, in this case, the midpoint of the bid ($120) and ask ($124.1) turns out to be $122.05.

Last Day of Trading: 6/17/2022

The last day of trading is the expiration date. In this case, the AAPL Jun17'22 $180 strike call's last day of trading, and its expiration is June 17, 2022.

Expiration Date: 6/17/2022

The expiration date is the last day the option contract can be exercised. In this case, June 17, 2022. Before expiration, the owner of the AAPL Jun17'22 $180 strike call has two choices: 1) exercise the option (acquire the underlying stock by buying them at the strike price), 2) close the position for a profit or loss.

Exercise Style: American

American options can be exercised on any trading day on or before expiration. European options can only be exercised on expiration. For this book, when we talk about options, we're referring to American options.

Options Multiplier: 100

The multiplier is unique to options and helps standardize the trading/pricing of options while making the options market more efficient. A 100 multiplier means 1 option contract controls 100 shares of the underlying stock, and an option price is multiplied by 100 to get the actual value. E.g., the AAPL Jun17'22 $180 strike call's last price was $119.84/contract, which means that the premium the buyer paid was $11,984 (119.84 * 100) less any brokerage fees. For standard US stocks, ETFs, and index option contracts, the multiplier is 100. If you're new to options, don't make the mistake of thinking the quoted option price is the actual price. E.g., buying 10 contracts at $119.84/contract costs $119,840 less any fees, not $1,198.40 less any fees—a big difference!

Option Quote Break Down – Part 3

UNDERLYING QUOTE

Symbol	Last Price	Today's Change	Bid (Size)	Ask (Size)
AAPL	293.80	+6.07 (+2.11%)	286.10 x2,000	286.30 x800

Day's Range	Volume
288.35 – 294.53	45,765,968

Last Price: $293.80

This is the last price that one share of the underlying stock was traded for. In this case, one share of AAPL stock last traded for $293.80/share.

Today's Change: +6.07 (+2.11%)

The amount the underlying stock price has increased or decreased. In this case, AAPL stock traded up 6.07 points or 2.11% from the last trade.

Bid (Size): $286.10 x2,000

The bid is the maximum price a buyer is willing to pay for a share of the underlying stock (investors are offering to buy 2,000 shares for $286.10/share).

Ask (Size): $286.30 x800

The ask is the minimum price a seller is willing to accept for a share of the underlying stock (investors are offering to sell 800 shares for $286.30/share). The difference between bid and ask ($0.20 in this case) is the spread and is the market makers' compensation for making a market for a particular stock. In general, the smaller the spread, the better the liquidity of the underlying stock.

Day's Range: $288.35 – $294.53

The day's range represents the range of prices that the underlying stock has traded for throughout the day. In this case, AAPL stock sold for no lower than $288.35/share or higher than $294.53/share.

Volume: 45,765,968

The number of shares of the underlying stock that have been traded.

Option Quote Break Down – Part 4

OPTION ANALYSIS
Days to Expiration   778

Delta	0.8552	Gamma	0.0011	Theta	-0.0307
Vega	1.0728	Rho	2.4618		
Theoretical Value		135.76	Implied Volatility		32.23%*

* Based on midpoint of bid/ask

Days to Expiration: 778

The number of days before the option contract expires. In this case, the AAPL Jun17'22 $180 strike call has 778 days (more than two years) before it expires. This call is a LEAPS due to the expiration being so far in the future.

Delta: 0.8552

Delta is how much an option price is expected to change for a $1 change in the underlying stock. In this case, if AAPL stock increases by $1, then the price of the AAPL Jun17'22 $180 strike call should increase by $0.8552 (1 * 0.8552).

Gamma: 0.0011

Gamma is how much the delta will change with a $1 change in the underlying stock. In this case, if AAPL stock increases by $1, then the delta for the AAPL Jun17'22 $180 strike call should increase by 0.0011 from 0.8552 to 0.8563 (0.8552 + 0.0011).

Theta: -0.0307

Theta is the dollar amount an option price will lose each day until expiration, assuming all other variables remain constant. Theta is negative for long positions and positive for short positions. In this case, each day, the AAPL Jun17'22 $180 strike call price should decrease by $0.0307, assuming everything else remains constant.

Vega: 1.0728

Vega is the dollar amount an option price will change in response to a 1% change in the IV of the underlying stock. In this case, if the IV of AAPL stock changes by 1%, the price of the AAPL Jun17'22 $180 strike call should change by $1.0728.

Rho: 2.4618

Rho measures the rate an option price changes relative to a 1% change in the risk-free interest rate (typically the 90-day US Treasury bill rate). In this case, if the risk-free interest rate changes by 1%, then the price of the AAPL Jun17'22 $180 strike call should change by $2.4618.

Theoretical Value: $135.76

The theoretical or fair value of an option is calculated using a mathematical option pricing model like Black-Scholes. Black-Scholes takes into account IV, underlying stock price, strike price, and time to expiration. The theoretical value will fluctuate over time because the inputs also change over time.

Implied Volatility: 32.23%

IV is an estimate of the future value of an option. It indicates how volatile the market expects the underlying stock to be. Volatility is driven by uncertainty.

IV is an input factor for option pricing models like Black-Scholes when calculating an option price.

Placing an Options Order

Once you decide which option you want to trade, you'll need to place a limit order with your brokerage. An opening transaction gets you into the market, whereas a closing transaction gets you out. There are four choices when placing an options order: buy-to-open (BTO), sell-to-close (STC), sell-to-open (STO), buy-to-close (BTC).

BTO

When you initiate a long position by buying a call or put option, you BTO. If your order is successfully executed, you pay the premium to the seller of the option and obtain the rights provided by the option contract. This transaction will result in a debit to your account. To close a BTO trade, you need to STC the call or put that you purchased. FYI, instead of saying, buy 1 AAPL Jun17'22 $180 strike call, I'll often say BTO 1 AAPL Jun17'22 $180C.

STC

When you close or sell an existing long position in a call or put option that you had previously purchased, you STC. A closing STC trade offsets an opening BTO trade. FYI, instead of saying close 1 AAPL Jun17'22 $180 call, I'll often say STC 1 AAPL Jun17'22 $180C.

STO

When you initiate a short position by selling a call or put option, you STO. This is commonly referred to as options writing. If your order is successfully executed and since you're the seller of the option, you'll collect the premium from the option buyer in exchange for the rights provided by the option contract that the buyer receives. This transaction will result in a credit to your account. For example, to sell (i.e., write) covered calls, you STO.

BTC

When you close an existing short position in a call or put option that you had previously sold, you BTC. A closing BTC trade offsets an opening STO trade. For example, to close a covered call before expiration, you BTC.

As I've previously mentioned, while I did try some of the more advanced options strategies such as straddles, strangles, spreads, and collars, I ultimately concluded that the easiest and most efficient way for me to consistently make money in the stock market was simply being long and leveraged by using LEAPS. And all that is needed to trade LEAPS are paired BTO-STC trades. In other words, after an opening BTO order is placed, and if the underlying stock moves in the direction predicted, at some point before expiration when the option is ITM (preferably deep-in-the-money (DITM)), a closing STC order will need to be executed to close out the option so you can lock in profit. Note, in general, an option is said to be DITM if it's ITM by more than $10; hence, a DITM call has a strike that's at least $10 less than the underlying stock price, and a DITM put has a strike that's at least $10 higher than the underlying stock price. Note, depending on the underlying stock price, DITM can be a lot more than $10 less than the current underlying stock price. E.g., it would be $100s less for stocks like AMZN, SHOP, or MELI.

Options Are Not Financial Weapons of Mass Destruction

To the uninitiated, options often get a bad rap as being financially dangerous akin to gambling. Many often cite what Warren Buffet wrote in his 2002 annual letter to Berkshire Hathaway shareholders when he said, "Derivatives are financial weapons of mass destruction." However, Russell Rhoads, director of program development for the CBOE's Options Institute, maintains this quote has been used out of context. Rhoads says that Buffet was commenting about Berkshire Hathaway's acquisition of General Re, where they had inherited a book of OTC (over-the-counter) derivatives. Buffet was expressing his frustration with trying to figure out what to do with these derivatives. On the page in the Berkshire Hathaway annual shareholder letter before calling derivatives financial weapons of mass destruction, Buffet stated that Berkshire Hathaway uses derivatives to execute some investment strategies. One of those strategies was between 2004-2007 when Buffet made $4.9 billion selling puts in a bullish bet before the financial crisis that later appeared in 2007-2008 due to the subprime mortgage housing crash. Options can be risky and dangerous if you don't know what you're doing. However,

I don't believe they're inherently risky—real risk comes with the actions an options trader takes or does not take. Patience, flexibility, discipline, common sense, and maintaining the right temperament are all essential to making the right decisions at the right time when buying and selling stocks and options.

Mark Cuban's Famous Costless Collar Trade

Let's look at an example of how options are not always risky and dangerous if you know what you're doing. This was a famous options trade that occurred over 20 years ago. The trade was executed by Mark Cuban or via someone on his behalf. Today, Cuban is most well known for being the billionaire owner of the NBA Dallas Mavericks basketball team and appearing regularly on the long-running ABC TV show *Shark Tank*.

Broadcast.com was originally founded as an Internet radio company in 1989 as Cameron Audio Networks. It was later renamed AudioNet.com in 1995 when Cuban took control of the company. In May 1998, AudioNet.com was renamed Broadcast.com. At this point, the company was streaming audio and video for radio, TV, and sports. On July 18, 1998, the company went public on Nasdaq, soaring 250% on its first trading day. After the IPO, Broadcast.com's market cap was $1 billion, and Cuban was worth $300 million. On April 1, 1999, YHOO acquired Broadcast.com for $5.7 billion in stock. Cuban received 14.6 million shares of YHOO worth around $1.4 billion; however, one of the acquisition restrictions was that Cuban wasn't allowed to sell the stock for three years.

Since Cuban's entire net worth was tied up in just one stock and he couldn't sell any stock for three years, he decided to protect his paper wealth by using a costless collar. A collar is used when you own stock and want to protect it from any downside risk. Here is what Cuban did. 1) he bought 146,000 puts at the $85 strike price with a 3-year expiration. 2) he sold 146,000 calls at the $205 strike with a 3-year expiration. The premium he paid for the puts was offset by the premium he received for selling the calls. This means he effectively paid nothing for this options trade except for any commissions the investment bank and/or brokerage firms charged; however, it's very likely that given the size of this trade, Cuban also negotiated any commissions to be included as part of the premiums. At this time, YHOO was $95/share; hence, if YHOO fell by 10.5% to $85/share or lower, he could sell all of his stock for $85/share, and he would still end up with $1.24 billion. If YHOO popped and surged past $205/share, then he would be forced to sell his shares and would end up with $2.99 billion. So, what actually happened? After the costless collar trade was made, nine months later, in January 2000, YHOO rocketed up to $237/share. This was later followed by the dot-com crash, with YHOO plummeting to just $13/share by late 2002. Cuban's costless collar trade enabled him to sell his shares for $85/share and protect the vast majority of his $1.4 billion in YHOO over the course of three years despite the dot-com bubble bursting. For what Cuban wanted to achieve, this was a classic textbook example of how options were used to manage downside risk. It wasn't a speculative, risky option bet like many investors often perceive options trading to be. And again, because this was a costless collar, the options trade didn't cost Cuban anything to put into play—a pretty savvy trade to protect his paper wealth.

Making Money Before Theoretical BE

When you trade options, an interesting phenomenon involving BE can sometimes occur. The value of an option can become profitable even though the theoretical BE for the trade has not been met yet. Here is an example. Before the market opened on January 23, 2019, Kerrisdale Capital issued a note saying QCOM was "teetering on the brink of disaster" and that they were shorting the stock and the price could get cut in half if QCOM loses the FTC (Federal Trade Commission) antitrust trial. At the time, QCOM was defending itself against an antitrust case filed by the FTC. I thought QCOM was facing a lot of market uncertainty, and there was a good chance the stock could decline further in the near term. So, I made an educated speculative options trade and paid $1.14/contract (i.e., $1,140 per contract), and BTO some short-term QCOM Mar1'19 $50 strike puts; hence, BE for this trade was $48.86 (50 − 1.14). By market close on January 23, 2019, QCOM was selling for $51.77/share. Two days later, when the market opened on January 25, 2020, QCOM was selling for around $50.93/share, and the puts had a bid price of

$1.54/contract and an ask of $2.08/contract. If I STC the puts for $1.81/contract (midpoint of the bid and ask), my trade would have produced an ROI of 58.8% in just two days. This was even though the theoretical BE ($48.86/share) for this put trade had not been achieved yet. I.e., QCOM was currently trading at $50.93/share and needed to decline another 4.06% or 2.07 points to reach BE for this put options trade. I ended up holding the puts a little longer and then sold them on January 29, 2020, for $2.05/contract (i.e., $2,050 per contract) for an ROI of 79.8%. Note, when I sold the puts, the BE ($48.86/share) for this put options trade still had not been reached yet (the daily low for the stock on January 29, 2020, was $49.34/share, and the stock closed at $49.40/share).

Tesla

To wrap up this chapter, I wanted to tell you a story about TSLA that's only possible with options. The story consists of three parts—The Rise, The Fall, and The Gamblers. I like stories like these because they dramatically illustrate the extremes of what can happen with options. However, remember when used properly, options can help achieve a variety of financial goals, whether protecting a substantial stock position like what Mark Cuban did with YHOO, generating income in a flat market by selling covered calls, getting paid to acquire stock at a lower price by selling puts, or doing what I like to do— amplifying potential ROI by buying DITM LEAPS calls as a stock replacement (we'll get to this shortly).

The Rise

On Friday, January 31, 2020, TSLA opened at $640/share and closed at $650.66/share. On February 3, 2020, in a note, Argus Research raised its target price from $556/share to $808/share, a 45.3% price increase, and TSLA gapped up and opened for trading at $673.65/share. TSLA soared 19.9%, the biggest single-day jump for the stock since May 2013 when it reported its first quarterly profit and increased 24.4%. Daily trading volume was 3x higher (47.2 million shares versus 15.7 million shares) than the prior trading day on January 31, 2020, and TSLA closed at $780/share while its market cap reached $140.6 billion. The chart below shows TSLA daily volume for the time period discussed in this story.

Date	Num of shares traded Million
Fri 1/31/20	15.72
Mon 2/3/20	47.23
Tue 2/4/20	60.94
Wed 2/5/20	48.42
Thu 2/6/20	39.88
Fri 2/7/20	17.06

TSLA's nearly 20% move up on February 3, 2020, triggered a short squeeze with *MarketWatch* reporting shorts losing $2.5 billion on a single day. Then, just after noon ET on February 4, 2020, the stock hit $916.34/share, up another 17.5% from the close the day before. In less than two days, TSLA increased 40.9% from market close on January 31, 2020. TSLA would later hit an intraday high of $969/share (up 49% from market close on January 31, 2020). The daily volume on February 4, 2020, was 60.9 million shares. If you were holding the Feb7'20 $800 strike call, it was selling for $0.25/contract at market open on February 3, 2020. When TSLA hit $916.34/share, the Feb7'20 $800 strike was selling for $103.41/contract. This means the Feb7'20 $800 strike call, which you only paid $25 (0.25 * 100) per contract, was now worth, wait for it, $10,341 (103.41 * 100) for an ROI of 41,264% in less than two days. I didn't track what the intraday premium high was for the Feb7'20 $800 strike call, but at one point, I did see it trading for $127.63/contract, which would be a 50,952% ROI. Add some zeroes and the dollar gains sound too good to be true. For example, if you bought 10 Feb7'20 $800 strike calls for $250 (10 * 0.25 * 100) those calls would now be worth $127,630 (10 * 127.63 * 100). If you had bought 100 Feb7'20 $800 strike calls for $2,500 (100 * 0.25 * 100) those calls would now be worth $1,276,300 (100 * 127.63 * 100), and while highly unlikely, but not impossible, given the OI was 10,438 and volume was 5,340, if you had bought 1,000 Feb7'20 $800 strike calls for $25,000 (1,000 * 0.25 * 100) those calls would now be worth $12,763,000 (1,000 * 127.63 * 100).

The Fall

As fast as options premium can rocket up, they can also just as quickly disappear in a flash. Returning to the TSLA Feb7'20 $800 strike calls, by February 5, 2020, once the epic short squeeze on the underlying stock and likely heavy profit-taking started to subside, COVID-19 news took center stage with TSLA announcing car deliveries in February in China would be delayed. By market close the next day, TSLA was selling for $748.95/share, and the Feb7'20 $800 strike call sold for $3.96/contract, which was still up 1,484% from $0.25/contract at market open on February 3, 2020, but nowhere close to when it sold for $127.63/contract just two days earlier on February 4, 2020. The hammer finally dropped on February 7, 2020, when the Feb7'20 $800 strike call expired. By market close, TSLA was selling for $748.05/share (i.e., below the $800 strike price). The last price someone unloaded their Feb7'20 $800 strike calls on February 7, 2020, was for $0.02/contract, which was down 92% from what it sold for ($0.25/contract) at the start of the week. Hence, in just one week, if you held the Feb7'20 $800 strike calls all the way to expiration, you would have seen the value of one call option go from $25 on Monday to over $12,763 on Tuesday to $2 on Friday. The Feb7'20 $800 strike call volume on February 5, 2020, was 22,780 contracts, and on February 6, 2020, it was 36,572, and on February 7, 2020, it was 31,636. To me, that looks like there were a lot of traders unloading and selling the Feb7'20 $800 strike calls after the stock price of TSLA started to turn down on February 5, 2020. Professional options traders, and possibly even a few savvy retailer traders, probably made money playing both sides by buying weekly calls on the way up and buying weekly puts on the way down.

The Gamblers

As wild as the TSLA stock and call options price action was between February 3-7, 2020, what is even crazier is that some traders were actually buying the Feb7'20 $1,550 and $1,880 strike calls hoping to hit the jackpot. The table below shows the stock price for TSLA between February 3-7, 2020.

Date	Open	Low	High	Close
2/3/20	673.69	673.52	786.14	780.00
2/4/20	882.96	833.88	968.99	887.06
2/5/20	823.26	704.11	845.98	734.70
2/6/20	699.92	687.00	795.83	748.96
2/7/20	730.55	730.00	769.75	748.07

Even if you ignore the call premium when calculating BE, which results in an even higher BE, this means someone holding the $1,550 strike or the $1,880 strike would need TSLA to go up 60% or 94%, respectively, just a day before expiration (February 7, 2020) from the intraday $968.99/share high on February 6, 2020, to BE. I will make educated speculative OOTM option trades, but these seem like totally foolish bets to me. At market close on February 7, 2020, OI on the $1,550 strike call was 13,179 contracts, and OI on the $1,880 strike call was 5,593 contracts. On February 5, 2020, when the $1,880 strike call first appeared, OI was 0, and volume was 6,294 contracts. On that same day, for the $1,550 strike call, OI was 10,442, and the volume was 10,207. Market makers were busy profiting by selling hope (aka the $1,550 strike and $1,880 strike calls) to retail investors. Someone was speculating big time by buying the $1,550 strike and $1,880 strike calls, which all ended up expiring worthless by February 7, 2020. Hopefully, these option gamblers learned their lesson the hard way. Sadly, you still see way OOTM options being sold by market makers and purchased by retail traders today. Charlie Munger, vice chairman of Berkshire Hathaway, said, "Success is not about being a genius, it's about not being stupid too often."

The Greeks and Then LEAPS

LEAPS are my very favorite type of options to trade. As mentioned, they are nothing more than standard options with expiration dates far in the future. However, the long expiration dates provide you with a cushion for your predicted moves and are exactly what makes them special, and the reason why I like to trade them. We will briefly cover the Greeks in the next chapter and then move onto LEAPS.

6

THE GREEKS

All the math you need in the stock market you get in the fourth grade.
—Peter Lynch

O PTIONS TRADERS REFER to a set of terms to describe the relationship between the underlying stock price and an option price. These terms include delta, theta, vega, gamma, rho, and are collectively known as the Greeks. The Greeks are not used to calculate the price of an option. They're theoretical numbers that are constantly changing and are based on complex mathematical option pricing models like Black-Scholes. Options traders use the Greeks to analyze and estimate how an option price might react to changes in the stock market and the underlying stock. When you look up an option quote, your brokerage will also display the current Greek values associated with that option. We'll briefly cover each of the Greeks, and then at the end of this chapter, I'll tell you how I use them in the real world when trading options.

Delta

Delta tells you how much an option price is expected to change for a $1 change in the underlying stock. Delta doesn't stay constant, and its value will change as the price of the underlying stock changes. While not mathematically accurate, some like to think of delta as the estimated probability an option expires ITM. Note, however, this doesn't necessarily mean the option will be profitable. Profitability will depend on the price the option was purchased and later sold at. A call option will have a positive delta with a value between 0 and 1, while a put option will have a negative delta with a value between -1 and 0. ATM calls typically have a delta of 0.5 or -0.5 for puts, DITM calls generally have deltas of 0.8 and higher or -0.8 or lower for puts, and far OOTM calls generally have deltas of 0.2 or less or -0.2 or higher for puts. The delta for 1 share of stock is always 1. Hence, if you own 100 shares of a stock, you have 100 deltas. The total delta of a position is equal to the number of contracts times the delta (e.g., if you own 20 contracts and delta is 0.85, then the total delta is 17 (20 * 0.85)). For every $1 the underlying stock increases, the total position value will increase using the following calculation.

$1 multiplied by 100 multiplied by the total delta of your position

For example, if the underlying stock goes up $3.33 and the total delta of your position is 17, then the total value of your position will increase to $5,661 (3.33 * 100 * 17)). Here is another example. An option with a delta of 0.7466 suggests that if the underlying stock moves up $1, the option price will move up $0.7466, and there's a 74.7% chance (0.7466 * 100) the option expires ITM. If a stock is selling for $241.41/share and the option is selling for $43.55/contract, then if the stock increases to $245.03/share, the option price will increase to $46.25/contract (((245.03 – 241.41) * 0.7466) + 43.55). It's important to note that while the stock price increased 1.5%, the option price increased 6.2% or slightly over 4x the percentage gain in the underlying stock price. This is the leverage options provide when the underlying stock moves in the predicted direction.

The table below shows the number of days to expiration, delta, and the cost per contract (aka premium) at the ask for three AAPL calls with three different expiration dates for the $245 strike, which is near where AAPL closed ($241.41/share) on April 4, 2020. There's one short-term weekly call (indicated by the "w") and two LEAPS.

Option	# days to expiration	Delta	Premium $
AAPL Apr9'20w $245 strike call	5	0.5116	5.10

AAPL Jun18'21 $245 strike call	441	0.7050	30.60
AAPL Jan21'22 $245 strike call	658	0.7466	43.55

The higher the delta, the higher the premium; however, this also means that in the case of DITM LEAPS calls, you have more downside protection if the underlying stock falls and more time for the underlying stock to turnaround and recover. DITM options are sensitive to changes in the underlying stock price whereas, OOTM options will be much less sensitive. When an option is DITM with a delta nearing or at 1, the option price will move practically dollar for dollar with the underlying stock. In other words, for every $1 increase for a call or decrease for a put in the underlying stock, the value of the option will increase by $100 for a call or decrease by $100 for a put because each standard stock option contract represents 100 shares of stock. If the underlying stock price has moved up significantly or down for a put, and if I own DITM LEAPS calls with a delta near or at 1 and the options were purchased over a year ago (meaning long-term capital gains when the options are sold if they're in a taxable account), I've hit the ROI sweet spot for options.

Theta

Theta (aka time decay or theta burn) is the dollar amount the price of an option will lose each day until the expiration date. Theta is a measurement of time decay, and hence, it's always a negative number for long positions and always positive for short positions. In other words, theta shows how sensitive the price of an option is to time. For example, an option with a theta of -0.0797 means the option will lose $0.0797/day assuming all other variables remain constant, which is highly unlikely. If an option is selling for $43.55/contract today, then tomorrow it'll be worth $43.47/contract (43.55 – 0.0797), and the following day it'll be selling for $43.39/contract (43.47 – 0.0797), and so on until the option reaches its expiration. Note, decay is not linear. For LEAPS, theta decay is small in the first few months. However, as the expiration date nears, theta increases for ATM options and decrease for ITM and OOTM options. For options that are far OOTM, theta is also high because the option is made up of mostly extrinsic value. Conversely, for DITM options, theta is low because the option is made up of mostly intrinsic value.

The table below shows the theta for the same three AAPL calls at the $245 strike previously mentioned above.

Option	# days to expiration	Theta	Premium $
AAPL Apr9'20w $245 strike call	5	-1.0406	5.10
AAPL Jun18'21 $245 strike call	441	-0.1049	30.60
AAPL Jan21'22 $245 strike call	658	-0.0797	43.55

Recall, the value of an option is made up of intrinsic value and extrinsic value. Only extrinsic value is affected by time decay. Intrinsic value is not. Hence, long options have negative theta, and for these options to be profitable, the intrinsic value needs to outweigh the loss of extrinsic value.

Vega

Vega is the dollar amount the price of an option will change in response to a 1% change in the IV of the underlying stock. Vega is not a Greek letter because they don't have the letter V/v in their alphabet. It was chosen because it sounded like a Greek letter and would fit with delta, theta, gamma, and rho. Options are not priced based upon the underlying stock's historical volatility. They're priced according to where the market thinks the underlying stock's volatility will be over the option's life. This is known as IV. IV indicates how much movement the market is expecting in the future. Increased volatility makes option prices more expensive, while decreased volatility lowers option prices. Options with high IV suggest that investors in the underlying stock expect a big move in one direction or the other. Seasoned options traders will often look for options with high IV to sell premium because it captures decay.

It's important to understand that volatility is not directional. If volatility is high, it just means the stock is fluctuating a lot around some long-term average. A stock with low volatility means that traders have a higher degree of confidence where they think the stock price will be in the future. In contrast, a stock with high volatility means that traders have low confidence and expect the stock price to move around a lot. A higher volatility means greater price swings in the underlying stock price, which in turn means there's a higher chance an option will be profitable by expiration.

If you know the current underlying stock price and the IV, you can estimate the expected range for the stock price before the options expiration date by using the following formula (note, 256 is the number of trading days in a calendar year and sqrt means square root):

Expected Change = (Stock Price x IV x sqrt(# Days to Expiration)) / sqrt(256)

E.g., if AAPL is currently trading at $241.41/share and the IV for the AAPL Apr9'20w $245 strike call is 53.46%, and there are five days before expiration, the expected change is $18.04.

$$\text{Expected Change} = (241.41 \times 0.5436 \times \text{sqrt}(5)) / 16 = \$18.04$$

Hence, the expected price per share range of AAPL over the next five days should be between $223.37 (241.41 − 18.04) and $259.45 (241.41 + 18.04). With an IV of 53.46%, you can see that traders are expecting AAPL to move around quite a bit in the next five days (in this example, AAPL stock may move up or down by 7.47%); however, remember, this is just a snapshot in time because both the stock price and IV will also be constantly changing.

An option price is driven by supply and demand for various strike prices and by the market expectation of the IV of the underlying stock. Vega is highest for ATM options and decreases the further the option moves away from the ATM strike price. ITM and OOTM options are not affected as much by volatility. DITM LEAPS calls with delta nearing or at 1 will have almost no vega. Note, however, since it's difficult to estimate volatility 2-3 years away, depending on the strike price, LEAPS may have high vega because they can be sensitive to changes in IV.

The table below shows the vega and IV for the same three AAPL call options at the $245 strike previously mentioned above.

Option	# days to expiration	Vega	IV	Premium $
AAPL Apr9'20w $245 strike call	5	0.1248	53.46%	5.10
AAPL Jun18'21 $245 strike call	441	0.9178	34.27%	30.60
AAPL Jan21'22 $245 strike call	658	1.0396	33.23%	43.55

Future-dated options will have positive vega, while options expiring shortly will have negative vega. Vega also decreases as an option nears expiration. Because it's difficult to price expected volatility 2-3 years in the future, the bid-ask spread for LEAPS is often wide. If the bid-ask spread is less than the vega, then the option is offering a competitive spread. Note, however, this says nothing about whether or not the option trade will be profitable. The table below shows the vega and bid-ask spreads for the same three AAPL calls at the $245 strike previously mentioned above.

Option	# days to expiration	Vega	Bid-ask spread	Premium $
AAPL Apr9'20w $245 strike call	5	0.1248	0.15	5.10
AAPL Jun18'21 $245 strike call	441	0.9178	2.40	30.60
AAPL Jan21'22 $245 strike call	658	1.0396	3.85	43.55

In general, the best time to purchase LEAPS is after the underlying stock has had a big decline in price; however, this also means IV has increased, which makes LEAPS more expensive. Volatility usually increases the value of LEAPS. This is because of the higher probability that the underlying stock will move in the predicted direction by the expiration date. This generates more intrinsic value. The higher an option price is above your strike price, the more ITM the option becomes, and the greater its intrinsic value. Recall, the value of an option, if exercised today, is known as intrinsic value. Extrinsic value is solely determined by volatility.

Gamma

Gamma measures how much delta will change with a $1 change in the underlying stock. In other words, if you think of delta as speed, then gamma is acceleration. For example, an option with a gamma of 0.0010 and a delta of 0.7466 means that if the underlying stock moves up $1, then the option's new delta will be 0.7476 (0.7466 + 0.0010). Hence, gamma will manufacture call deltas if a stock increases and put deltas if the stock decreases. Options with high gamma react the most to changes in the underlying stock price. When an option is near-the-money or ATM, gamma is highest. Options that are DITM or far OOTM have small gamma. As delta nears 1 or -1, gamma decreases and approaches 0 the deeper ITM or further OOTM the option is. Gamma for a stock is 0 because its delta is always 1. The table below shows the gamma for the same three AAPL calls at the $245 strike previously mentioned above.

Option	# days to expiration	Gamma	Premium $
AAPL Apr9'20w $245 strike call	5	0.0130	5.10
AAPL Jun18'21 $245 strike call	441	0.0013	30.60
AAPL Jan21'22 $245 strike call	658	0.0010	43.55

The more time an option has before it expires, the smaller the gamma. Conversely, the closer to expiration that an option contract is, the higher the gamma. Hence, since LEAPS have expirations 2-3 years in the future, LEAPS will have small gamma. All long options have positive gamma, while all short options have negative gamma.

Rho

Rho is one of the least-used Greeks. It measures the rate that the price of an option changes relative to a 1% change in the risk-free interest rate (typically the 90-day US Treasury bill rate). Calls generally rise in price as interest rates increase while puts decrease. Hence, calls have positive rho and puts have negative rho. For example, for a call priced at $43.55 with a rho of 1.0876, if the risk-free interest rate increased from 1% to 2%, the call value will increase from $43.55 to $44.64 (43.55 + 1.0876). For a put priced at $31.50 with a rho of -2.2842, if the risk-free interest rate decreased from 2% to 1%, the value of the put will decrease from $31.50 to $29.22 (31.5 + (-2.2842)). The table below shows the rho for the same three AAPL calls at the $245 strike previously mentioned above.

Option	# days to expiration	Rho	Premium $
AAPL Apr9'20w $245 strike call	5	0.0173	5.10
AAPL Jun18'21 $245 strike call	441	0.8446	30.60
AAPL Jan21'22 $245 strike call	658	1.0876	43.55

Rho is higher for ITM options, and it decreases as options go OOTM. The options that are the most sensitive to changes in interest rates are those that are either ATM or those with the longest amount of time before expiration. Hence, LEAPS have larger rho than shorter-term options. Note, the change in an option's price based on a 1% change in interest rates is usually small. Furthermore, interest rates don't normally change by 1% during the life of an option. However, because LEAPS don't expire for 2-3 years, interest rates have a higher chance of changing, especially if a macro-level event occurs like when the US Fed cut short-term interest rates to near 0 on March 15, 2020, to combat the economic damage caused by the COVID-19 pandemic.

What I Really Think About the Greeks

Professional traders understand that an option price is driven by market expectation. More specifically, it's driven by the IV of an underlying stock. Furthermore, they also understand that the two most important factors that affect an option price are the underlying stock price and the amount of time before an option expires. Hence, for professional options traders who use the Greeks to decide which options to buy or sell, they are important. However, average retail investors will often find the Greeks technical, intimidating, and confusing, and they are not quite sure how to use them. An all too familiar refrain heard from retail investors is that trading options sound too complex. Combine this with the commonly-accepted belief among non-options traders that options are super risky, and it is easy to see why so many never trade options. When I first started trading options, I used to study the Greeks to try and figure out how to use them to help me decide which options to buy. What I quickly learned is that based on how I trade options, the only Greek of any real interest to me is delta. I trade primarily based on the long-term direction I think a stock is moving and not on its volatility. Therefore, I ignore the other Greeks (theta, vega, gamma, rho) because they provide no assistance in my decision-making process determining which option to buy. Certainly, understanding what the Greeks are is not a bad thing. However, from a practical options trading standpoint, I do not use them. Bottom line, if you trade options the way I do, there is no need to understand the Greeks.

7

LEAPS

If you can dream, you can do it. Always remember that this whole thing was started by a mouse.

—*Walt Disney*

MICHAEL JORDAN ONCE said, "I mean we all fly. Once you leave the ground, you fly. Some people fly longer than others." Despite the elaborate name, Long-term Equity Anticipation Securities, LEAPS are nothing more than options with expiration dates up to 2-3 years in the future. LEAPS enable you to fly longer due to their longer expiration dates. They behave like any other options, and they're not without risk—remember, LEAPS are still options. To be successful with options, you not only have to be correct about the direction of a stock's movement, but you also have to be right about the timing and size of the movement.

LEAPS Enable Long-Term Options Investors

Options were first introduced in the US by the CBOE in 1973. They were initially created with expiration dates of three, six, and nine months. The CBOE introduced weekly options in October 2005, and in October 1990, they introduced LEAPS. What I like about LEAPS is they provide you with the time to be a long-term investor and not just a short-term trader. Unlike short-term options, LEAPS enable you to make long-term leveraged bets on the future movement of stocks, indices, or ETFs.

LEAPS are available for about 2,500 stocks and 20 indices such as the S&P 500 (SPY, VOO), Nasdaq 100 (QQQ), Russell 2000 (IWM), and Gold (GLD). LEAPS are also available for many ETFs such as the Technology Select Sector SPDR ETF (XLK), iShares PHLX Semiconductor ETF (SOXX), and the First Trust Cloud Computing ETF (SKYY). Stock LEAPS enable you to take a bullish or bearish position on an individual company. Index and ETF LEAPS allow you to do the same on the entire market, a specific S&P 500 sector such as information technology, or a particular industry like semiconductors.

LEAPS Are Not Popular

A *Barron's* article titled "How to Make Sense of the Stock Market in the Ages of Algorithmic Trading" published on April 25, 2019, stated, "On any given day, the options market represents about 55% of the stock market's average daily volume." This trend is even more significant in some stocks such as AMZN, AAPL, Boeing (BA), BKNG, FB, GOOG, TSLA, and Wynn Resorts (WYNN). In these stocks, options volumes often exceed daily stock volumes. *Barron's* article states, "At a minimum, it means investors are increasingly using options to trade and control stocks—not the other way around, as has been true for decades." According to the OIC (Options Industry Council), LEAPS only account for 10% of all options listed for trading. Hence, they're still not that popular versus shorter-term options, which still make up the vast majority of options traded in the market today.

When stock options are first listed for trading, LEAPS are usually not immediately available because they're difficult to price due to expirations much further out than short-term options. In particular, interest rates are hard to predict in the future. Therefore, before LEAPS are listed for trading, exchanges need to ensure sufficient market demand exists, and market makers or specialists are prepared to price and trade LEAPS once they're listed. Consequently, LEAPS are not always available for every stock, even if shorter-term options are available. If a stock's price closes below the lowest listed strike price or above the highest listed strike price before expiration, market makers or specialists will introduce new option strike prices. Hence, the range of option strike prices available for any particular stock may change over time.

How I Classify LEAPS

Historically, options with expirations of more than nine months in the future were considered LEAPS. However, to align with the timing of long-term capital gains from a tax perspective, I personally consider LEAPS to be options with expirations of more than a year in the future. For example, if we looked at the options chain for AAPL on March 25, 2020, we would have seen the following expiration dates for call options ("w" indicates a weekly option). Hence, based on how I classify LEAPS, 4 out of 17 are AAPL LEAPS (Jun18'21, Sep17'21, Jan21'22, Jun17'22) as of March 25, 2020.

<u>2020</u>
Mar27'20w, Apr3'20w, Apr9'20w, Apr17'20, Apr24'20w, May1'20w, May15'20w, Jun19'20, Jul17'20, Sep18'20, Oct16'20, Dec18'20

<u>2021</u>
Jan15'21, Jun18'21, Sep17'21

<u>2022</u>
Jan21'22, Jun17'22

LEAPS Provide More Cushion

Just like with stocks, LEAPS allow you to go long or go short. I go long significantly more often than I go short because I'm intuitively better at predicting up movements than down. Expiration dates 2-3 years out provide you with not only more time for the underlying stock to move in the predicted direction but also more time to build up some cushion, assuming the stock moves in your predicted direction, to absorb any unforeseen events that may impact the stock price later in the future. However, due to the longer time until expiration, LEAPS costs more than shorter-term options because they have a greater probability of being ITM over time. Like any other call option, at or before expiration, you can decide to sell LEAPS to lock in any realized gains or exercise them at the strike price and take (i.e., acquire) the shares.

LEAPS Can Be Used in Advanced Option Strategies

If desired, LEAPS can also be used in more advanced options strategies like standard options. This includes strategies such as the following. 1) calendar spread (buy a long call and sell a short call at the same strike price with different expiration dates). 2) bull call spread (buy a long call at a lower strike price and sell a short call at a higher strike price with the same expiration dates). 3) collar (you own stock and buy a put at a lower strike price and sell a call at a higher strike price with the same expiration dates). 4) diagonal ratio spread (this is a diagonal spread where you buy and sell an unequal number of put options and call options, often done in a 2:1 ratio, which means two short options to one long option). In general, spreads limit risk and improve the probability of making money on an options trade, but in exchange for less risk, the upside is also limited.

Options Trading Levels

There are four options trading levels available via your brokerage. You apply by answering a short questionnaire requesting approval to trade options at each specific level. Each subsequent level enables access to additional options strategies and is based on the experience and resources available to the trader. The table below shows the options trading strategies that are available for each level once approved. Level 2 approval is required to trade LEAPS (i.e., calls and puts). Level 4 approval is required to trade naked calls and puts. Selling naked calls (i.e., you don't own shares of the underlying stock when assigned) is one reason why options are often given a bad name and are perceived as being financially dangerous. Brokerages will also require you to have a margin account to sell naked calls.

Options trading level	Options trading strategies allowed
Level 1	Covered calls, cash-secured puts
Level 2	Calls, puts, straddles, strangles
Level 3	Spreads
Level 4	Naked calls, naked puts

If you don't know what you're doing, you can suffer huge losses trading on margin, and in the worst-case scenario, quickly wipe out your portfolio. I'm approved for Level 3 and have made spread trades over the years. I have not requested Level 4 approval and highly doubt I'll ever trade naked calls and puts. I also never trade on margin.

Dividends and Voting Rights

Similar to short-term options, if you buy LEAPS instead of shares of stock, you'll forfeit shareholder benefits such as dividends and voting rights. As an investor, these benefits may or may not be important to you. For me, they're not that important. First, other than some large-cap tech stocks like AAPL, AVGO, MSFT, NVDA, or QCOM, many tech stocks don't pay dividends, and even when they do, they tend to have low dividend yields. Second, if I purchase the stock outright, the reality is that unlike a hedge fund or mutual fund, the number of shares I buy is too small to have any real influence on shareholder voting results. I'm perfectly willing to forgo dividend payments in exchange for the increased leverage that LEAPS provide.

If a dividend has been announced and you own an ITM call for the underlying stock, and you decide to exercise the option early, it's probably better to exercise the call before the ex-dividend date to capture the dividend. This is because on an ex-dividend date, the dividend amount is deducted from the underlying stock price, and this will probably put some near-term downward pressure on the option's value. Two rules of thumb: 1) if the underlying stock isn't paying a dividend, it's not to your advantage to exercise earlier than required because you'll throw away the extrinsic value of the option, 2) if a call option's extrinsic value is greater than the dividend payment, it's also not to your advantage to exercise the option early.

Using LEAPS for Diversification

If desired, investors can also choose to use LEAPS to diversify their portfolios. In other words, instead of committing more money upfront buying shares of individual stocks in several different companies, you can effectively achieve the same thing at a much lower cost by buying LEAPS. And if you're interested in sector diversification, you can buy index LEAPS. However, using LEAPS in this manner will only provide potential diversification for a period of 2-3 years unless you roll the LEAPS.

LEAPS Strategies for Long-Term Investors

Long-term investors use LEAPS in one of two ways. The first is as a stock replacement (aka stock substitute), and the second is for long-term hedging.

Stock Replacement

Rather than spending a lot of cash upfront to buy shares of stock outright, investors betting on the long-term growth or decline of a stock 2-3 years in the future can buy LEAPS instead. If you predict the direction the underlying stock moves, you can also achieve a much larger ROI. For example, see the table below for the options chain for the AAPL Jun18'21 calls for 11 strike prices near $245.52, which is the price AAPL closed on March 25, 2020.

Strike price $	Bid $	Ask $	Last $	Net change $	Volume	OI
220.00	51.05	53.40	59.50	9.50	14	1,847
225.00	48.15	51.20	55.00	9.00	18	775
230.00	45.30	48.40	51.21	7.47	3	807
235.00	42.60	44.70	49.75	7.75	2	1,328
240.00	40.00	42.05	46.11	6.11	39	940
245.00	37.50	39.55	42.50	5.75	63	863
250.00	35.10	37.15	36.00	1.00	410	2,842
260.00	30.60	32.60	36.90	7.32	30	1,000
270.00	26.55	28.50	32.00	5.00	55	2,751
275.00	24.65	26.50	29.84	7.39	15	169
280.00	22.85	24.75	24.00	2.30	92	2,173

If 100 shares of AAPL were purchased on March 25, 2020, at $245.52/share, it would cost $24,552 (245.52 * 100). If 1 Jun18'21 $245 strike call is purchased at the ask, it would cost $39.55/contract or $3,955 (39.55 * 100) less any fees, and if a similar amount of money was spent buying Jun18'21 $245 strike calls instead of 100 shares of AAPL, you could buy 6 calls, which would cost $23,730 (6 * 39.55 * 100) less any fees. Note, buying 6 calls is still $822 or 3.4% less than $24,552, which is the amount needed to buy 100 AAPL shares.

	Cost per share $	Total cost $
100 AAPL shares	245.52	24,552

	Cost per contract $	Total cost $
1 AAPL Jun18'21 $245 strike call	39.55	3,955
6 AAPL Jun18'21 $245 strike calls	39.55	23,730

Purchasing one Jun18'21 $245 strike call on March 25, 2020, enables you to control 100 shares of AAPL stock for about 15 months for 16.1% of the cost of buying 100 shares outright. In other words, you can substitute purchasing 100 shares of AAPL by buying one AAPL Jun18'21 $245 strike call instead, and at a much lower cost. If AAPL goes up 10% from $245.52/share to $270.07/share, then 100 shares of AAPL will increase in value from $24,552 to $27,007.20 (a $2,455.20 gain). LEAPS enable you to capture as much profit as the delta of those LEAPS will provide. Delta for the AAPL Jun18'21 $245 strike call is 0.7224. Therefore, if AAPL stock goes up 10% or 24.552 points, the price of the AAPL Jun18'21 $245 strike call will increase by $17.74 (24.552 * 0.7224). I.e., the premium will increase from $39.55/contract to $57.29/contract (39.55 + 17.74) and the AAPL Jun18'21 $245 strike call will increase from $3,955 to $5,728.64 for a gain of 44.8%. The three tables below summarize the percentage and dollar gains if the price of AAPL stock goes up 10%, 20%, and 30% for 100 shares of AAPL, one AAPL Jun18'21 $245 strike call, and 6 AAPL Jun18'21 $245 strike calls.

	Value if AAPL up 10% $	Gain %	Gain $
100 AAPL shares	27,007.20	10	2,445.20
1 AAPL Jun18'21 $245 strike call	5,728.64	44.85	1,773.64
6 AAPL Jun18'21 $245 strike calls	34,371.82	44.85	10,641.82

	Value if AAPL up 20% $	Gain %	Gain $
100 AAPL shares	29,462.40	20	4,910.40
1 AAPL Jun18'21 $245 strike call	7,502.27	89.69	3,547.27
6 AAPL Jun18'21 $245 strike calls	45,013.64	89.69	21,282.63

	Value if AAPL up 30% $	Gain %	Gain $
100 AAPL shares	31,917.60	30	7,365.60
1 AAPL Jun18'21 $245 strike call	9,275.91	134.54	5,320.91
6 AAPL Jun18'21 $245 strike calls	55,655.46	134.54	31,925.46

The results above show the leverage that's possible when using options. If the price of AAPL stock increases by 10% or 24.552 points (245.52 * 0.1), the price of the AAPL Jun18'21 $245 strike call increases by 44.9% to $57.29/contract ((24.552 * 0.7224) + 39.55). If the price of AAPL stock increases by 20% or 49.104 points (245.52 * 0.2), the price of the AAPL Jun18'21 $245 strike call increase by 89.7% to $75.02/contract ((49.104 * 0.7224) + 39.55). And if the price of AAPL stock increases by 30% or 73.656 points (245.52 * 0.3), the price of the AAPL Jun18'21 $245 strike call increases by 134.5% to $92.76/contract ((73.656 * 0.7224) + 39.55). In this example, the percentage gain of the 6 AAPL LEAPS increased at 4.5x the percentage gain of owning 100 shares of the underlying AAPL stock.

Next, let's compare the dollar gains between 100 shares of AAPL and 6 AAPL Jun18'21 $245 strike calls. If 6 AAPL Jun18'21 $245 strike calls are purchased for $23,730 (6 * 39.55 * 100), and the price of AAPL stock increases by 10%, owning 100 shares of AAPL stock would result in a gain of $2,455.20 (((245.52 * 1.1) – 245.52) * 100) whereas owning 6 AAPL LEAPS it would be $10,641.82 (((((24.552 * 0.7224) + 39.55) – 39.55) * 100) * 6). If the price of AAPL stock increases by 20%, owning 100 shares of AAPL stock would result in a gain of $4,910.40 (((245.52 * 1.2) – 245.52) * 100) whereas owning 6 AAPL LEAPS it would be $21,283.64 (((((49.104 * 0.7224) + 39.55) – 39.55) * 100) * 6). And lastly, if the price of AAPL stock increases by 30%, 100 shares of AAPL stock would result in a gain of $7,365.60 (((245.52 * 1.3) – 245.52) * 100) whereas owning 6 AAPL LEAPS it would be $31,925.46 (((((73.656 * 0.7224) + 39.55) – 39.55) * 100) * 6). In this example, the dollar gain of owning 6 AAPL LEAPS is about 4.3x the gain of owning 100 shares of the underlying AAPL stock.

One final comment regarding using LEAPS as a stock replacement. To reduce the risk exposure of only buying LEAPS, a mix of stock and LEAPS could be purchased instead. For example, instead of buying 3 AAPL Jun18'21 $245 strike calls at a cost of $11,865 (3 * 39.55 * 100), 1 AAPL Jun18'21 $245 strike call and 25 shares of AAPL stock could be purchased for a total combined cost of $10,093 ((39.55 * 100) + 25 * 245.52)). This reduces overall potential risk versus only buying options, but it also reduces potential upside. Like all trades, it always comes down to a risk-reward tradeoff.

Buying LEAPS enables control of an equal or greater number of shares while using a smaller or near equal amount of money versus buying only stock. Furthermore, LEAPS can also produce a percentage and dollar gain that's a multiple of what can be achieved buying the underlying stock. That's the real power of options and the leverage that they provide.

Long-Term Hedging

If you own stocks, you could sell OOTM LEAPS covered calls to generate income from premiums collected; however, this only provides very moderate downside protection for your stock holdings. Furthermore, if the underlying stock moves above the strike, you'll forfeit any gains and are also obligated to provide 100 shares of stock at the strike price for each contract if the buyer decides to exercise. Selling covered calls is a neutral strategy. It assumes small movements in the underlying stock for the remaining life of the option before it expires. If you're bullish or bearish, a covered call strategy is not recommended. If you're bullish, you're better off holding stock, and if you're bearish, you're better off selling.

Alternatively, you could buy LEAPS puts as insurance to protect your stock holdings against any future stock price declines. If you own a stock that has gone up a lot and remain bullish for the long term, consider buying a protective put (aka a covered put). This will protect your stock gains if you're worried about the stock price in the short or immediate time frame. For example, there's an unexpected slowdown in earnings, or the economy more broadly, or perhaps you want to be very conservative, and you're just hedging for an unforeseen event that is yet to happen. Purchasing LEAPS puts can help hedge against a price decline in stock for up to 2-3 years in the future. Buying index LEAPS puts can be used as a protective put for an entire portfolio or a more focused hedge against sector-specific headwinds. Note, buying LEAPS puts may also bolster an investor's confidence to stay in the market since it's less likely an investor will immediately exit a stock position in the short term because of the insurance the puts provide. Finally, if you're planning a long-term hedge, don't use short term puts. This will only result in more trades and fees to maintain the protection you're looking for.

Beyond the Scope

This book is not intended to cover more advanced options strategies. However, if desired, you can set up these trades after making the initial DITM LEAPS trade. One that works well with DITM LEAPS calls is a long call diagonal spread. This net debit spread consists of two legs: 1) you buy a longer-term ITM call that will not expire for a few months (i.e., this is the back-month leg), 2) you sell a shorter-term call with an OOTM strike that expires in about a month (i.e., this is the front-month leg), which will reduce the cost basis of the longer-term ITM call. A diagonal spread is often described as a combination of a calendar spread and a vertical spread. As an option strategy, it can be thought of as creating a synthetic covered call where the longer-term ITM call is used in place of stock. Setting up a long call diagonal spread is what advanced options traders will consider putting in play if they're: 1) predicting that a stock price will increase, 2) they have a target price in mind, and 3) they want to manage risk. Similar to a vertical spread, this trade increases your chances of making money while lowering risk, but your upside is limited if the underlying stock price rises above the strike of the shorter-term call. Hence, why it's important to have a target price in mind (any profits generated above the strike of the shorter-term call will not be captured). The ideal result for this trade is the stock price approaches the shorter-term call strike but doesn't exceed it, and then the shorter-term call expires worthless. At this point, the simplest thing to do would be to close the entire long call diagonal spread trade; however, what experienced traders will often do instead is roll the strategy by setting up another front-month leg (i.e., sell another shorter-term call) and continue to repeat this every month until expiration of the back-month leg. After the entire trade is closed, then another long call diagonal spread can be put in play. Alternatively, the options trader could do nothing after the shorter-term call expires worthless and just bet on the stock continuing to go up. If this happens, then the longer-term call will also go up in value, and more profit will be realized once this back-month leg is eventually closed by an STC order.

Summary

For option buyers, the maximum amount that can be lost is 100% of the premium paid. Buyers of LEAPS require more cash upfront than buyers of short-term options. For investors who are not fully comfortable with options, LEAPS are probably best used as long-term hedges against stock they own that have significantly gone up in value or by trading them in conjunction with stocks they own to magnify returns. However, for investors who are comfortable with options, I think using LEAPS as stock replacement is a powerful strategy. It can potentially amplify returns several times more than what is possible from just purchasing shares of stock. This is true whether the underlying tech stock is a well-known large-cap like AAPL or a high-flyer like TSLA, where potential return amplification is even greater.

Most options traders incur losses not because they incorrectly analyzed a bull or bear thesis but because the option expired before the underlying stock had enough time to move in the predicted direction. By using LEAPS that expire 2-3 years in the future, a long-term investor is not affected by short-term fluctuations and has more time to see if the predicted move plays out. The extended time before expiration makes LEAPS special if you can identify the right underlying tech stocks. In other words, you don't have to be right about the direction in terms of days or weeks. You only have to be right about the direction in terms of years. I think LEAPS are ideal for long-term options investors (not traders) who are skillful at predicting industry, company, market, technology, platform, product, and/or services trends over an extended period of time. I believe the secret to consistently making money in the market is being long and leveraged, and buying and selling LEAPS are my absolute favorite options trade.

8

CHECKPOINT TWO

A man who dares to waste one hour of time has not discovered the value of life.

—*Charles Darwin*

THIS IS THE second of three checkpoints that review key takeaways as we progress through the book. When you know what you're doing, and if used appropriately, options are not financial weapons of mass destruction. Quite the opposite. Options are unique equity-based financial instruments that can help you achieve and accelerate your financial goals due to the inherent leverage they provide.

Although delta is interesting, if you trade options like me, which we'll discuss in the next part of the book, then the good news is you don't have to worry about the Greeks (theta, vega, gamma, rho). It's certainly not a bad thing to understand the Greeks and what they're intended to be used for, but from a real-world options trading standpoint, as you'll find out shortly, they're not needed when deciding which options to buy if you trade options the way I do.

LEAPS are nothing more than options with expiration dates 2-3 years in the future. They only account for about 10% of all options listed for trading, so they're not that popular versus shorter-term options, which still make up the vast majority of options traded in the market today. Note, you'll need to be approved for Level 2 options trading in your brokerage account to trade LEAPS. Historically, options with future expirations of more than nine months were considered LEAPS. However, from a tax perspective, to align with the timing of long-term capital gains, I consider LEAPS options with expirations of more than a year in the future.

What makes LEAPS special is that they enable you to be a long-term investor and not just a short-term trader. By using LEAPS that expire 2-3 years away, a long-term options investor is not affected as much by short-term market fluctuations, can wait and see if the predicted move plays out, and has more time to build up a cushion. LEAPS are my absolute favorite way to make money in the stock market. They allow you to go long with leverage and can be used as a stock replacement to amplify ROIs if the underlying stock moves in the expected direction.

Advanced options strategies are beyond the scope of this book. However, one trade I like is setting up a long call diagonal spread after buying DITM LEAPS calls.

Part Four

WHERE THE RUBBER MEETS THE ROAD

A plan without action is not a plan. It's a speech.
—*T. Boone Pickens*

9

DRUMROLL PLEASE

Risk comes from not knowing what you're doing.
—Warren Buffet

THERE IS A common misconception that 80-90% of all options expire worthless, and therefore it's better to sell options like the pros than to buy options like what amateurs often do. This is not true and it also builds upon the myth that options are dangerous and should be avoided. In 2015, according to the OCC, 7% of options were exercised, 21.7% of options expired worthless, and 71.3% of options were bought or sold to close the position. The reality is most open option trades don't expire worthless and are closed by either a BTC or STC order. Many in the options industry believe that buying options is generally favored by retail investors and they're playing a game of hope because the odds are stacked against them. This is also the reason why there are so many books, courses, and systems on how to get rich trading options—they're all selling the hope of making lots of money. In his 2002 book titled *Come Into My Trading Room*, Alexander Elder wrote, "A woman who was a market maker on the floor of the American Exchange once said to me: 'Options are a hope business. You can buy hope or sell hope. I am a professional—I sell hope. I come to the floor in the morning, find out what people hope for, price that hope, and sell it to them.'" Elder goes on to say, "Profits in the options business are in the writing, not in buying. When you write options, you begin every trade by taking in someone else's money. A hopeful buyer forks over some money to a writer who is almost always a much more experienced trader." With all due respect to the pros on the other side of my trades, I'm proof that an amateur can make money buying options. I never enter option trades buying hope. I enter option trades to make money.

The Big Reveal

Making money buying options ultimately comes down to one simple question. Which option do I buy? My secret is: I buy DITM LEAPS calls with a BE no higher than 5% of the current underlying stock price when the option order executes. Remember, BE for a call is calculated by adding the premium to the strike price (the BE for a put is calculated by subtracting premium from the strike price). BE is the theoretical price the underlying stock needs to reach for you to breakeven on your options trade. After buying DTIM LEAPS calls and assuming I've picked the right underlying stock, I keep calm, remain patient, and wait for the underlying stock to go up. While past performance is never a guarantee for future results, this simple options trading strategy has consistently worked for me. Does it always work? No. However, after making over 90 options trades in the 3.75 years since retiring, my winning (i.e., profitable) call options trade percentage is 89%. This is the strategy I used to achieve my retirement number and retire early. Even if I buy DITM LEAPS calls with a BE no higher than 10% of the current underlying stock price when the option order executes, my winning call options trade percentage over the past 3.75 years is still 86%.

Recall, LEAPS are just options with expirations 2-3 years in the future. I like to trade calls more than puts because I have a more intuitive feel for stocks going up than down. Hence, buying DITM LEAPS calls is nothing more than buying calls with DITM strikes and expirations 2-3 years in the future. The value of these calls is almost all intrinsic value with little extrinsic value. In general, an option is said to be DITM if it's ITM by more than $10; hence, a DITM call has a strike that's at least $10 less than the underlying stock price, and a DITM put has a strike that's at least $10 higher than the underlying stock price. DITM also means the calls will have a high delta, and if it's near or at 1, the call will move practically 1-for-1 with the underlying stock—an impressive thing to watch when the underlying stock is moving in the direction you predicted. Buying DITM LEAPS calls is essentially investing in the underlying stock for the next 2-3 years except with leverage. This leverage provides the opportunity for potentially higher ROI versus simply owning shares of the underlying stock outright.

Ideally, the current price of the underlying stock, at the time the option order executes, is 5-10% or more below its 52-week high. This makes for a better options trade entry point. However, this is not always possible, and even if a stock is near its 52-week high, this will not prevent me from buying DITM LEAPS calls if I like the company. The best options trade entry points typically appear after there's a market correction (i.e., 10% down) or during a bear market (i.e., 20% down) when high-quality stocks often go on sale.

MSFT DITM LEAPS Example

Let's look at an actual example to be sure it's clear what I mean when I say buy DITM LEAPS calls with a BE no higher than 5% of the current underlying stock price when the option order executes.

On January 22, 2019, I bought MSFT Jan15'21 $70 strike calls and paid a premium of $40.10 (i.e., $4,010 per contract). Recall, the premium is just another name for the option price. When the option order was executed, MSFT was trading for $106.75/share, so buying a $70 strike call, which was $36.75 less than the underlying stock price, is for sure DITM. With an expiration date of January 15, 2021 (725 days to expiration), this call option is

127

also a LEAPS. Finally, BE for this call option is $110.10 (70 + 40.10), which is 3.1% (((110.10 / 106.75) – 1) * 100) higher than the current underlying stock price. Recall, BE for a call is calculated by adding the premium to the strike price. BE is the theoretical price the underlying stock needs to reach to breakeven on your options trade. Hence, buying MSFT Jan15'21 $70 strike calls for $40.10/contract satisfies all of the requirements of buying DITM LEAPS calls with a BE no higher than 5% of the current underlying stock price when the option order executes. About five months later, as of market close on June 30, 2020, the stock price of MSFT was $203.51/share, the premium for the MSFT Jan15'21 $70 strike call was $133.78/contract (i.e., $13,378 per contract), and the delta was 1. Hence, the option will move 1-for-1 with the underlying stock (i.e., for every $1 move up or down in MSFT stock, the call will move up or down $100 (1 * 100)). The current ROI on the MSFT Jan15'21 $70 strike call is 233.6% (133.78 / 40.1) compared to the 90.6% (203.51 / 106.75) increase in the underlying stock from when I first bought the options on January 22, 2019. With 200 days remaining before expiration, there are more than six months left for the MSFT Jan15'21 $70 strike call to continue to climb in value if MSFT stock keeps going up. Alternatively, if a negative catalyst appears that causes MSFT to decline, there are over six months for the stock and the Jan15'21 $70 strike call to recover. There is a built-in cushion now (from the existing 233.6% option ROI) to absorb the blow and still result in a winning (i.e., profitable) trade when the call is closed out (assuming I don't do anything stupid like let the ROI return to 0%). Note, building up a cushion (i.e., positive ROI) early such that there are many days left (preferably over a year) before the option expiration date is the ideal situation you want to be in after you buy DITM LEAPS calls. When I like a stock, I'll trade it repeatedly using DITM LEAPS calls. Here are three additional examples of buying MSFT DITM LEAPS calls with a BE no higher than 5% of the current underlying stock price when the option order was executed. 1) Nov3'17 $79 strike call BE was 3.5% higher, and when the call was closed, it produced a 431.8% ROI. 2) Jan17'20 $70 strike call BE was 5.3% higher, and when the call was closed, it produced a 394.8% ROI. 3) Jan17'20 $70 strike call BE was 4.6% higher, and when the call was closed, it produced a 178.2% ROI.

As mentioned, I like to buy DITM LEAPS calls with a BE no higher than 5% of the current underlying stock price when the option order executes. However, from time to time, I will go beyond 5%. It depends on the current situation of the underlying stock and the broader market in general. Here are some examples. 1) FB Jan19'18 $95 strike call BE was 10.1% higher, and when the call was closed, it produced a 201.4% ROI. 2) NXPI Jan19'18 $105 strike call BE was 12.3% higher, and when the call was closed, it produced a 417.2% ROI. 3) NFLX Jan18'19 $105 strike call BE was 25.3% higher, and when the call was closed, it produced a 246.8% ROI. Anything above 5% increases the risk from my perspective, so, as you can see, I'm very conservative versus other options traders who regularly buy ATM or OOTM options and/or short-term options that expire within a few months, weeks, or days. FYI, the reason why so many retail traders gravitate towards far OOTM options is that they're cheap, and they hope to hit the jackpot and make a lot of money. Don't be tempted by hope and far OOTM options. The odds are stacked against you.

90 Option Trades and Counting

As of June 2020, and since retiring in January 2017, I've made over 90 options trades. Of the underlying stocks that I traded options in, 74% were tech. When compiling this data, I was surprised the percentage of options trades in non-tech stocks was so high—a percentage that I've since adjusted down. Based on my personal investing and risk-reward profile as well as my focus and interest in tech, what didn't surprise me was that all of the trades in non-tech stocks were speculative in nature in industries such as biotech (e.g., MRNA calls), healthcare (e.g., UNH calls), packaged foods (e.g., BYND calls), discount stores (e.g., SHLD puts), and others. Despite being net profitable in these trades, I wandered off the range with these non-tech options trades.

Options Profit and Loss Diagrams

Profit and loss diagrams (aka risk graphs) help investors visualize a strategy before investing. They are used for simple/complex options and short/long positions. I don't look at risk graphs because I primarily buy the same type of option every time. However, if you find risk graphs helpful, please use them. The risk graph for a long call (i.e., DITM LEAPS call) is shown below.

Long Call Profit and Loss Diagram

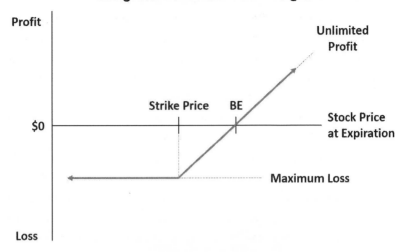

Technical Indicators

Technical indicators are used to try and identify market trends and signals. There are hundreds of technical indicators, but only four major types: 1) trend (EMA (exponential moving average), MACD (moving average convergence divergence), etc.), 2) momentum (stochastic oscillator, RSI (relative strength index), etc.), 3) volume (OBV (on-balance volume), Chaikin oscillator, etc.), 4) volatility (standard deviation, Bollinger bands, etc.). Indicators can be further categorized as leading (used to predict future price movements) or lagging (used to confirm long-term trends). I'm not a technical trader, and when it comes to options, I never use technical indicators when determining which underlying stock to buy DITM LEAPS calls in. Some indicators are more applicable to options, such as OI or PCR (put-call ratio), but again, never enough to directly influence my decision on which ones to buy. For better or for worse, I ignore all technical indicators. This simplifies my options trading decisions and saves me time.

Why I Pay No Attention to the Greeks

Here is a summary of the Greeks vis-à-vis DITM LEAPS calls. 1) delta will be high. 2) theta will be low because they are made up of mostly intrinsic value.

3) if delta is nearing or at 1, there will be almost no vega; however, since it is difficult to estimate volatility 2-3 years in the future, depending on the strike, vega may be high because these types of options can be sensitive to changes in IV. 4) gamma will be small. 5) rho will be larger than shorter-term options because interest rates have a higher probability of changing in a meaningful way. Got that? Remember at the end of the chapter on the Greeks when I said besides delta, I ignore the Greeks (theta, vega, gamma, rho)? Here is why. The value of an option is made up of intrinsic and extrinsic value. DITM LEAPS are comprised of nearly all intrinsic value; hence, the Greeks have very little influence on the value of the option since they are primarily used to estimate extrinsic value. Thus, it does not matter what values the Greeks are. Take theta as an example. Only extrinsic value decays, not intrinsic value. Therefore, the negative impact of time decay (i.e., theta) on the value of an option premium is minimized when buying DITM LEAPS. And if the option continues to stay DITM and as expiration nears, the extrinsic value eventually goes to 0 such that by expiration, the option is made up of entirely intrinsic value. Because I am buying DITM LEAPS calls, even delta does not matter. DITM means delta will be high, which is what I want anyway. However, in practice, I like to know what delta is since it gives me a rough idea of how the option value will move relative to how the stock moves. Recall, delta tells you how much an option price is expected to change for a $1 change in the underlying stock. E.g., if the delta is 0.95, then for every $1 that the stock goes up, the option value will increase by $95 (0.95 * 100). Now you know why I pay no attention to the Greeks. From a real-world practical options trading standpoint, they are not needed when deciding which options to buy. This greatly simplifies the process I go through when picking which DITM LEAPS to buy. Since I do not use the Greeks regularly, except for delta, I often forget what they mean. As Albert Einstein once said, "Don't memorize something you can look up."

Picking the Underlying Stock

Obviously, buying DITM LEAPS calls can only be successful if the right underlying stock is chosen first. For any DITM LEAPS calls that you're willing to buy, you should be willing to buy and hold the underlying stock for the same time frame that the DITM LEAPS calls have before expiration. If you're not willing to do this, then you shouldn't be buying DITM LEAPS. For example, if you're willing to buy TTD DITM LEAPS calls that don't expire for the next 2½ years, then you should have no problem buying and holding TTD stock for the next 2½ years. I buy DITM LEAPS calls as a stock replacement instead of buying the underlying stock. This allows me to go long, obtain leverage, and amplify my ROI several times the stock price increase if the stock moves as predicted.

I have no fear buying options in underlying tech stocks with rich valuations sporting high PE (price-to-earnings), high revenue multiples, or negative EPS (earnings per share). For example, as of July 14, 2020, AMZN's PE was 148.3, while its stock price was $3,084/share, and its ROI over the past five years was 562.4%, NFLX's PE was 112.9, while its stock price was $524.88/share, and its ROI over the past five years was 423%, SHOP's EPS was -$1.162, while its stock price was $974.41/share, and its ROI over the past five years was 3,057.5%, and TSLA's EPS was -$0.871, while its stock price was $1,516.80/share, and its ROI over the past five years was 471%. I have had call options in AMZN, NFLX, SHOP, and TSLA in the past and currently have calls in SHOP and TSLA, both of which have ROIs that have more than doubled since I initially purchased the options.

I always take what Wall Street analysts say regarding a tech stock with a grain of salt—they often can't even agree on a company's future outlook. The table below shows the target prices analysts from some of Wall Street's largest firms had for TSLA as of July 14, 2020 (note, TSLA closed at $1,516.80/share on this day).

Firm	Analyst(s)	1-year target price $	% away from current price ($1,516.80)
Piper Sandler	Alex Potter	2,322	53.09
JMP Securities	Joe Osha	1,500	-1.11
Credit Suisse	Dan Levy, AJ Denham	1,400	-7.70
Wedbush Securities	Dan Ives	1,250	-17.59
Jefferies	Philip Houchois	1,200	-20.89
Goldman Sachs	Mark Delaney	864	-43.04
Morgan Stanley	Adam Jonas	740	-51.21
Baird	Ben Kallo	700	-53.85

RBC Capital Markets	Joseph Spak	615	-59.45
Citi	Itay Michaeli	450	-70.33
Barclay	Brian Johnson	300	-80.22
Cowen	Jeffery Osborne	300	-80.22
J.P. Morgan	Ryan Brinkman	295	-80.55

A bull-bear analyst target price spread of $2,027 (2,322 – 295) among the 13 analysts above is wide. According to *TipRanks*, there are currently 27 analysts (7 have buy ratings, 11 have hold ratings, 9 have sell ratings) that cover TSLA with an average 1-year target price of $954.70/share, which is 37% lower than where the stock is currently trading at today ($1,516.80/share). Nevertheless, if an analyst issues a report with a change in rating and target price, this can sometimes cause the stock price to move. Note, I'll pay attention when analysts increase target multiples, boost target prices, or raise their estimates, particularly after a solid earnings report beat. In this case, the market is either in the process of driving the price of a stock up, or it has already done so. Analyst upgrades help reset the baseline for an underlying stock at a higher price. This drives the premium up for DITM LEAPS calls. Finally, note that since DITM LEAPS calls typically have expirations 2-3 years in the future, this provides analysts 8-12 opportunities (i.e., earnings reports) to issue future upgrades on the underlying stock.

Up and To the Right Over Long Periods of Time

I like tech stocks that have charts that go up and to the right over long periods. For me, this means a minimum of 2-3 years, which is the same amount of time DITM LEAPS calls usually have before expiration. Preferably, it is for 10 or more years, but this is not always possible with some of the newer tech companies which have recently gone public. I especially like large-cap tech stocks like AAPL and MSFT that are reliable winners over the long run. I have also had success with FANG (FB, AMZN, NFLX, GOOG) in the past, although I have not actively traded GOOG for some time now. FB is a dominant platform that I have made profitable trades in the past. However, I have some concerns with the current regulatory and political headwinds that the company constantly faces (GOOG is facing a similar situation). As of June 2020, tech stocks that have gone public in the past five years that I currently have open DITM LEAPS calls include COUP, DOCU, NET, SHOP, and TTD. I also have open DITM LEAPS calls in TSLA, which went public 10 years ago, and MELI, which went public 13 years ago. As of June 2020, tech stocks that I have bought and sold DITM LEAPS calls in the past few years but do not currently have open trades include AVGO, BABA, NVDA, OLED, ROKU. Finally, as of June 2020, some stocks that I do not currently have open DITM LEAPS calls, but I have been watching include ADBE, ANSS, ETSY, OKTA, PYPL, SE, SNPS, SQ, and TTWO.

Let's look at the charts for AAPL and MSFT, so it's clear what I mean by charts that go up and to the right over long periods of time. The chart below is for AAPL for the past 30 years from 1990-2020.

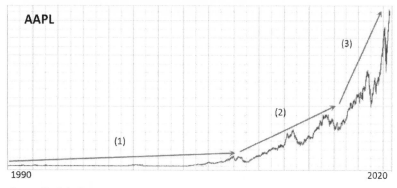

Source: Stockcharts.com.

In my simple mind, here's what I see. (1) from 1990-2009 the long-term trend line is sloping slightly up, and to the right, with initially a very long period of being essentially flat. (2) from 2009-2016 the long-term trend line is sloping up, and to the right, with an increased slope. (3) from 2016-2020 the long-term trend line for the stock is still sloping up, and to the right, except for this time period, the slope has become much steeper. Something else that I see is that if you pick any low point between 2004-2020 (except 2007-2009) and if you go back 2-3 years earlier, the stock at the low point was still higher (this wasn't true of 2007-2009, but was true for 2006-2009). For example, in September 2012, AAPL began a 6-month slide before turning around in April 2013. The price of AAPL in April 2013 was higher than in April 2011 (two years earlier) and April 2010 (three years earlier). Or at the end of September 2018, AAPL began a 3-month slide before turning around in January 2019. The price of AAPL in January 2019 was higher than in January 2017 (two years earlier) and January 2016 (three years earlier).

Now let's look at MSFT. Below is the stock chart for MSFT for the past 30 years from 1990-2020. In my simple mind, here's what I see. (1) from 1990-1996 the long-term trend line is sloping slightly up and to the right., (2) from 1996-2000 the long-term trend is up, and to the right, with an increased slope. (3) after the dot-com crash in 2000 from 2001-2012, the long-term trend is essentially flat, (4) from 2012-2017, the long-term trend line for the stock is sloping up, and to the right, with an increased slope. (5) from 2017-2020 the long-term trend line for the stock is still sloping up, and to the right, except for this time period, the slope has become much steeper. Also, similar to the AAPL stock chart, if you pick any low point between 2012-2020, and if you go back 2-3 years earlier, the stock price at the low point was still higher.

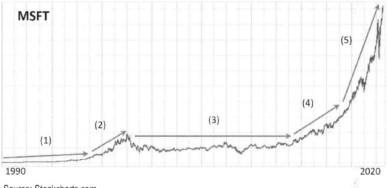

Source: Stockcharts.com.

Why is it important the stock price at a low point is higher than the stock price 2-3 years earlier? The reason why is because I buy DITM LEAPS calls that don't expire for 2-3 years. In other words, I'm willing to pay a higher premium for these calls in exchange for the longer expiration. DITM LEAPS calls provide 2-3 years to ride out any negative movements in the underlying stock. If you buy DITM LEAPS calls, and as long as the underlying stock is moving up and to the right, you have to remain patient and wait for the calls to work. If you've picked a high-quality company with a history of going up over long periods of time, and if the stock goes through some rough patches when you first buy the DITM LEAPS calls, relax and don't panic, and don't sell unless something has fundamentally gone wrong with the company. A strong tech stock has a high probability it'll recover from early downturns and end up at a higher price 2-3 years later. As Charlie Munger said, "The big money is not in buying and selling, but in waiting."

What DITM LEAPS Calls Would I Buy?

Below is the data I quickly scan for in the underlying stock quote and option quote before deciding which DITM LEAPS calls I buy. I look to see if there's anything unusual that warrants attention. Assuming nothing stands out and I like the underlying stock, and its long-term chart is up and to the right for long periods of time, then I'll make the BTO decision quickly. I track key data for each trade in a trading book, which can also be tracked in a spreadsheet.

Underlying Stock	Call Option
Stock price	Expiration date
Bid / ask price	Strike price
Day range	Last / bid / ask price
52-week range and dates	Midpoint of bid/ask
% 52-week high is from stock price	BE
Number of shares outstanding	% BE is above stock price
Average volume	% BE is from 52-week high
Market cap	OI /volume
Date of next earnings report	Delta
Are past earnings reports strong beats	Number of days to expiration
Did stock react positively to earnings results	IV

Let's use a real-world example to test your new knowledge of buying DITM LEAPS calls with a BE no higher than 5% of the current underlying stock price when the option order executes. As of July 2, 2020, listed below are the expiration dates currently available for AAPL calls.

Jul2'20	Aug7'20	Dec18'20	Jun17'22
Jul10'20	Aug21'20	Jan15'21	Sep16'22
Jul17'20	Sep18'20	Jun18'21	
Jul24'20	Oct16'20	Sep17'21	
Jul31'20	Nov20'20	Jan21'22	

If I bought an AAPL call option, which expiration, from the dates listed above, do you think I would pick? If you've been paying attention, this should be an easy question to answer. I would pick an AAPL call option with an expiration date of Sep16'22 (i.e., September 16, 2022). It's the last expiration among the 17 calls available. Remember, I'm interested in LEAPS, which have expiration dates 2-3 years in the future. Hence, I would pick the Sep16'22 call, which has the largest number of days remaining before expiration. In this case, 807 days from the current date of July 2, 2020. AAPL closed at $364.11/share on July 2, 2020. The table below shows the AAPL options chain for calls expiring on September 16, 2022, and the strike prices that were available along with the OI, volume, last, bid, and ask prices.

Strike price $	OI	Volume	Last $	Bid $	Ask $
160.00	48	1	210.00	205.00	210.00
165.00	8	0	207.00	200.50	205.50
170.00	4	0	202.80	196.00	201.00
175.00	3	0	197.50	192.00	196.50
180.00	13	0	192.00	187.50	192.50
185.00	1	0	152.18	183.00	188.00
190.00	6	0	180.75	179.00	183.50
195.00	1	0	164.04	174.50	179.50
200.00	122	0	177.00	170.50	175.50
210.00	16	0	158.00	162.00	167.00
220.00	35	21	159.95	154.25	159.00
230.00	28	0	151.15	146.00	151.00
240.00	98	11	147.25	138.50	143.50
250.00	80	0	135.14	131.50	136.00
260.00	59	0	128.00	124.10	129.00
270.00	190	1	122.18	117.00	122.00
280.00	29	0	115.16	110.50	115.00
290.00	35	33	109.00	104.00	108.50
300.00	370	4	102.94	97.50	102.50
305.00	94	2	101.67	94.00	97.60
310.00	110	3	93.70	91.50	96.00
315.00	49	2	94.12	88.50	93.25
320.00	227	1	90.39	85.50	90.50
325.00	60	0	88.45	83.00	87.50
330.00	157	0	85.25	80.00	85.00
335.00	166	4	81.00	77.50	82.50
340.00	102	8	77.85	74.50	79.50

345.00	71	0	77.76	72.00	77.00
350.00	558	8	72.00	69.50	74.50
360.00	994	52	67.72	65.00	70.00
370.00	599	19	64.31	60.00	63.90
380.00	280	2	60.60	56.00	61.00
390.00	58	32	55.50	52.00	57.00
400.00	536	136	52.00	50.00	52.75
410.00	92	6	49.95	44.50	49.50
420.00	46	3	44.82	43.50	46.50
430.00	130	10	42.00	38.00	43.00
440.00	56	9	39.25	35.00	40.00
450.00	206	106	36.25	32.50	37.00
460.00	89	9	31.70	29.50	34.50
470.00	119	29	29.10	27.50	32.00
480.00	72	46	28.00	25.00	30.00
490.00	27	0	26.28	23.00	28.00
500.00	4,260	19	24.00	22.85	26.00
520.00	485	5	20.00	19.50	22.20
540.00	335	36	18.00	16.50	19.25

If I was buying an AAPL call, what strike price from the ones listed in the table above do you think I would pick? For this question, to calculate the premium for a specific strike, don't use the last price. Instead, use the midpoint between the bid and ask. For example, if the bid is 19.50 and the ask is 22.20, then the midpoint is 20.85 ((19.5 + 22.2) / 2)). Also, an order placed near the midpoint is likely to be executed (the theoretical value of an option based on an options pricing model like Black-Scholes is usually somewhere near the midpoint). Note, for some options, the order price entered must be in increments of $0.05 or $0.10, so the midpoint price may need to be adjusted slightly up or down for the order to be accepted by your brokerage. See the table below for some of the calculations that I would have made to answer the question above regarding which strike price I would pick. 13 call strikes might work based on LEAPS being DITM and BE being no more than 5% higher ($382.32/share) than the current underlying stock price ($364.11/share) when the option order executes. In other words, any call strike with a BE less than $382.32 could be a potential AAPL DITM LEAPS to buy. Remember, for a call, BE is the strike price plus the premium, and in this case, the premium is the midpoint.

Strike price $	% strike is below current price $364.11	Bid $	Ask $	Midpoint $	BE $	% BE is above current underlying stock price
160.00	-56.06	205.00	210.00	207.50	367.50	0.93
165.00	-54.68	200.50	205.50	203.00	368.00	1.07
170.00	-53.31	196.00	201.00	198.50	368.50	1.21
175.00	-51.94	192.00	196.50	194.25	369.25	1.41
180.00	-50.56	187.50	192.50	190.00	370.00	1.62
185.00	-49.19	183.00	188.00	185.50	370.50	1.75
190.00	-47.82	179.00	183.50	181.25	371.25	1.96
195.00	-46.44	174.50	179.50	177.00	372.00	2.17
200.00	-45.07	170.50	175.50	173.00	373.00	2.44
210.00	-42.33	162.00	167.00	164.50	374.50	2.85
220.00	-39.58	154.25	159.00	156.63	376.63	3.44
230.00	-36.83	146.00	151.00	148.50	378.50	3.95
240.00	-34.09	138.50	143.50	141.00	381.00	4.64

Hence, there's no obvious answer to the question of which strike price from the strikes listed in the table above do you think I would pick. It would depend on how risk-averse you think I would be for this particular options trade, which leads to how much you think I would be willing to pay per call contract. For example, if I were risk-averse, I would probably pay a higher premium to buy a lower strike price call. The $160 strike costs at the midpoint $207.50/contract (i.e., $20,750 per contract) versus the $240 strike is 32% cheaper and costs at the midpoint $141/contract (i.e., $14,100 per contract). However, while the $160 strike is more expensive, it's practically at BE already (just 0.93% higher) versus the $240 strike is 4.64% higher. The more bullish I am in the company, the higher the strike I'd buy because premium would be cheaper and potential ROI would be increased. In contrast, the less bullish I am in the company, the lower the strike I'd buy because although I'm paying more premium and potential ROI would be lower, I'm also buying more cushion. So, once again, like any trade, it comes down to a decision of what risk-reward balance you're most comfortable with.

Let's say you planned to spend $100,000 buying AAPL DITM LEAPS calls on July 2, 2020. You could buy 5 $160 strike calls for $103,750 (5 * 207.50 * 100) less fees or 7 $240 strike calls for $98,700 (7 * 141 * 100) less fees. The delta for the $160 strike is 0.9778, and the delta for the $240 strike is 0.8783. Let's assume AAPL stock goes up 100 points or 27.5% to $464.11/share within the next 807 days before expiration (September 16, 2022). This means the $160 strike call would be worth $305.28 (207.50 + (100 * 0.9778)) per contract (i.e., $30,528 per contract) and the $240 strike call would be worth $228.83 (141 + (100 * 0.8783)) per contract (i.e., $22,883 per contract). Hence, 5 $160 strike calls would now be worth $152,640 (5 * 305.28 * 100) for an ROI of 47.12%, while the 7 $240 strike calls would now be worth $160,181 (7 * 228.83 * 100) for an ROI of 62.29%. Both the $160 strike call and the $240 strike call produced ROIs (47.12% and 62.29%, respectively) that beat the 27.46% ROI if only shares of the stock were purchased (274 shares at $364.11/share would cost $99,766.14, 274 shares at $464.11/share would be worth $127,166.14). As expected, the $160 strike call, which was much closer to BE than the $240 strike call (0.93% higher versus 4.64% higher), would provide more cushion for any potential declines, but its ROI is lower. The $160 strike call also cost $5,050 (103,750 − 98,700) more to enter the trade than the $240 strike call. To answer the original question of what AAPL call I would buy, I would pick the $240 strike.

Lastly, while this is not a requirement for me to place a BTO call option order, I will check to see how far away the DITM LEAPS calls BE is from the 52-week high for the stock. Ideally, but again not a requirement, the BE is 5-10% or more below the 52-week high. This provides more cushion versus the underlying stock having to break out and push higher from its 52-week high. However, for fast-moving tech stocks, this is not always possible, and rather than sitting on the sidelines waiting for big dips, sometimes I'll buy high with the expectation of selling higher 2-3 years in the future.

Why I Pay No Attention to OI and Volume

Notice that I made no mention of the OI or volume above when deciding which strike price to select for DITM LEAPS calls that I would consider buying. Unless I'm attempting to trade on unusual options activity, it doesn't matter if there are low OI and low or no volume in an option I'm going to buy. Furthermore, when there's also a wide bid-ask spread, this generally indicates very low liquidity, and some traders will stay away from these options. This has never been a concern for me. The reason why is that as long as a fair price is offered, market makers and ECNs (electronic communication networks) will step in and make the market. I think a fair price is the midpoint of the bid and ask, and I find that my limit orders generally execute if I set my price at the midpoint or slightly above. I've never had a liquidity issue when buying or selling options, even if I'm the only person doing the buying or selling for a particular option. In fact, there have been many times when 100% of the volume in a specific option strike trading during the day is due to only my trading and no other options traders. A tighter bid-ask spread would be nice, which means that I'm probably getting a better price if my limit order executes, but if I'm successful with the trade, in the long run, it doesn't matter to me if I missed out on a few percentage points due to a wide bid-ask spread.

Exiting A Call Option

After you buy a call, at some point, you'll need to decide what to do with this open options trade. If you BTO a call, there are four main things you can do. First, you can STC the call at any time after the call is purchased and before expiration. This is the most common way of exiting a call. Second, as the call option holder, you have the right, but not obligation, to exercise the call. Exercising the call means you'll buy the stock at the strike price, and the shares will be delivered to your brokerage account. Third, you can let the call expire. If the call is OOTM when it expires, the option will be worthless. However, if the underlying stock price is above the strike price by at least $0.01 or more, the call will automatically be exercised at expiration, and shares will be delivered to your brokerage account. Fourth, you can roll the call to obtain more time for the predicted outcome to play out.

Exercising A Call Option

Some investors decide to exercise a call option when the underlying stock price is above the strike price. This is typically done when the investor wants to own shares of the underlying stock as a longer-term investment. Note, the overwhelming majority of calls are closed and not exercised. The decision to exercise lets you buy shares at the lower strike price, resulting in an immediate paper profit. Note, if you haven't sold the option and the stock price is above the strike price by $0.01 or more when the option expires, the option is automatically exercised. The shares will then be purchased and delivered to your brokerage account on the Monday following the Friday expiration. SEC settlement rules allow you two business days to pay for the shares the day after the order executes. Note, mutual funds and other financial products, settle on different timelines than stocks. The settlement date is commonly referred to as T+2 where "T" stands for trade date, which is the date the trade took place, and the number "2" denotes how many business days after the trade date the settlement or transfer of money must occur. For example, if you executed a trade order on Thursday, trade settlement will occur on Monday the following week. If you have a margin account, you can borrow half the amount due on margin from your brokerage and will have to deposit the other half (if it's not already in your account) before the trade settles. Note, I never trade or borrow on margin and I always have 100% of the cash required in my account by the time I plan to exercise if my plan is to acquire the shares. With two days to pay for the shares, you might be thinking you could outsmart your brokerage and flip the shares without having to pay for them and keep the gain (less any fees and capital gain taxes). In a cash account, this is known as freeriding, and you would violate Federal Reserve Board Regulation T. Your brokerage may freeze your account for 90 days as well as assess other penalties. If you have enough cash to cover half the trade cost in a margin account, you could flip the shares. However, if you don't have enough, you would again violate Federal Reserve Board Regulation T.

Rolling Options

Rolling an option means closing an open option and opening a new position. Rolling up means the new strike price for the new option is higher, and the expiration date is the same. Rolling down means the new strike price for the new option is lower, and the expiration date is the same. Rolling out means the expiration is for a later date, and the new strike price for the new option is the same. Also known as rolling over or rolling forward. Rolling up and out means the new strike price for the new option is higher, and the date expiration is for a later date. Rolling is a powerful tool available to options traders. It's something that can be done with options, but not with shares of stock. You can roll both short-term and long-term options; however, they're most often done with short-term options near expiration to avoid assignment of ITM options, to continue to generate income, or to adjust a position because of movement in the underlying stock. Covered calls and cash-secured puts are two of the most common types of options that traders roll. One thing you should pay special attention to is that if your options trade has definitively gone against you, it's better to close out your option now and take your losses sooner rather than later. Continuing to roll a losing option to delay an inevitable loss will only result in digging a deeper hole for yourself. If I like a particular stock that I repeatedly buy and sell DITM LEAPS calls, I'm essentially going long the stock with leverage for a period longer than 2-3 years; however, I'm doing this with options versus shares of the stock. Hence, LEAPS calls give buy and hold investors the ability to build long-term leveraged portfolios. Substituting a financial derivative such as an option for a stock is a stock replacement strategy and is used not only for leverage but also to improve overall capital efficiency.

Simplified Stock Replacement Strategy with Increased Leverage
At its most basic level, stock replacement means you're replicating a long position in a stock with derivatives such as options (i.e., you're substituting buying shares of stock by buying options instead). One of the often-cited advantages of a stock replacement strategy is that you're able to control shares of stock with less money at risk (i.e., your potential downside exposure is reduced) versus buying the stock with cash outright. For example, on July 22, 2020, for $388/share, you could buy 100 shares of AAPL that would cost $38,800 (388.00 * 100), or you could buy 1 AAPL Sep16'22 $260 strike call option for $147.50/contract (i.e., $14,750 per contract) and also control 100 shares of AAPL albeit only until expiration on September 16, 2022. Note, I picked the AAPL Sep16'22 $260 strike call because buying this DITM LEAPS call would have a BE of $407.50/share (260 + 147.50), which is 5.03% higher (407.50 / 388) than the current underlying stock price ($388.00/share).

Buying DITM LEAPS calls is a stock replacement strategy. However, when I implement this strategy, I use a simplified form versus what is typically employed by more advanced options traders. In my case, I use any excess cash saved from buying options instead of shares of stock to buy more options to increase my leverage. Increasing leverage increases potential gains, but it also increases potential risk. Professional traders are usually more interested in managing and reducing risk and volatility. They accomplish this by using hedging activities such as selling OOTM calls against the existing DITM LEAPS calls to create a bull call spread, shorting the underlying stock (this will protect profits already made in the position against a large downwards correction), and/or buying OOTM puts (this is another way to short the underlying stock).

Unlike more advanced options traders, when I buy DITM LEAPS calls, I perform no hedging as the trade progresses and un-hedging (i.e., selling the hedges for profit) when the hedges are no longer needed. Hence, in the AAPL Sep16'22 $260 strike call mentioned above, I would buy not one contract but two contracts for $29,500 (2 * 147.50 * 100). Buying two contracts enables me to control twice as many shares (200 versus 100), and it would still cost me $9,300 less than buying 100 shares of APPL outright ($38,800). The delta for the AAPL Sep16'22 $260 strike call is currently 0.9029, so I would be capturing about 90% of any APPL stock price increases. In other words, the upside potential of any AAPL stock price has almost been replaced by the use of the AAPL Sep16'22 $260 strike call option. And if AAPL stock continues to go up and the AAPL Sep16'22 $260 strike call goes deeper ITM, the delta will begin to approach 1. If delta gets to 1, then the option will be increasing 1-for-1 with the underlying stock (100% of the upside will have been replaced by the option). However, keep in mind that leverage cuts both ways. If delta is 1 and the stock falls, the option will also fall 1-for-1. Depending on how much you have in play with your DITM LEAPS, this can mean the total dollar value of your options can swing four, five, six, or even seven figures in a single day. Please read that last sentence again. On a big up day, you'll feel totally euphoric, but on a big down day, it may be a gut-wrenching experience for some—having the right temperament is critical. For the example above, in the worst-case scenario, the maximum loss is incurred if the options expire worthless (100% of the cost (i.e., total premium paid) to buy the two call options would be lost, which would be $29,500).

There are 787 days from July 22, 2020, until the AAPL Sep16'22 $260 strike call expires. Let's assume AAPL stock increases 30% or 116.4 points from $388/share to $504.40/share before the September 16, 2022, option expiration. If this happens, the AAPL Sep16'22 $260 strike call premium would increase from $147.50/contract to $252.60/contract (147.50 + (116.4 * 0.9029)) assuming delta remains 0.9029. Note, the delta would actually be higher, likely nearing 1 because the AAPL Sep16'22 $260 strike call would have gone deeper ITM. In this example, 100 shares of AAPL would have gained $11,640 (116.4 * 100) versus 2 AAPL Sep16'22 $260 strike calls would have gained $21,020 (2 * (252.6 – 147.5) * 100), and this is even though buying the two calls cost $9,300 less than buying the 100 shares. The results of these two trades are shown in the table below.

	Cost $	Final value $	Total gain $	ROI %
100 shares AAPL	38,800	50,440	11,640	30
2 AAPL Sep16'22 $260 strike calls	29,500	50,520	21,020	71.25

The options trade ROI was 71.25% versus 30% for the pure stock trade. FYI, if the delta were 1 instead of 0.9029, the final value would have been $52,780, the total gain would have been $23,280, the ROI would have been 78.92%, and again, the trade would have cost $9,300 less than buying the stock outright.

It Takes Money to Make Money

If you had a $1 million portfolio and achieved the S&P 500 historical 9.8% AR, it would take 18 years to grow your portfolio to over $5 million ($5,380,741) less any fees/taxes. To grow faster, you either have to increase AR, start with a larger portfolio value, or do both. The four tables below summarize how many years are required to grow a portfolio to $5 million for various ARs and beginning portfolio values. If you increase AR from 9.8% to 20%, you can cut the time in half from 18 years to 9 years.

Starting portfolio value: $1 million

AR %	# years	Ending portfolio value $
9.8	18	5,380,741
20	9	5,159,780

25	8	5,960,464
30	7	6,274,852
35	6	6,053,445
40	5	5,378,240
45	5	6,409,734
50	4	5,062,500

If you start with a $1.5 million instead of $1 million, and your AR is 9.8%, you can reduce the time needed to grow a $1.5 million portfolio to $5 million from 18 years to 13 years.

Starting portfolio value: $1.5 million

AR %	# years	Ending portfolio value $
9.8	13	5,057,335
20	7	5,374,771
25	6	5,722,046
30	5	5,569,395
35	5	6,762,050
40	4	5,762,400
45	4	6,630,759
50	3	5,062,500

If you start with a beginning portfolio value of $2 million instead of $1 million, and your AR is 9.8%, you can reduce the time needed to grow a $2 million portfolio to $5 million from 18 years to 10 years. If you increase AR from 9.8% to 20%, you can grow a $2 million portfolio to $5 million in 6 years.

Starting portfolio value: $2 million

AR %	# years	Ending portfolio value $
9.8	10	5,093,935
20	6	5,971,968
25	5	6,103,516
30	4	5,712,200
35	4	6,643,013
40	3	5,488,000
45	3	6,097,250
50	3	6,750,000

Finally, if you start with a beginning portfolio value of $2.5 million instead of $1 million, and if you increase AR from 9.8% to 20%, you can grow a $2.5

million portfolio to $5 million in just four years. As Albert Einstein famously said, "Compound interest is the eighth wonder of the world. He who understands it, earns it. He who doesn't, pays it."

Starting portfolio value: $2.5 million

AR %	# years	Ending portfolio value $
9.8	8	5,281,518
20	4	5,184,000
25	4	6,103,516
30	3	5,492,500
35	3	6,150,938
40	3	6,860,000
45	2	5,256,250
50	2	5,625,000

Ultimately, you have to be comfortable investing in the market and pursuing higher ARs if you want to reduce the number of years required to grow your portfolio to your retirement number. Sitting in savings accounts, money market accounts, CDs, and/or US Treasury savings bonds will not help you achieve your financial retirement goals. And if you do this for years on end, this is lost time you'll never get back. Before retiring, I routinely put in play six-figure option trades and continue to do so today in retirement. The bottom line is it takes money to make money.

Trading Book

I keep track of all of my option trades along with any other trades (e.g., stocks, ETFs, or cryptocurrency) in a trading notebook so that I have a snapshot of what happened and a trading history. This can also be done via spreadsheet. When an options order executes, I'll capture the data listed below.

- Account number the order was made from, date and time the order executed
- Order type (usually BTO since I primarily buy calls)
- Expiration date and number of days to expiration
- Strike price and executed price (i.e., the premium paid per contract)
- Last / bid / ask / midpoint (of bid and ask) prices
- OI, volume, and delta
- Current underlying stock ticker and price when order executes
- 52-week low and high for underlying stock and dates they occurred

147

- BE and how far away percentage and points-wise BE is from the current underlying stock price when order is executed
- Total cost of order and brokerage fees paid and how much cash is remaining in the account after the order executes

What I'll do is capture the data above via multiple lines of text. For example, one line of text you might see scribbled in my trading book might be BTO 35 ROKU JAN17'20 25C @ 28.50 $99,750. This means buy-to-open 35 Roku calls expiring on January 17, 2020, with a strike price of $25 for $28.50 per contract for a total trade cost of $99,750 less any fees. When a position is closed, I pair it up with the opening position logged in my trading book, and I'll capture the data listed below.

- Date and time the order executed
- Order type (usually STC since I primarily buy calls)
- Executed price (i.e., the premium received per contract)
- ROI for the trade (i.e., percentage gain/loss, cash gain/loss)
- Current underlying stock price at the time the order executed
- How much was charged in fees, how much is in cash in the account after the order executes

Finally, I also make marks in my trading book to indicate the current status of each trade. For example, if I'm buying a call, I make a mark when the order is placed, I make a second mark when the order executes, and the position is opened, and I make a mark when the position is closed. I also use a yellow highlighter (or color the applicable spreadsheet cells) since it makes it easy to find key bits of data in my trading book.

Long-Term Capital Gains

I always try to hold my options in my taxable brokerage account for at least 12 months before selling. Depending on the expiration date, I usually hold for much longer since DITM LEAPS typically expire 2-3 years in the future. This means I pay long-term capital gains of either 15% or 20% and not short-term capital gains of 35%. For example, assume I bought $100,000 in call options and doubled my investment to $200,000 in 11 months. If I sold in less than 12 months, I would pay $35,000 (100,000 * 0.35) in taxes with a net gain less any brokerage fees of $65,000 (100,000 – 35,000). However, if instead I held for 13 months or longer before selling, I would pay either $15,000 (100,000 * 0.15) or

$20,000 (100,000 * 0.20) depending on my income bracket with a net gain less brokerage fees of either $85,000 (100,000 – 15,000) or $80,000 (100,000 – 20,000). Hence, I come out ahead paying long-term capital gains versus paying short-term capital gains. This also doesn't account for any additional gains that I may realize if the options continue to go up before they're sold.

The Power Hours

Professional traders like to trade during the power hours when the market is open. The first power hour is from 9:30 to 10:30 AM ET. It's the first hour of trading after the market opens and is when the market tends to be the most volatile and active. The first hour of a trading day is also when retail investors regularly trade after reacting hastily to news and stock movements from the market close the prior day. Smart money likes to swoop in and take advantage of retail investors at this time if they can. By late morning when professional traders take lunch (generally anywhere between 11:30 AM and 2 PM ET), volume and volatility tend to taper off. This is when algo's (i.e., computerized AI-based algorithms) typically take the lead in trading. The second power hour is the last hour of a trading day from 3:00 to 4:00 PM ET. By this time, professional traders have had time to fully digest any news and price action for the day and will make their final moves. If the market rallies into the close, this is considered a bullish sign. Typically, trading activity during the last hour on Friday is also different compared to other weekdays. Since it's the last trading hour of the week, sometimes there will be large moves because traders don't want to be stuck in certain positions over the weekend.

Don't Make Foolish Bets

Certainly, you're free to make any options trade you want. However, my advice is, do not gamble and buy cheap far OOTM short-term options hoping to hit the jackpot like in the TSLA story I told you about earlier in the book. Once in a while, way OOTM short-term options hit the jackpot and make an extreme amount of money. However, it's mostly due to circumstances completely out of control of the buyer of the options (e.g., unexpected M&A (mergers and acquisitions), major partnership, litigation, or discovery of accounting irregularities or fraud). Despite the odds being heavily stacked against them, this type of trade is what option rookies make too often and are attracted to. Most retail options traders lose money because they're on the wrong side of a statistically unfavorable trade. Guess who is on the other side? Market-makers such as Citadel and Susquehanna, who are constantly in search of rookies. Don't make rookie mistakes by making foolish bets.

Don't Get Greedy

If you're up several times on your original investment and you have been holding DITM LEAPS calls for more than 12 months, know when to take money off the table and close out your open options trade. Having a pre-defined exit plan for each trade, adjusting it as needed, and sticking to it instills discipline and keeps you honest. In general, I try to sell profitable DITM LEAPS calls 30-45 days before expiration at the very latest to lock in gains; however, if I'm up significantly (3-5x or more), then I'll seriously consider selling well in advance of expiration to lock in gains. Here's an example of greed is not good. I was holding AMZN Jan18'19 $990 strike calls, which I had originally purchased on June 6, 2017, for $154.30/contract (i.e., $15,430 per contract). I sold these calls on the expiration date for $668/contract (i.e., $66,800 per contract) for a 332.9% ROI. Not a bad return by any measure, but a few months earlier, the calls were selling for $1,000/contract (548.1% ROI). I distinctly remember this trade because I had set my exit point at $1,000/contract (i.e., $100,000 per contract), and you don't often see a six-figure option contract; however, I didn't exit the trade when I should have. I got greedy, and with about three months before expiration, I decided to let it all ride to see if I could make more (as if making about 6.5x my original investment wasn't enough). Once the premium turned down, I then waited until expiration to see if it would turn around to regain what I had lost. It didn't. By not selling when I hit my exit point, I gave up an additional $33,200 gain per contract. Don't get greedy.

Now You Know the Answer

I like using simple options trading strategies versus complex ones. Thus far, buying DITM LEAPS calls as a stock replacement with increased leverage is a simple options strategy that has consistently worked for me for as long as I've been trading options. John Bogle, the late founder of Vanguard, once said, "Successful investing doesn't require sophistication and complexity; all that's necessary is a healthy dose of common sense." Warren Buffet said, "Success in investing doesn't correlate with IQ. Once you have ordinary intelligence, what you need is the temperament to control the urges that get other people into trouble in investing." Recall, when I retired early, I was often asked the question, "How did you do it?" Now you know the answer to the question. I buy DITM LEAPS calls with a BE no higher than 5% of the current underlying stock price when the option order executes. After that, I keep calm, remain patient, and wait for the underlying stock to go up. Simplicity and patience do work. As of August 2020, underlying stocks that I currently have open DITM LEAPS calls in include AAPL, AMD, COUP, DOCU, MELI, MSFT, NET, SHOP, TSLA, and TTD. I plan to close these trades either in 2021 or 2022 based on my exit points and the expiration date for each of the open call positions. Some underlying stocks I may buy DITM LEAPS calls in the future include ADBE, ETSY, OKTA, PYPL, SNPS, SQ, and a few others. While past performance is never a guarantee of future results, I think the DITM LEAPS calls strategy I use is absolutely within the grasp of a non-professional retail investor. It worked for me and helped enable me to retire early. It continues to work for me today. Maybe it'll work for you too.

10

BUT DOES IT WORK?

Amateurs want to be right. Professionals want to make money.
—Alan Greenspan

WHILE I WAS writing this book, I continued to trade options. I thought it would be helpful to show you a few of the trades that I made. However, as mentioned in the Introduction, I will not reveal the exact number of option contracts I've bought and sold or the actual dollar amounts I've paid in premiums because I think these aspects of the trades should remain private. Two of the trades were made in January 2020, four in February 2020, and one in April 2020. Five of the trades were DITM LEAPS calls; however, to show some variation, the last two trades I made were more speculative versus what I normally do. One was OOTM LEAPS calls, and the other was short-term DITM calls that expired in July 2020. By showing you some of the options trades I made, you'll be able to see how the ROI changed from the time I first bought the options up to me completing the final manuscript of this book in September 2020.

COVID-19 Fear Grips Wall Street

On February 12, 2020, the DJIA hit an all-time high of 29,568.57. Seven days later, on February 19, 2020, both the S&P 500 and Nasdaq also hit all-time highs of 3,393.52 and 9,838.37, respectively. RSI, a bullish/bearish price momentum indicator used by technical traders that measures whether an asset is overbought or oversold, still had not reached overvalued levels for the three indices. However, with an RSI of 68.67, Nasdaq was getting close (traditionally, an RSI over 70 is considered overbought). By March 23, 2020, all three major stock indices hit 52-week lows as COVID-19 pandemic fear took hold. The S&P 500 declined by 33.9%, the Nasdaq fell 30.2%, and the DJIA fell 37.1%. Wall Street had lost about one-third of its value, and US stocks suffered the quickest fall in history from all-time highs to a bear market.

Trade #1 (January 2020) – TTD DITM LEAPS Calls

Summarized below are the details for the TTD Jan21'22 $100 strike call trade, which I made on January 9, 2020. This is an example of buying DITM LEAPS calls with a BE no higher than 5% of the current underlying stock price when the option order executes.

Options trade date:	January 9, 2020
Company / ticker symbol:	The Trade Desk / TTD
Stock price / 52-week high:	$286.64 / $286.64
Stock price % below 52-week high:	0%
Option order / type / strike:	BTO / call / $100
Option strike $ below stock price:	$186.64 (this option is DITM)
Option strike % below 52-week high:	65.11%
Option price:	$195.50/contract (i.e., $19,550 per contract)
BE / % higher than stock price:	$295.50 (100 + 195.50) / 3.09% (less than 5%)
Option expiration date:	January 21, 2022 (this option is a LEAPS)

Despite TTD stock currently trading at a 52-week high, I bought the TTD Jan21'22 $100 strike calls. This trade is an example of buying high and expecting to sell higher in the future. Positive TTD factors include the global digital advertising market is expected to reach $360 billion by 2021 (which is nearly half the total advertising market), programmatic advertising growth, built-in contractual switching costs due to TTD's use of master service agreements instead of campaign-specific agreements.

On March 23, 2020, when all three major stock indices hit 52-week lows due to COVID-19, TTD closed at $176.67/share, down 38.4% from its $286.64/share closing price on January 9, 2020, when I first bought the TTD DITM LEAPS calls. And since I had purchased DITM LEAPS calls, which means high delta, the value of the TTD Jan21'22 $100 strike calls were down even more. They were selling for $93.83/contract (i.e., $9,383 per contract), which was 52% below the $195.50/contract that I had paid on January 9, 2020. I had lost about half of my initial investment 74 days after buying the TTD Jan21'22 $100 strike calls; however, there was no panic and no thought of selling. Fundamentally, I didn't think there was anything wrong. The TTD Jan21'22 $100 strike calls don't expire for another 669 days, and I still had a lot of time for TTD to recover and start moving in the right direction.

On June 3, 2020, TTD closed at $354.98/share, and the TTD Jan21'22 $100 strike call was selling for $261.50/contract (i.e., $26,150 per contract), which is the midpoint between the bid ($259) and the ask ($264). I selected the midpoint because it's likely an order placed near this price (note, for some options, the price entered must be in increments of $0.05 or $0.10) will be executed, and there were no sales (i.e., last price) of the TTD Jan21'22 $100 strike call on June 3, 2020. Both TTD stock and the TTD Jan21'22 $100 strike calls had not only recovered after having been down 38.4% and 52% respectively on March 23, 2020, but they're now both up. This shows how volatile the market can be when unexpected catalysts appear, and options with high delta can swing in either direction when big changes in the stock price occur. The TTD Jan21'22 $100 strike call premium had gone up 33.8% since first purchased for $195.50/contract. On June 3, 2020, the delta for the TTD Jan21'22 $100 strike call was 0.9947. I don't mind paying a higher premium for LEAPS because the expiration is far in the future, which provides more cushion to ride out unforeseen negative events.

The table below shows the price of TTD stock and the TTD Jan21'22 $100 strike call and ROI for a few more dates up to the point of completing the final manuscript of this book. Note, I'm still holding the TTD Jan21'22 $100 strike calls and haven't closed the trade out via an STC order. I plan to hold the calls for more than a year to ensure capital gains will be long term and I'll most likely STC sometime in late 2021 or early 2022.

Date	Call option price $	Call ROI from $195.50 %	Stock price $	Stock ROI from $286.64 %
6/03/20	261.50	33.76	354.98	23.84
6/19/20	303.75*	55.37	394.78	37.73
7/02/20	347.50*	77.75	442.93	54.52

7/17/20	338.75*	73.27	433.03	51.07
7/31/20	354.75*	81.46	451.32	57.45
8/14/20	368.25*	88.36	465.60	62.43
8/28/20	388.50*	98.72	485.70	69.45

* Midpoint of bid and ask used for call price due to no last price.

For the dates that I captured the data in the table above, the TTD Jan21'22 100C had a low price per contract of $261.50 and ROI of 33.8% on June 3, 2020, and a high price per contract of $388.50 and ROI of 98.7% on August 28, 2020. For the final entry in the table above, you can also compare the ROI between the TTD Jan21'22 100C and how far the underlying stock rose from the initial call purchase. The TTD Jan21'22 100C is currently beating the stock 98.7% versus 69.5%.

Trade #2 (January 2020) – MSFT DITM LEAPS Calls

Summarized below are the details for the MSFT Jan21'22 $95 strike call trade, which I made on January 24, 2020. This is an example of buying DITM LEAPS calls with a BE no higher than 5% of the current underlying stock price when the option order executes.

Options trade date:	January 24, 2020
Company / ticker symbol:	Microsoft / MSFT
Stock price / 52-week high:	$165.04 / $167.10
Stock price % below 52-week high:	1.23%
Option order / type / strike:	BTO / call / $95
Option strike $ below stock price:	$70.04 (this option is DITM)
Option strike % below 52-week high:	43.15%
Option price:	$74.60/contract (i.e., $7,460 per contract)
BE / % higher than stock price:	$169.60 (95 + 74.60) / 2.76% (less than 5%)
Option expiration date:	January 21, 2022 (this option is a LEAPS)

Although MSFT stock is just 1.23% below its 52-week high, I bought the MSFT Jan21'22 $95 strike calls. Like TTD, this trade is also buying high and expecting to sell higher in the future. Positive MSFT factors: 1) Satya Nadella, 2) Azure, 3) SaaS, 4) Office 365, Teams, 5) Xbox Series X/S, xCloud.

On March 23, 2020, when all three major stock indices hit 52-week lows due to COVID-19, MSFT closed at $135.98/share, down 17.6% from its $165.04/share closing price on January 24, 2020, when I first bought the MSFT

DITM LEAPS calls. The MSFT Jan21'22 $95 strike calls were down an even greater amount. They were selling for $52.50/contract (i.e., $5,250 per contract), which was 29.6% below the $74.60/contract that I had paid on January 24, 2020. Even though I was down 30% on my initial investment 59 days after buying the MSFT Jan21'22 $95 strike calls, again, no panic and no thought of selling. Fundamentally, I didn't think there was anything wrong. The MSFT Jan21'22 $95 strike calls don't expire for another 669 days, and I had a lot of time for MSFT to recover and start moving in the right direction.

On June 3, 2020, MSFT closed at $185.36/share, and the MSFT Jan21'22 $95 strike call was selling for $96.63/contract (i.e., $9,662.50 per contract), which is the midpoint between the bid ($94.50) and the ask ($98.75). I selected the midpoint because it's likely an order placed near this price (note, for some options, the price entered must be in increments of $0.05 or $0.10) will be executed, and there were no sales (i.e., last price) of the MSFT Jan21'22 $95 strike call on June 3, 2020. Both MSFT stock and the MSFT Jan21'22 $95 strike calls had not only recovered after having been down 17.6% and 29.6% respectively on March 23, 2020, but they're now both up. The MSFT Jan21'22 $95 strike call premium had gone up 29.5% since first purchased for $74.60/contract. On June 3, 2020, the delta for MSFT Jan21'22 $95 strike call was 0.9995. I don't mind paying a higher premium for LEAPS because the expiration is far in the future, which provides more cushion to ride out unforeseen negative events.

The table below shows the price of MSFT stock and the MSFT Jan21'22 $95 strike call and ROI for a few more dates up to the point of completing the final manuscript of this book. Note, I'm still holding the MSFT Jan21'22 $95 strike calls and haven't closed the trade out via an STC order. I plan to hold the calls for more than a year to ensure capital gains will be long term and I'll most likely STC sometime in late 2021 or early 2022.

Date	Call option price $	Call ROI from $74.60 %	Stock price $	Stock ROI from $165.04 %
6/03/20	96.63	29.53	185.36	12.31
6/19/20	101.50*	36.06	195.15	18.24
7/02/20	112.00*	50.13	206.26	24.98
7/17/20	108.68*	45.68	202.88	22.93

7/31/20	110.65*	48.32	205.01	24.22
8/14/20	115.78	55.20	208.90	26.58
8/28/20	134.00	79.62	228.91	38.70

* Midpoint of bid and ask used for call price due to no last price.

For the dates that I captured the data in the table above, the MSFT Jan21'22 95C had a low price per contract of $96.63 and ROI of 29.5% on June 3, 2020, and a high price per contract of $134 and ROI of 79.6% on August 28, 2020. For the final entry in the table above, you can also compare the ROI between the MSFT Jan21'22 95C and how far the underlying stock rose from the initial call purchase. The MSFT Jan21'22 95C is currently beating the stock 79.6% versus 38.7%.

Trade #3 (February 2020) – TSLA OOTM LEAPS Calls

Summarized below are the details for the TSLA Jun17'22 $1,010 strike call trade, which I made on February 10, 2020.

Options trade date:	February 10, 2020
Company / ticker symbol:	Tesla / TSLA
Stock price / 52-week high:	$771.28 / $887.06
Stock price % below 52-week high:	13.05%
Option order / type / strike:	BTO / call / $1,010
Option strike $ above stock price:	$238.72 (this option is OOTM)
Option strike $ above 52-week high:	$122.94
Option strike % above 52-week high:	13.86%
Option price:	$156.55/contract (i.e., $15,655 per contract)
BE / % higher than stock price:	$1,166.55 (1,010 + 156.55) / 51.25% (this is speculative, way higher than 5%)
Option expiration date:	June 17, 2022 (this option is a LEAPS)

I normally buy DITM LEAPS calls, but once in a while, as an educated speculative options trade, I'll buy OOTM LEAPS calls. Buying the TSLA Jun17'22 $1,010 strike call trade is an example of this type of trade. Positive TSLA factors include Elon Musk, potential TSLA inclusion into the S&P 500, Gigafactory (Shanghai, Berlin, Austin), Model 3, Model X, Cybertruck, Roadster, Plaid mode, SaaS (over-the-air feature updates, self-driving package subscription service), battery tech, solar battery farms, and positive SpaceX indirect halo on TSLA. This is a speculative but educated trade because the BE is way higher (51.3%) than the underlying stock price when I purchased the options. Remember, my conservative threshold is usually the BE is no higher than 5% (up to 10%) of the current underlying stock price when the option is purchased.

On March 23, 2020, when all three major stock indices hit 52-week lows due to COVID-19, TSLA closed at $434.29/share, down 43.7% from its $771.28/share closing price on February 10, 2020, when I first bought the TSLA OOTM LEAPS calls. The TSLA Jun17'22 $1,010 strike calls were down even more. They were selling for $75.00/contract (i.e., $7,500 per contract), which was 52.1% below the $156.55/contract that I had paid on February 10, 2020. I had lost just over half of my initial investment 42 days after buying the TSLA Jun17'22 $1,010 strike calls; however, there was no panic and no thought of selling. Even though TSLA was volatile and again, this was a speculative play, fundamentally, I didn't think there was anything wrong. The TSLA Jun17'22 $1,010 strike calls don't expire for another 816 days, and I still had a lot of time for TSLA to recover and start moving in the right direction.

On June 3, 2020, TSLA closed at $882.96/share, and the TSLA Jun17'22 $1,010 strike call was selling for $254.48/contract (i.e., $25,448 per contract), which is the midpoint between the bid ($249) and the ask ($259.95). I selected the midpoint because it's likely an order placed near this price (note, for some options, the price entered must be in increments of $0.05 or $0.10) will be executed, and there were no sales (i.e., last price) of the TSLA Jun17'22 $1,010 strike call on June 3, 2020. Both TSLA stock and the TSLA Jun17'22 $1,010 strike calls had not only recovered after having been down 43.7% and 52% respectively on March 23, 2020, but they're now both up. The TSLA Jun17'22 $1,010 strike calls had gone up 62.6% since first purchased 114 days earlier for $156.55/contract. There are also 744 days left before the TSLA Jun17'22 $1,010 strike calls expire, so a lot of time for the premium to go higher. On June 3, 2020, the delta for TSLA Jun17'22 $1,010 strike call was 0.5467.

The table below shows the price of TSLA stock and the TSLA Jun17'22 $1,010 strike call and ROI for a few more dates up to the point of completing the final manuscript of this book. Note, I'm still holding the TSLA Jun17'22 $1,010 strike calls and haven't closed the trade out via an STC order. I plan to hold the calls for more than a year to ensure capital gains will be long term and I'll most likely STC sometime in late 2021 or early 2022.

Date	Call option price $	Call ROI from $156.55 %	Stock price $	Stock ROI from $771.28 %
6/03/20	254.48	62.56	882.96	14.48
6/19/20	338.45*	116.19	1,000.90	29.77
7/02/20	489.38	212.60	1,208.66	56.71
7/17/20	777.25*	396.49	1,500.84	94.59
7/31/20	687.73*	339.30	1,430.76	85.50
8/14/20	864.28*	452.08	1,650.71	114.02
8/28/20	1,371.25*	775.92	2,213.40	186.98

* Midpoint of bid and ask used for call price due to no last price.

For the dates that I captured the data in the table above, the TSLA Jun17'22 1,010C had a low price per contract of $254.48 and ROI of 62.56% on June 3, 2020, and a high price per contract of $1,371.25 (i.e., $137,125 per contract) and ROI of 775.92% on August 28, 2020. For the final entry in the table above, you can also compare the ROI between the TSLA Jun17'22 1,010C and how far the underlying stock rose from the initial call purchase. The TSLA Jun17'22 1,010C is currently beating the stock 775.9% versus 187%.

Trade #4 and #5 (February 2020) – AAPL DITM LEAPS Calls

Summarized below are the details for the AAPL Jun17'22 $180 strike call trade, which I made on February 10, 2020. This is an example of buying DITM LEAPS calls with a BE no higher than 5% of the current underlying stock price when the option order executes.

Options trade date:	February 10, 2020
Company / ticker symbol:	Apple / AAPL
Stock price / 52-week high:	$321.55 / $327.85
Stock price % below 52-week high:	1.92%
Option order / type / strike:	BTO / call / $180
Option strike $ below stock price:	$141.55 (this option is DITM)
Option strike % below 52-week high:	45.1%
Option price:	$146/contract (i.e., $14,600 per contract)
BE / % higher than stock price:	$326 (180 + 146) / 1.38% (less than 5%)
Option expiration date:	June 17, 2022 (this option is a LEAPS)

Despite both AAPL stock and the market being near their 52-week highs, I moved forward with buying the AAPL Jun17'22 $180 strike calls. This trade is buying high and expecting to sell higher in the future. Positive AAPL factors include services, iPhone 5G, iPhone SE (emerging markets especially India), wearables (watch, AirPods, healthcare), app store, and Apple Glass.

On March 23, 2020, when all three major stock indices hit 52-week lows due to COVID-19, AAPL closed at $224.37/share, down almost one-third (30.2%) from its $321.55/share closing price on February 10, 2020, when I first bought the AAPL DITM LEAPS calls. And since I had purchased DITM LEAPS calls, which means high delta, the AAPL Jun17'22 $180 strike calls were down even more. They were selling for $68/contract (i.e., $6,800 per contract), which was 53.4% below the $146/contract that I had paid on February 10, 2020. I had lost just over half of my initial investment 42 days after buying the AAPL Jun17'22 $180 strike calls; however, there was no panic and again no thought of selling. You should be noticing a familiar pattern for how I manage my options trades if the value declines significantly due to factors outside company control, and I still fundamentally believe in the company. If there's a lot of time left before expiration (816 days in the case of the AAPL Jun17'22 $180 strike calls), I'll wait patiently for the underlying stock to reverse, recover, and start moving up again.

On June 3, 2020, AAPL closed at $325.12/share and the AAPL Jun17'22 $180 strike call was selling for $152/contract (i.e., $15,200 per contract). Both AAPL stock and the AAPL Jun17'22 $180 strike calls had not only recovered after having been down 30.2% and 53.4% respectively on March 23, 2020, but they're now both slightly up. This shows how volatile the market can be when unexpected catalysts like COVID-19 appear and how options with high delta can swing in either direction when big changes in the underlying stock price occur. As of June 3, 2020, the AAPL Jun17'22 $180 strike call premium has increased just 4.1% since first purchased for $146/contract, and the delta was 0.9951. As previously stated, I don't mind paying a higher premium for LEAPS because the expiration is far in the future, which gives me more cushion to ride out unforeseen negative events.

The table below shows the price of AAPL stock and the AAPL Jun17′22 $180 strike call and ROI for a few more dates up to the point of completing the final manuscript of this book. Note, I'm still holding the AAPL Jun17′22 $180 strike calls and haven't closed the trade out via an STC order. I plan to hold the calls for more than a year to ensure capital gains will be long term and I'll most likely STC sometime in late 2021 or early 2022.

Date	Call option price $	Call ROI from $146.00 %	Stock price $	Stock ROI from $321.55 %
6/03/20	152.00	4.11	325.12	1.11
6/19/20	175.93*	20.50	349.72	8.76
7/02/20	189.50*	29.79	364.11	13.24
7/17/20	210.25*	44.01	385.31	19.83
7/31/20	246.30	68.70	425.04	32.18
8/14/20	282.95*	93.80	459.63	42.94
8/28/20	322.00*	120.55	499.23	55.26

* Midpoint of bid and ask used for call price due to no last price.

For the dates that I captured the data in the table above, the AAPL Jun17′22 180C had a low price per contract of $152 and ROI of 4.1% on June 3, 2020, and a high price per contract of $322 and ROI of 120.6% on August 28, 2020. For the final entry in the table above, you can also compare the ROI between the AAPL Jun17′22 180C and how far the underlying stock rose from the initial call purchase. The AAPL Jun17′22 180C is currently beating the stock 120.6% versus 55.3%.

On February 28, 2020, as the market started to decline from its all-time high, AAPL stock had fallen 15% from $321.55/share to $273.36/share, and I decided to purchase more AAPL Jun17′22 $180 strike calls. This time I paid $95/contract (i.e., $9,500 per contract), which was $51 per contract less (34.9% less) than the $146/contract that I paid for the same contracts on February 10, 2020, when I first bought AAPL Jun17′22 $180 strike calls. As mentioned, on June 3, 2020, the AAPL Jun17′22 $180 strike call was selling for $152/contract, which was 60% higher than the $95/contract that I originally paid when buying more of the AAPL Jun17′22 $180 strike calls on February 28, 2020. The BE is $275/share (180 + 95), which is 0.6% higher (less than 5%) than the $273.36/share stock price for AAPL.

The table below shows the price of AAPL stock and the AAPL Jun17'22 $180 strike call (the ones I purchased on February 28, 2020) and ROI for a few more dates up to the point of completing the final manuscript of this book. Like the AAPL Jun17'22 $180 strike calls I bought on February 10, 2020, I have not closed out the additional AAPL DITM LEAPS calls I bought on February 28, 2020. I plan to hold both sets of calls for more than a year to ensure capital gains will be long term and I'll most likely STC both sets of calls sometime in late 2021 or early 2022.

Date	Call option price $	Call ROI from $95.00 %	Stock price $	Stock ROI from $273.36 %
6/03/20	152.00	60.00	325.12	18.93
6/19/20	175.93	85.19	349.72	27.93
7/02/20	189.50*	99.47	364.11	33.20
7/17/20	210.25*	121.32	385.31	40.95
7/31/20	246.30	159.26	425.04	55.49
8/14/20	282.95*	197.84	459.63	68.14
8/28/20	322.00*	238.95	499.23	82.63

* Midpoint of bid and ask used for call price due to no last price.

For the dates that I captured the data in the table above, the AAPL Jun17'22 180C (the ones I purchased on February 28, 2020) had a low price per contract of $152 and an ROI of 60% on June 3, 2020, and high price per contract of $322 and ROI of 239% on August 28, 2020. For the final entry in the table above, you can also compare the ROI between the AAPL Jun17'22 180C (the ones I bought on February 28, 2020) and how far the underlying stock rose from the initial call purchase. The AAPL Jun17'22 180C (the ones I bought on February 28, 2020) is currently beating the stock 239% versus 82.6%.

Trade #6 (February 2020) – MRNA DITM Short-Term Calls

Summarized below are the details for the MRNA Jul17'20 $10 strike call trade, which I made on February 26, 2020. This is not a LEAPS trade. This is a DITM short-term trade.

Options trade date:	February 26, 2020
Company / ticker symbol:	Moderna / MRNA
Stock price / 52-week high:	$29.16 / $29.16
Stock price % below 52-week high:	0%

Option order / type / strike:	BTO / call / $10
Option strike $ below stock price:	$19.16 (this option is DITM)
Option strike % below 52-week high:	65.71%
Option price:	$17.80/contract (i.e., $1,780 per contract)
BE / % lower than stock price:	$27.80 (10 + 17.80) / 4.66%
Option expiration date:	July 17, 2020

When I decide to make non-LEAPS trades, it's not always in the technology sector in companies I'm familiar with. Such is the case with the MRNA Jul17'20 $10 strike calls trade, which is in the biotech industry, an industry I have no real experience or expertise in, nor do I really follow. However, for the MRNA Jul17'20 $10 strike calls trade, I was intrigued by Moderna. When I bought the calls, they were an early front-runner in potentially developing a COVID-19 vaccine. Moderna's mRNA-1273 candidate is based on a new technology known as mRNA (messenger RNA), which is supposedly a much faster way to develop vaccines, a process that can traditionally take up to a decade to develop and test. Two days before I bought the MRNA Jul17'20 $10 strike calls on February 26, 2020, Moderna shipped the first clinical batch of mRNA-1273 to the NIH (National Institutes of Health) for their COVID-19 Phase 1 clinical study. This was just a mere 44 days after January 11, 2020, the date the Chinese authorities shared the genetic sequence for COVID-19. In addition to the NIH, Moderna is also working closely with NIAID (National Institute of Allergy and Infectious Diseases) and VRC (Vaccine Research Center). When I bought the MRNA Jul17'20 $10 strike calls, the stock was trading for $29.16/share, so I also bought DITM calls to reduce risk. I moved forward with an educated speculative trade of buying the MRNA Jul17'20 $10 strike calls on February 26, 2020, with 142 days left before expiration.

On March 23, 2020, when all three major stock indices hit 52-week lows due to COVID-19, MRNA closed at $26.57/share, only down only 8.9% from the $29.16/share closing price on February 26, 2020, when I first bought the MRNA DITM calls. MRNA wasn't as impacted as many other stocks since it could potentially be a solution to COVID-19. The MRNA Jul17'20 $10 strike calls were selling for $19.60/contract (i.e., $1,960 per contract), which is 10.1% higher than the $17.80/contract I had paid on February 26, 2020.

On June 3, 2020, MRNA closed at $59.89/share, and the MRNA Jul17'20 $10 strike call was selling for $49.65/contract (i.e., $4,965 per contract), which is the midpoint between the bid ($47.80) and the ask ($51.50). I selected the midpoint because it's likely an order placed near this price (note, for some options, the price entered must be in increments of $0.05 or $0.10) will be executed, and there were no sales (i.e., last price) of the MRNA Jul17'20 $10 strike call on June 3, 2020. The MRNA Jul17'20 $10 strike calls had increased 178.9% from when they were first purchased 98 days earlier on February 26, 2020, for $17.80/contract. There were also 34 days left before the MRNA Jul17'20 $10 strike calls expired, so it's possible the premium could go higher or lower. On June 3, 2020, the delta for MRNA Jul17'20 $10 strike call was 1.

The table below shows the MRNA stock price and the MRNA Jul17'20 $10 strike call and ROI for a few more dates. Note, I thought about exercising the calls and acquiring MRNA stock at $10/share but ending up closing the trade out and taking profits via an STC order for $57.95/contract on July 13, 2020, for a 225.6% ROI. Note, the day after, July 14, 2020, MRNA announced that it would begin late-stage trial testing on July 27, 2020. The stock continued to climb, and during the trading day, the Jul17'20 $10 strike call was trading for around $71.65/contract, up another 23.6% from when I sold the day before and 302.5% from when I first bought the calls. By July 17, 2020, the Jul17'20 $10 strike was selling for around $84.35/contract, up 573.9% from $17.80/contract when I originally bought the calls. You can't win them all, and my trade still returned 3.26x the initial investment.

Date	Call option price $	Call ROI from $17.80 %	Stock price $	Stock ROI from $29.16 %
6/03/20	49.65	178.93	59.89	105.38
6/19/20	56.80*	219.10	66.35	127.54
7/02/20	49.25*	176.69	58.57	100.86
7/13/20	57.95	225.56	68.41	134.60

* Midpoint of bid and ask used for call price due to no last price.

For the dates that I captured the data in the table above, the MRNA Jul17'20 10C had a low price per contract of $49.25 and ROI of 176.7% on July 2, 2020, and a high price per contract of $57.95 and ROI of 225.6% on July 13, 2020. For the final entry in the table above, you can also compare the ROI between the MRNA Jul17'20 10C and how far the underlying stock rose from the initial call purchase. The MRNA Jul17'20 10C outperformed the stock 225.6% versus 134.6% and was an example of a successful, educated speculative short-term options trade. Note, I bought a DITM call to reduce the potential risk of making this trade. If I had purchased a call with a higher strike price or even speculated even more by buying an OOTM call, the ROI would have been much higher.

Trade #7 (April 2020) – SHOP DITM LEAPS Calls

Summarized below are the details for the SHOP Jan21'22 $150 strike call trade, which I made on April 6, 2020. This is an example of buying DITM LEAPS calls with a BE no higher than 5% of the current underlying stock price when the option order executes.

Options trade date:	April 6, 2020
Company / ticker symbol:	Shopify / SHOP
Stock price / 52-week high:	$392.65 / $543.21
Stock price % below 52-week high:	27.72%
Option order / type / strike:	BTO / call / $150
Option strike $ below stock price:	$242.65 (this option is DITM)
Option strike % below 52-week high:	72.39%
Option price:	$249.30/contract (i.e., $24,930 per contract)
BE / % higher than stock price:	$399.30 (150 + 249.30) / 1.69% (less than 5%)
Option expiration date:	January 21, 2022 (this option is a LEAPS)

I bought the SHOP Jan21'22 $150 strike calls. This trade is buying high and expecting to sell higher in the future. Positive SHOP factors include:

- SHOP will benefit from the COVID-19 pandemic as home-bound consumers avoid going to physical retail stores and shift the majority of their essential and non-essential purchases online (on April 17, 2020, SHOP CTO Jean-Michel Lemieux's said, "...our platform is now handling Black Friday level traffic every day!").
- Amazon won't be the only e-commerce winner as brick-and-mortar stores continue to fall victim to online shopping (per Digital Commerce 360's analysis of the US Department of Commerce's quarterly e-commerce published figures, online spending represented only 16% of total retail sales in 2019, up from 9.7% five years ago in 2014).
- SHOP is a key partner in helping Facebook Shops enable e-commerce on Instagram.
- Over one million customers worldwide with larger businesses appearing on Shopify's platform like Hasbro, Heinz, and Nestle, in addition to youth-oriented brands such as Kylie Cosmetics.
- The launch of the consumer-facing Shopify Shop mobile app.

On June 3, 2020, SHOP closed at $762.02/share, and the SHOP Jan21'22 $150 strike call was selling for $618.50/contract (i.e., $61,850 per contract). The SHOP Jan21'22 $150 strike calls had gone up 148.1% from when they were initially purchased 58 days earlier on April 6, 2020, for $249.30/contract. There were also 597 days left before the SHOP Jan21'22 $150 strike calls expired, so there's the possibility the premium could go higher. On June 3, 2020, the delta for SHOP Jan21'22 $150 strike call was 0.9961.

The table below shows the price of SHOP stock and the SHOP Jan21'22 $150 strike call as well as ROI for a few more dates up to the point of me completing the final manuscript of this book. Note, I'm still holding the SHOP Jan21'22 $150 strike calls and haven't closed the trade out via an STC order. I plan to hold the calls for more than a year to ensure capital gains taxes will be long term and I'll most likely STC sometime in late 2021 or early 2022.

Date	Call option price $	Call ROI from $249.30 %	Stock price $	Stock ROI from $392.65 %
6/03/20	618.50	148.09	762.02	94.07
6/19/20	739.75*	196.73	881.00	124.37
7/02/20	885.95*	255.38	1,029.97	162.31
7/17/20	784.60*	214.72	928.13	136.38
7/31/20	879.00*	252.59	1024.00	160.79
8/14/20	842.25*	237.85	987.90	151.60
8/28/20	897.25*	259.91	1,042.06	165.39

* Midpoint of bid and ask used for close price due to no last price.

For the dates that I captured the data in the table above, the SHOP Jan21'22 150C had a low price per contract of $618.50 and ROI of 148.1% on June 3, 2020, and a high price per contract of $897.25 and ROI of 259.9% on August 28, 2020. For the final entry in the table above, you can also compare the ROI between the SHOP Jan21'22 150C and how far the underlying stock rose from the initial call option purchase. The SHOP Jan21'22 150C is currently beating the stock 259.9% to 165.4%.

The Current Scorecard

The table below shows current ROIs as of August 28, 2020, for the trades described above up to the completion of the final manuscript for this book.

Call option	Strike price $	Call option BE % higher than stock price at options order execution	# days to expiration	Option ROI %	Stock ROI %
TTD Jan21'22 DITM	100	3.09	511	98.72	69.45
MSFT Jan21'22 DITM	95	2.76	511	79.62	38.70
TSLA Jun17'22 OOTM	1,010	51.25	658	775.92	186.98
AAPL Jun17'22 DITM	180	1.38	658	120.55	55.26
AAPL Jun17'22 DITM	180	0.6	658	238.95	82.63
MRNA Jul17'20 DITM	10	N/A, not DITM LEAPS call	0	225.56	134.60
SHOP Jan21'22 DITM	150	1.69	511	259.91	165.39

To recap, two trades were made in January 2020, four in February 2020, and one in April 2020. Five trades were DITM LEAPS calls (TTD Jan21'22 100C, MSFT Jan21'22 95C, AAPL Jun17'22 180C (bought on two different dates), SHOP Jan21'22 150C), one was an educated speculative OOTM LEAPS calls (TSLA Jun17'22 1,010C), and one was an educated speculative short-term DITM call (MRNA Jul17'20 10C) expiring in July 2020. Having expirations dates far in the future allowed the DITM LEAPS and OOTM LEAPS trades to absorb and recover from the COVID-19 market decline in March 2020. And despite paying higher premiums for these LEAPS, buying options with strike prices that are DITM means the BEs for the trades were all no higher than 5% from the prices of the underlying stocks when the option orders executed. All five open DITM LEAPS calls and the open OOTM LEAPS calls are currently profitable and have ROIs that have outperformed their underlying stocks thus far. The closed short-term DITM call also produced an ROI that outperformed the underlying stock. The DITM LEAPS calls don't expire for another 511 or 658 days, and the OOTM LEAPS calls don't expire for another 658 days. Hence, there's plenty of time for the open calls to potentially further appreciate. Since all of these DITM LEAPS calls expire in either January 2022 or June 2022, unless something fundamentally changes in the underlying stocks, my expectation is their ROIs will be higher by the time I sell them. Alternatively, if I didn't care about paying short-term capital gains, I could STC the calls and lock in the profits now. The bottom line is: buying DITM LEAPS calls with a BE no higher than 5% of the current underlying stock price when the option order executes appears to be working for all six of the open option trades I discussed above.

11

CHECKPOINT THREE

You miss 100 percent of the shots you don't take.
—Wayne Gretzky

THIS IS THE third and final checkpoint that reviews key takeaways as we progress through the book. DITM LEAPS are comprised of nearly all intrinsic value; hence, the Greeks have little influence on the value of these types of options since they're primarily used to estimate extrinsic value. Therefore, I don't use any Greeks when making decisions on which options to buy. I also don't use any technical indicators such as EMA, MACD, RSI, etc.

I primarily buy DITM LEAPS calls with a BE no higher than 5% of the current underlying stock price when the option order executes. After that, I keep calm, remain patient, and wait for the underlying stock to go up. Note, sometimes I'll buy DITM LEAPS calls with a BE 10% above the current underlying stock price, and I'll also occasionally make educated speculative option trades such as OOTM LEAPS calls and short-term non-LEAPS calls. In addition to ignoring the Greeks, I also don't pay attention to OI and volume. The reason why is that as long as a fair price is offered, there are market makers and ECNs that will step in and make the market. I find that my limit orders generally execute if I set my price at the midpoint of the bid and ask or slightly above. Lastly, I keep track of all of my option trades in a trading book.

Buying DITM LEAPS calls is a stock replacement strategy. However, unlike more advanced options traders, when I buy DITM LEAPS calls, I perform no hedging during the trade and un-hedging (i.e., selling the hedges for profit) when the hedges are no longer needed. Instead, I use a simplified strategy of using any excess cash saved from buying options instead of stock to buy more options to increase my leverage. Increasing leverage increases potential gains, but it also increases potential risk. Depending on how much you have in play with your DITM LEAPS and if delta is near or at 1, this means the total dollar value of your options can swing four, five, six, or even seven figures in a single day. Please read that last sentence again. On a big up day in the stock market, you'll feel totally euphoric, but on a big down day, it may be a gut-wrenching experience for some—having the right temperament is critical.

A good options trading entry point is if the current price of the underlying stock when the trade order executes is 5-10% below its 52-week high, but this is not always possible. The best options trading entry points often appear after a market correction (i.e., the stock market is 10% down) or during a bear market (i.e., the stock market is 20% down) when high-quality stocks go on sale. However, even if a tech stock is near its 52-week high, this will not prevent me from buying DITM LEAPS calls based on the stock if I like the company and its long-term prospects. In other words, I'm not afraid of buying high today with the expectation of selling higher tomorrow. Sometimes it's not about where the stock came from but where it's headed.

This simple options trading strategy of buying DITM LEAPS calls with a BE no higher than 5% of the current underlying stock price when the option order executes consistently works for me over and over again. Furthermore, when I find a tech stock I like, such as AAPL or MSFT, with charts that go up and to the right over long periods of time (preferably 10 years or more), I'll trade the underlying stock repeatedly using DITM LEAPS calls. From my experience, going long with leverage is the best way for a non-professional retail investor to make money trading options. If you pick the right underlying stocks that go up and to the right over long periods of time, your options will also do the same.

I always try to hold my options in my taxable brokerage account for at least 12 months to avoid paying short-term capital gains. If I'm up several times on my original investment, I try not to get greedy and take some or all of the money off the table to ensure profits are realized and locked in. As Bernard Baruch once said, "Nobody ever lost money taking a profit." Lastly, having a pre-defined exit plan for each trade, adjusting it as needed, and sticking to it instills discipline and keeps you honest.

12

OTHER STUFF

A clever person solves a problem. A wise person avoids it.
—Albert Einstein

BELOW ARE MY thoughts regarding some additional financial topics, which you may find of interest. Fair warning. How I manage and invest my money works for me, but some things I do might be controversial and something you disagree with. That's OK. I'm sure there are plenty of professional financial advisors who will also not agree with me. Therefore, your mileage may vary depending on your specific individual situation. As always, take what you find useful and discard the rest.

401(k) Plan – Enable Self-Directed Investing
Created in 1978, a 401(k) allows an employee to invest a portion of their salary up to an annual limit into long-term investments for retirement purposes. An employer may also match part of an employee's contribution up to a certain predefined limit. According to Fidelity Investments, the most common match is 100% on the first 3% contributed and 50% on the next 2%. Like a traditional IRA, employees cannot withdraw money without incurring a tax penalty until they're 59½ years old. The 401(k) plan is now the most popular employer-sponsored retirement plan in America.

Most 401(k) plans are set up by default to offer only a limited number of funds. A BrightScope study found that the average 401(k) plan offered just 22 different funds to invest in. Over time some of the funds offered will underperform, and the plan administrator will replace them with new choices. This means that the 401(k) accounts for any employees invested in these funds also underperformed. From my own experience, many of the funds offered in a 401(k) plan like target date and bond funds consistently underperform the market (i.e., S&P 500) over time.

According to a 2018 report from PLANSPONSOR, only 20.3% of all employers offered an SDBA (self-directed brokerage account). An SDBA will enable you to buy and sell individual stocks, bonds, options, ETFs, futures, etc. An SDBA enables you to have more control over how you invest your money in workplace retirement plans, and you're not restricted to the limited number of funds offered. Note, companies typically don't promote SDBAs even if they're available because employees who don't know what they're doing can incur large losses or take unnecessary risks in their 401(k) retirement plans.

Qualcomm uses Fidelity Investments, and here's what I did with my 401(k) account before I retired. I setup Fidelity BrokerageLink to turn on self-directed investing. However, when I was enrolled in Qualcomm's 401(k), I could only transfer $1,000 or more into BrokerageLink; hence, if my contributions didn't reach this threshold after each paycheck, I would have to wait to accumulate more before I could initiate a transfer. Another requirement was a minimum of 5% had to be invested in one of the standard pre-selected investment options that my employer's plan offered. I picked a fund like Fidelity OTC (FOCPX) or Fidelity Contrafund (FCNKX) that would hopefully, at a minimum, match and exceed the performance of the S&P 500. I then put the remaining 95% into BrokerageLink. If there were no restrictions from my employer, then I would have put 100%. Once the money was in BrokerageLink, I started trading individual tech stocks like AAPL in the account, which quickly evolved to trading only DITM LEAPS calls. If you can enable an SDBA with your 401(k), be sure to ask your employer if there are any restrictions.

Every paycheck, I contributed the maximum amount to secure the maximum employer match, which I consider free money. If you're risk-averse, step 1 is to invest in an S&P 500 ETF like VOO or Nasdaq 100 ETF like QQQ. Step 2 would be to invest in high-quality tech stocks like AAPL, MSFT, or AMZN. Step 3 would be to invest the employer match in DITM LEAPS calls, and the rest would be in individual tech stocks. Finally, step 4 would be to do what I did—trade only DITM LEAPS calls in your SDBA.

529 Plan – A Complete Waste of Time

A 529 is a popular tax-advantaged savings account designed to help parents save and pay for their kids' K-12 and college expenses. Individual states sponsor their own 529 plans. You're not required to select your home state's plan, although some states offer state income tax incentives, deductions, and tax credits for contributions to their state's 529 plan. A 529 can also be used to cover qualified educational expenses in any state, not just your home state. There's no annual contribution limit, but each state does specify a maximum aggregate contribution limit per beneficiary, which currently ranges from $235,000-$529,000. 529 contributions are considered gifts for federal tax purposes. In 2019, up to $15,000 per donor per beneficiary qualifies for the annual gift tax exclusion, and any excess contributions above $15,000 must be reported to the IRS (Internal Revenue Service) and count against a taxpayer's lifetime estate and gift tax exemption, which as of June 2020, is $11.58 million per person.

There are two main types of 529 plans. They include savings plans (these are tax-deferred with no capital gains taxes and withdrawals are tax-free) and prepaid tuition plans where you pay tuition in advance at a limited number of designated colleges and universities by locking in the cost at today's rates (room and board are not covered). The funds you contribute to a 529 are always 100% yours, and you can withdraw them at any time for any reason; however, any non-qualified distribution will be subject to ordinary income taxes and a 10% withdrawal tax penalty with some exceptions.

I set up a Fidelity 529 for my son when he was 16 months old. After a few years, I paid the taxes and penalty for withdrawing the money and closing the account. Despite tax advantages provided by a 529, the ROI was horrible. I could do much better if I invested the money myself, even if it was in a taxable account. A 529 plan is like a 401(k) plan, except with no ability to set up an SDBA. I looked up what was offered by my home state's 529 plan (California ScholarShare) as of June 2020. Besides target age-based choices, ScholarShare also offered static and individual investment choices to select from. Among the 12 static investment choices, the best-performing selection (Passive Diversified Fixed Income Investment Portfolio) returned 6.2% over the past year, and the worst-performing selection (Index International Equity Investment Portfolio) returned -15.5%. Among the five individual investment choices, the best-performing selection (Index Bond Investment Portfolio) returned 8.7% over the past year, and the worst-performing selection (Index US Equity Investment Portfolio) returned -9.2%. Not only were the best-performing selections unable to beat the performance of an S&P 500 ETF like VOO, which returned 28.6% over the past year, but even worse, if you selected the wrong investment, you would have lost money in your 529 plan. My guess is the performance results for other states' 529 plans wouldn't have been much better than California. In hindsight, I should have pulled the plug on my son's 529 sooner and not even set up the 529, and instead, invest money earmarked for my son's college education myself like I'm doing now.

In summary, I think 529s are a complete waste of time because the ROI is so low. It's better to invest your money in a taxable account where you can buy and sell DITM LEAPS calls, individual tech stocks, or at minimum park money in the S&P 500 (VOO) or Nasdaq 100 (QQQ). The table below shows the results (adjusted for dividends and splits) of investing an initial amount of $15,000 for 18 years (August 1, 2002, to July 31, 2020) in SPY (Vanguard didn't launch VOO until September 7, 2010), QQQ, AAPL, AMZN, and MSFT. The total gains and ROIs over 18 years for each of the investments speak for themselves.

Investment	Ending value $	Total gain $	AR %	ROI %
SPDR S&P 500 ETF SPY	78,720	63,720	9.65	425
Nasdaq 100 ETF Invesco QQQ	201,153	186,153	15.51	1,241
AAPL	6,905,870	6,890,870	40.59	45,939
AMZN	3,352,415	3,337,415	35.06	22,249
MSFT	210,144	195,144	15.8	1,301

Affordable Care Act (ACA) – No Asset Test

If you buy health care coverage through your ACA-based state marketplace (e.g., Covered California if you reside in California), you may qualify for a discount on your monthly premium. Eligibility for premium subsidies is only based on income. There's no asset test. In other words, it doesn't matter how much your stock portfolio is worth, how much your home or other real estate properties are worth, or how much cash you have in the bank. Federal assistance is determined solely based on your annual income. Medicaid eligibility in the states that have expanded Medicaid can also be based on monthly income, which is useful for people who experience income drops during the year. To determine eligibility, an ACA-specific MAGI (modified adjusted gross income) is calculated, which is made up of AGI (adjusted gross income) from your IRS Form 1040 income tax return plus non-taxable Social Security income, tax-exempt interest income, and/or foreign earned income and housing expenses for Americans living abroad.

If you have a substantial stock portfolio and you're consistently generating capital gains from buying and selling stocks and options on an annual basis, then it's unlikely you'll qualify for any health insurance discounts. However, it's possible to take advantage of the ACA no asset test if you decide to sell stocks or options biannually. In other words, if you don't sell any stocks or options for an entire tax year and if the total annual amount of money earned from any interest-bearing accounts or dividend payments you receive is low enough and you earn minimal or no income, then you may qualify for discounts for the health insurance you have purchased through your state's marketplace if your annual income is below certain threshold levels. For 2020, you may qualify for a discount if you're single and your annual income is between $12,490 and $49,960, or for a family of three if your household income is between $21,330 and $85,320 (the range differs for families of different sizes). Additionally, if you buy a health insurance plan through your state's marketplace and your income is between $12,490 and $31,225 for a single person or $21,330 and $53,325 for a family of three, you may also qualify for help with cost-sharing via certain plans.

The bottom line is if you decide to use an on/off stock and option biannual selling strategy, then you may qualify for discounts and cost-sharing assistance. ACA opponents think this is unfair and is a loophole that high net worth individuals and families can potentially take advantage of depending on how they report their income for a particular tax year. If your current tax situation allows you to take advantage of how the law is currently written, my recommendation is to go for it.

Coverdell ESA – Self-Directed Investing

A Coverdell ESA (Education Savings Account) is not the same as a 529 plan; however, it's another option that some parents use to save for their children's higher education expenses. ESAs were first introduced in 1998 as Education IRAs before being renamed to Coverdell in 2002. Like a 529, Coverdell contributions grow tax-deferred, and money can be withdrawn tax-free for qualified educational expenses. Similar to a 529, unused amounts can be transferred to another family member beneficiary. However, a Coverdell is age-limited while a 529 is not. Contributions to a Coverdell must end when the beneficiary reaches 18, and withdrawals must be distributed by the time the beneficiary is 30.

There's one very significant difference between a 529 and a Coverdell, and that is with the latter, you're allowed self-directed investing just like in a 401(k) if your employer allows it in your plan or an IRA. Note, a $2,000 maximum annual contribution limit per beneficiary for a Coverdell may apply depending on your income level. The $2,000 maximum contribution is phased out for joint filers with a MAGI between $190,000-$220,000 (between $95,000-$110,00 for single fliers).

I think a Coverdell is superior to a 529 due to self-directed investing; however, assuming you qualify to open a Coverdell account, it's constrained due to an annual contribution limit. For example, assume your son started college when he was 18, and you also set up a Coverdell the first year he was born. This means the maximum you would be able to contribute to a Coverdell would be $36,000 (2,000 * 18). Perhaps the most optimal strategy is to use both a self-directed Coverdell (if you qualify) and a regular taxable account where you can have complete control over both accounts.

Diversification – Protection Against Ignorance

By diversifying a stock portfolio, investors can reduce their exposure to risk and construct a potentially more profitable long-term portfolio. A diversified portfolio will contain many asset classes and diversity within those asset classes and investments with different risk profiles. Such a portfolio would typically include stocks (large-cap, small-cap, domestic, international, emerging market, different industries, and sectors), bonds (government, municipalities, corporations), cash and cash equivalents (including CDs and money market accounts), and alternative investments (real estate, commodities, private equity, cryptocurrency, etc.). While diversification doesn't guarantee against loss, most investment professionals believe that by investing in different areas that react differently to the same market event, a portfolio's returns can be maximized over time. Diversification is considered one of the most important strategies for investors to follow to achieve their long-term financial goals while minimizing risk and reducing volatility.

Let's take a look at FANG, FAANG, and FAANGM. The table below shows the ROI adjusted for dividends and splits (where applicable) and AR for the past eight years (FB went public on May 18, 2012) for FANG, FAANG, and FAANGM as well as the S&P 500, DJIA, Nasdaq, and Nasdaq 100 (QQQ). If you had invested in nothing more than FANG, FAANG, or FAANGM over the past eight years, you would have beaten the performance of all three major indices (S&P 500, DJIA, Nasdaq) and even outperformed the more tech-heavy Nasdaq 100 (QQQ).

Investment	Value 5/18/12 $	Value 5/18/20 $	ROI %	AR %
DJIA	12,369.38	24,597.37	98.86	8.97
S&P 500	1,295.22	2,953.91	128.06	10.86
Nasdaq	2,778.79	9,234.83	232.33	16.2
Nasdaq 100 (QQQ)	55.77	227.43	307.8	19.21
FAANGM	651.07	4,975.33	664.18	28.94
FAANG	626.74	4,790.93	664.42	28.95
FANG	561.15	4,475.97	697.64	29.64

American steel tycoon Andrew Carnegie once said, "Concentrate your energies, your thoughts and your capital. The wise man puts all his eggs in one basket and watches the basket." At the 1996 Berkshire Hathaway annual shareholder meeting, responding to an audience question on why in some years BRK.A reported only three stocks in its public equity portfolio, Warren Buffet replied, "We think diversification makes very little sense for anyone that knows what they're doing…diversification is protection against ignorance." Buffet continued, "…for investors and analysts who think they know and understand how to evaluate businesses, diversification is 'crazy'…and to have some super-wonderful business and then put money in number 30 or 35 on your list of attractiveness and forego putting more money into No. one, just strikes Charlie [Charlie Munger, vice chairman of BRK.A] and me as madness." Has anything changed since Buffet responded to that shareholder in 1996? The answer is no. According to Motley Fool, as of May 21, 2020, Buffet's $196 billion portfolio consisted of 46 securities, and 67.8% of the portfolio was in four stocks (AAPL ($79.5 billion, 40.6%), Bank of America (BAC)($21.7 billion, 11.1%), KO ($18.1 billion, 9.2%), American Express (AXP)($13.6 billion, 6.9%)). AAPL alone was 40.6% of Buffet's entire portfolio. By any measure, this is not a diversified portfolio.

For over 25 years, through both bull and bear markets, I have invested in tech. To beat the market (i.e., S&P 500), I do not think you need to be diversified. Ever since I started investing in individual tech stocks in 1993, I have never been diversified across industries, sectors, or asset classes. However, I will invest in different tech stock industries such as software, hardware, semiconductors, services, platforms, etc. If you know what you are doing, there is no need to diversify your portfolio. Returning to Buffet, "…if I had to bet the next 30 years on the fortunes of my family that would be dependent upon the income from a given group of businesses, I would rather pick three businesses from those we own than own a diversified group of 50."

Do Not Miss the Forest for the Trees

Stocks generally fall faster and more dramatically than they go up. When there is bad news on Wall Street, it spreads faster than good news. Investor fear can lead to panic selling when the prudent move is to hold tight and ride it out. If stock prices for great companies go on sale, you should buy more stock, not sell. If you were willing to buy a stock at a certain price, and now it is cheaper because the market went down, do not second guess yourself on whether you should still buy. Warren Buffet famously said, "Be fearful when others are greedy. Be greedy when others are fearful." Have conviction in your decisions, and if you are investing for the long run, do not miss the forest for the trees.

For example, let's look at a 2016 stock chart for AAPL adjusted for both dividends and splits. Let's also assume you had been holding AAPL stock for the past five years. On April 14, 2011, AAPL closed at $41.11/share. On April 14, 2016, AAPL closed at $104.79/share, a 154.9% (((104.79 / 41.11) – 1) * 100) ROI and a 20.6% AR over five years. On April 26, 2016, AAPL reported its fiscal Q2 earnings after market close. AAPL announced its first quarter-over-quarter revenue decline since 2003 and first-ever year-over-year iPhone decline in sales. Twenty-eight days later, on May 12, 2016, AAPL had fallen 18.9% or 19.83 points to close at $84.96/share. However, despite the near 20% drop from April 14, 2016, to May 12, 2016, AAPL still produced an ROI of 106.7% (((84.96 / 41.11) – 1) * 100) and a 15.6% AR from April 14, 2011, to May 12, 2016. Now assume you panicked and didn't want to lose any more money, so you decided to sell all of your shares the next day to lock in profits to protect against AAPL continuing to slide further. If you had sold AAPL on May 13, 2016, you missed the forest for the trees.

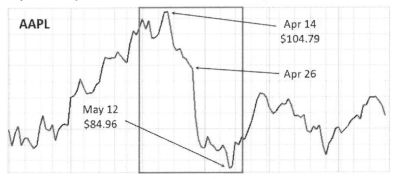

Source: StockCharts.com.

The chart below shows AAPL stock extended about 2½ years past May 13, 2016. The stock is up and to the right. By August 31, 2018, AAPL was selling for $222.35/share, which is 161.7% (((222.35 / 84.96) – 1) * 100) higher than what AAPL closed at on May 12, 2016. Furthermore, the ROI from April 14, 2011, would have been 440.9% (((222.35 / 41.11) – 1) * 100) with a 25.9% AR over 7.33 years.

Source: StockCharts.com.

Do not let short-term fear in the market derail your goals of building wealth if you are invested in high-quality companies for the long-term. Being invested in the right companies for the long haul far outweighs sitting on the sidelines waiting to buy at precisely the best time. Inevitably, what happens in the latter case is you end up watching the stock price go up and up and up and never buy. The stock market will often alternate between stages of fear and greed. Peter Lynch, the legendary former manager of the Fidelity Magellan Fund, is absolutely correct when he said, "You get recessions, you have stock market declines. If you don't understand that's going to happen, then you're not ready, you won't do well in the markets." He further added, "Everyone has the brainpower to make money in stocks. Not everyone has the stomach." When it comes to trading options, this is especially true where the ups and downs can be amplified several times compared to stocks.

Emergency Fund – I Do Not Have One Anymore

An emergency fund is typically a federally-insured high-yield bank savings account (or a money market account or no-penalty CDs) with readily-accessible money set aside to cover life's large, unexpected financial surprises such as loss of a job, unforeseen medical expenses, major home, and home appliance repairs, and needed car repairs. In other words, an emergency fund is a safety net of cash and other highly liquid assets that can be used for emergency purposes. It also reduces the need to access high-interest debt such as credit cards and high-interest loans and possibly go further into debt or derail your future financial security by prematurely tapping into retirement funds. Depending on your specific situation, financial planners recommend having enough set aside in an emergency fund to cover 3-6 months of expenses. The most conservative financial planners often recommend setting aside 9-12 months. An easy way to get started in saving for an emergency fund is to use any tax refunds and other cash windfalls you may receive (e.g., work bonus or cash gifts) to start building an emergency fund.

When I first started working full time in my early 20s, I set up a 3-month emergency fund. If you're financially disciplined, this is something you're supposed to do, and my parents beat it into my head too. However, as the years continued to roll on by, I later concluded that it wasn't a good ROI. My cash was effectively just "dead" money sitting in a bank account waiting to be used if needed. After diligently maintaining an emergency fund for about 13 years, when I was 36 and started working at Qualcomm in 2001, I decided to invest my emergency fund into the stock market. I've never set up a new emergency fund since and don't have one today. By 2001, I had been investing in tech stocks for about eight years, and my rationale was if I really needed money for an emergency, then I would sell some of my appreciated stock holdings to generate cash. While it's never ideal to sell stocks if you need to versus when you want to, even if I did, I still would have come out way ahead financially compared to if I had money earning next to nothing in an emergency fund bank account.

After closing my emergency fund, I took the balance and invested it in individual tech stocks like MSFT and others. Each year that I didn't tap into this balance (i.e., no emergency) meant it could grow, and at a much faster rate than if the money were sitting in a bank account. For example, assume you have a 3-month emergency fund with a balance of $30,000. The S&P 500 has historically returned about 9.8% annually over the past 90 years. That means after eight years, a $30,000 investment in an S&P 500 ETF like VOO would grow to $63,378. Hence, if you didn't tap into this investment during these eight years, you would have more than doubled your initial investment, which means if an emergency finally did arise, you would have twice as much money to address the situation if needed. Viewed another way, you have the entire $30,000 you had originally allocated to address emergencies, and you would have another $33,378 to continue to stay invested in the market. And if you can achieve higher ROI, it just shortens the double-time. For example, a 15% AR means $30,000 becomes $60,341 in five years, a 20% AR means $30,000 becomes $62,208 in four years, and a 30% AR turns $30,000 into $65,910 after just three years. I wouldn't do this, but if you're conservative, after building up enough cushion by doubling your initial investment, you could take half off the table and park it into a bank account, and leave the rest invested in the market

In my opinion, if your stock holdings have appreciated to a certain amount, an emergency fund is no longer required. You can generate far superior ROI by investing the cash you would have set aside for an emergency fund elsewhere (e.g., in individual tech stocks, VOO, or a Nasdaq 100 ETF (QQQ)) than in a low-interest bank account. Again, I have no emergency fund. If a major emergency popped up, I would sell some appreciated stock. Whether you're comfortable doing what I do is a question only you can answer.

Financial Advisors – Be Sure They Beat The S&P 500

I'm not a big fan of paying financial advisors to manage your investment portfolio. They typically charge clients using one of four different fee structures: 1) percentage of AUM (usually 0.25-0.50% for a robo-advisor and 1-2% for in-person), 2) flat annual retainer fee (usually $2,000-$7,500, 3) hourly fee ($100-$400), 4) per plan ($1,000-$3,000). There are two ROI thresholds to consider here. The first threshold is financial advisors must be able to consistently beat the market (i.e., S&P 500) over the long term less the fees they charge. If they can't do this, why bother using them. You would have been better off investing in an S&P 500 ETF (VOO), a Nasdaq ETF like Fidelity Nasdaq Composite Index Tracking Stock (ONEQ), or Nasdaq 100 ETF (QQQ). The second threshold is if your own AR over the long run outperforms the market, then financial advisors need to be able to beat your ROI, again, less the fees they charge. Otherwise, you would be better off continuing to invest your money yourself.

Secondary Market – Investing in Pre-IPO Tech Companies

In the past five years, there has been a trend for companies in the US to stay private longer before going public. Not surprisingly, the private market value of these companies has also increased. Today, dozens of unicorns (a privately held startup valued at over $1 billion) exist in the US. Some of these unicorns include Airbnb, Bird, Coinbase, DoorDash, Instacart, Robinhood, and SpaceX. Until a liquidity event occurs, the trend of pre-IPO US startup companies staying private longer means founders, owners, management, and employees holding vested stock options will not be able to convert illiquid options into cash. The most common liquidity event is an IPO. However, it could also be a sale to a publicly-traded company, in which case the startup's private company shares are converted into publicly-traded shares. As the company value continues to rise, it's also not uncommon for a significant percentage of a startup employee's overall net worth to become tied up with a single company, with no guarantee it'll go public.

The pre-IPO marketplace has historically been dominated by venture capital firms, investment banks, private placement agents, and brokers. As a result, a secondary market has emerged, consisting of private company marketplaces operated by companies such as Forge Global (SharesPost), Nasdaq Private Market, Oceanic, Scenic Advisement, Section Partners, and others. These marketplaces help facilitate private transactions between qualified buyers and startup founders, employees, and/or early-stage investors desiring to liquidate some of their vested stock holdings. Qualified buyers include high net worth individuals (accredited investors, qualified clients, qualified purchasers), venture capital firms, hedge funds, private equity firms, and other institutional investors.

I first purchased shares in pre-IPO tech companies via the secondary market in 2011. I acquired fund units in FB and LNKD as an LP in dedicated single-asset SPVs, the structure most commonly used for these types of investments. Fund units represent ownership interest in shares in the pre-IPO company and generally correspond 1:1 with the company shares held by the fund. Shares, which are acquired from existing employees or shareholders, are later transferred to investors once they become freely transferrable due to a liquidity event. After FB and LNKD went public and the lock-up period expired, I later sold my shares for a profit.

If you are an accredited investor, and you are interested, consider participating in the secondary market and direct private company investments. If you invest in the right pre-IPO companies at the right valuations, the secondary market can be an additional investment vehicle to generate superior ROI. However, these investments are not for the faint of heart. 1) you will be required to invest a minimum amount of capital (typically $100,000). 2) you will be charged very high transaction fees to purchase units in an SPV (lower fees can be negotiated). 3) you will not be able to withdraw your money from an SPV until a liquidity event occurs (an IPO or possibly an acquisition by a publicly-traded company), so you should assume whatever money you invest will not be accessible—you are willing to accept the opportunity cost for this dead money. 4) you will be subject to lock-up periods (usually 90-180 days or longer) just like employees of the company holding vested pre-IPO shares; hence, you cannot immediately flip your shares if a big pop occurs when the stock goes public.

Over the years, due to valuation, I passed on investing in companies such as Airbnb, Cloudera, Impossible Foods, Palantir, Robinhood, Snap, Unity, and others. Snap, Cloudera (CLDR), Palantir (PLTR), and Unity (U) have since gone public. Currently, I'm holding SPV units in two private tech companies. Often dubbed the Amazon of South Korea, the first is Coupang. The second is Space Exploration Technologies Corp. (better known as SpaceX). I'm patiently waiting for these two companies to go public. Coupang is likely to go public in the next 2-3 years, while SpaceX is not likely to IPO until they successfully send a crewed mission to Mars in 2026. SpaceX may, however, spinoff and IPO its Starlink space-Internet business sooner. If you're financially comfortable with the risk-reward profile of investing in pre-IPO companies and the valuation you can buy shares at, you should go for it. Just remember that any invested capital via the secondary market is "dead" money until a liquidity event occurs, which may take years.

Selling Covered Calls to Sell Stock

If you're interested in selling stock you own, you could put in a limit order at the bid or slightly above (e.g., at the bid/ask midpoint) and wait to see if the order executes. There's a second way to sell stock using options where you get paid for selling your shares. In this case, you write or sell covered calls slightly above what the stock is currently selling for. For example, let's say you own 100 shares of DOCU. DOCU last sold for $161.42/share, and the bid is $161.40, so you could sell 100 shares of DOCU for $16,140 (100 * 161.4) assuming the order executes at the bid. Looking at the options chain, there's a call contract one strike away at $162.50 with a bid of $2.70/contract and an ask of $6.40/contract, and it last sold for $4.50/contract, which is near the bid/ask midpoint of $4.55/contract (2.7 + 6.4) / 2). If you sold a weekly covered call at $4.50, and the stock moves up $1.08 (162.5 – 161.42) or 0.67% (((162.5 / 161.42) – 1) * 100), then the stock would be called away from you at the $162.50 strike price. Hence, options were used to sell 100 shares of stock for $162.50/share while allowing you to also collecting a premium of $4.50/contract. This means you actually sold the stock for $167/share (162.5 + 4.5).

If you don't need to sell immediately, then selling covered calls to sell your stock will help bring in a little extra money for something you intended to do anyway. In the example above, if you were OK with selling 100 shares of DOCU for $161.40/share, why not sell it for $167/share (3.47% higher) and make an extra $560 ((167 – 161.4) * 100). If DOCU stock goes down and doesn't hit your strike price, then your covered call will expire worthless, in which case you get to keep the premium ($4.50/contract or $450 per contract), and you can decide if you want to sell a covered call again to try to sell the stock. Note, as you keep repeating this process, you'll continue to generate income (effectively selling for a price higher than the current stock price) until you actually sell the stock. If DOCU stock goes up, then as discussed, the person you sold the covered call contract to will more than likely exercise, and you'll have to give up your 100 shares of stock; however, if expiration hasn't occurred yet, you could also decide you no longer want to sell the stock in which case you would need to buy back the covered call you sold to exit the trade.

Selling Puts and Getting Paid to Buy Stock

If you're interested in owning a stock, you could put in a limit order at the ask or slightly below (e.g., at the bid/ask midpoint) and wait to see if the order executes. There's a second lesser-used way to buy stock using put options where you can effectively lower the cost basis of acquiring the shares. In other words, you'll get paid to do something you wanted to do anyway. You do this by selling cash-covered puts ATM or slightly below. Cash-covered (aka cash-secured) means you have 100% of the cash in your account to buy the stock at the strike price if required. Note, if you don't have the cash in your account to buy the shares, if they're assigned, this would be called a "naked" put and is not recommended. For example, let's say you want to own 100 shares of DOCU. The ask for DOCU is $161.80, so you could buy 100 shares of DOCU for $16,180 (100 * 161.8). Looking at the options chain, there's no put ATM. The closest put is the $160 strike, which has a bid of $3.10/contract. If you sold this weekly put contract, you're committing to buy 100 shares of DOCU at $160/share if the stock falls to $160 or lower (i.e., the person you sold the put contract to will likely exercise the put, and you'll be assigned meaning you'll be required to buy the shares), but, in return, you get to collect a premium of $3.10/contract (i.e., $310 per contract) for selling the put. If DOCU falls to $160 or lower, you have effectively lowered the cost basis for buying 100 shares of DOCU to $156.90/share (160 – 3.10). If you were OK with buying 100 shares of DOCU for $161.80/share, why not buy it for $156.90/share (3% lower) and save $490 ((161.8 – 156.9) * 100). If DOCU stock goes up and doesn't hit your strike price, then your put will expire worthless, in which case you keep the premium ($3.10/contract or $310 per contract), and you can decide if you want to sell a put again to try to acquire the stock. Your effective cost basis for this trade will continue to go down until you acquire the stock. If DOCU stock goes down, then as discussed, the person you sold the put contract to will more than likely exercise, and you'll have to buy the 100 shares of stock; however, if expiration hasn't occurred yet, you could also decide you no longer want to own the stock in which case you would need to buy back the put you sold to exit the trade.

Instead of acquiring the stock via selling puts, you could also pick a strike price that is several strikes below the current underlying stock price of a stock you wouldn't mind owning (if it came to that) and repeatedly sell cash-secured puts with an expiration of 1-2 weeks. Picking a strike price several strikes below the current underlying stock price increases the probability that the strike is not hit. Selling puts works well in a flat, sideways-moving market and would generate a recurring weekly/monthly income (assuming you don't have to buy the shares). This is particularly advantageous in a tax-deferred or tax-free account where you will not have to pay any short-term capital gains tax. Furthermore, depending on what percentage return you received for selling the puts, and if you successfully repeated this trade several more times over the course of a year, your AR might compare favorably, or perhaps even beat, the 9.8% historical performance of the S&P 500.

Social Security

If you haven't set up an account at www.ssa.gov/myaccount, you should do this so that you can track your work earnings over the course of your career compared to what the SSA (Social Security Administration) has in their records. The SSA will also provide estimates of expected monthly payouts depending on the age you decide to start receiving payments. The estimates the SSA provides include early payout at age 62, at the full retirement age of either 66 or 67 (depends on the year you were born), and at a maximum payout at age 70. If you were to pass away, the SSA also shows estimated survivor benefits that your child, spouse caring for a child, and spouse at full retirement age would receive. Once you have obtained this data, you can use a spreadsheet to determine the optimal age for you to start taking Social

Security payments. I also like to run two other scenarios. 1) if I take payments early at age 62 and then invest 100% of the payouts in the market (e.g., in VOO, QQQ, individual tech stocks, or DITM LEAPS calls), assuming various ARs, will I come out ahead versus waiting to either full retirement age at 66 or 67 (i.e., investing payouts from the ages of 62-66 or 62-67) or maximum payout age at 70 (i.e., investing payouts from the ages of 62-70). 2) if I take payments at full retirement age at 66 or 67 and then invest 100% of the payouts in the market, will I come out ahead versus waiting to maximum payout age at 70 (i.e., investing payouts from the ages of 66-70 or 67-70). Lastly, if you want to be very conservative in your retirement planning, do what I did, don't include Social Security. If you can achieve your retirement number with no dependency on Social Security, then you'll automatically build in extra cushion, and anything you receive from Social Security in the future will be the icing on the cake.

Unusual Options Activity

Millions of options are traded daily on Wall Street. Unusual options activity occurs when there is abnormally high volume in a near-term option relative to its average daily volume. Option alert services provide alerts to paid subscribers when unusual options activity occurs. Sometimes abnormally high volume means nothing more than a protective hedge is being put in place by an institutional investor. However, what is most likely happening is smart money (e.g., a hedge fund manager) knows or suspects something that the average retail investor does not and is anticipating a big stock move (i.e., they are using options to place big bets to amplify profit due to the increased leverage that options provide). While smart money has an information and speed advantage over the retail investor, they're not always right, or as David Tepper put it, "For better or worse we're a herd leader. We're at the front of the pack, we are one of the first movers. First movers are interesting; you get to the good grass first, or sometimes the lion eats you."

When the volume exceeds the OI, this generally indicates a new position is being opened. Furthermore, if the volume is occurring in large blocks of 100 contracts or more, this usually indicates institutional investor buying rather than retail investors. Lastly, if the volume is 3-5x larger than the prior day's volume, this is another sign the activity is unusual. *CNBC* contributors Jon and Pete Najarian are well-known proponents of trading on unusual options activity. Some of the key takeaways from their book *Follow the Smart Money* include: 1) inside information leaks quickly and shows up in options first, 2) since it's based on publicly-available data, trading on unusual options activity is not illegal, 3) people trading on inside information want into the market, this usually means aggressive options buying at the ask, 4) if an order is larger than the current OI, it's an opening trade, 5) if a large trade is executed that appears to be tied to a spread, this is most likely not a trade based on inside information because a spread will limit upside (someone trading on inside information will try to maximize profit by buying OOTM options), 6) if there is unusual options activity in a specific option, the option price tends to increase, which increases its IV.

Upstream Planning

This book is not about estate tax planning, but I thought I'd mention something pretty cool if you're in a position to take advantage of it. When it comes to estate planning, most people focus on downstream planning (i.e., from old to young), but you can also perform upstream planning, in which case your assets first flow from young to old before round-tripping and coming back to you. Upstreaming is an old tax-savings strategy that the wealthy are familiar with but wasn't used very often. This is because people didn't want to use up their estate tax exemption, and instead, would rather preserve it until death. However, this has changed in recent years since, as of June 2020, the amount an individual can give away in assets while alive or after death has been doubled to $11.58 million. For a husband and wife, this means a total of $23.16 million can be transferred tax-free in estate, gift, and generation-skipping tax to their children and grandchildren. If new tax law is not passed, the increased exemption to $11.58 million per person is scheduled to expire on December 31, 2025, at which time the exemption will be reduced to $5 million per person.

Here is the basic concept. 1) you give a highly appreciated asset such as stock, real estate, or a business (hard-to-value assets such as artwork or collectibles should be avoided since they would require appraisals and their value may be open to challenge by the IRS) to an elderly parent or trusted elder with the understanding that it'll be bequeathed back to you. 2) the highly appreciated asset then gets a step-up in cost basis, which effectively wipes out the substantial tax obligations on the appreciated asset. 3) the asset is returned to you upon the death of the elderly parent or trusted elder. For example, you own NVDA stock, which you had initially purchased for $250,000 a long time ago, and it's now worth $2.5 million. If you sold the stock, you would have to pay long-term capital gains on $2.25 million. Assuming your elderly parent's net worth, including the $2.5 million in NVDA stock, is less than $11.58 million, upon your parent's death, no federal estate tax would be due. Furthermore, if your parent's estate is also less than the state tax exemption, there would also be no state estate tax due either. Hence, by upstreaming the $2.5 million in NVDA you have shielded it from taxes at potentially both the federal and state level.

As interesting as upstreaming sounds, there are, however, some important caveats to consider. 1) for upstreaming to work, both parties have to be under the estate tax exemption. 2) you have to 100% trust the person you're gifting your assets to because after the assets have been transferred, you'll no longer have control anymore (e.g., the worst-case scenario is they can be bequeathed to someone else). 3) if you die before the person you're upstreaming to, who now owns your appreciated assets, those assets cannot be legally relied upon to help provide support for your spouse and children. 4) if the person you're upstreaming to dies within 12 months of receiving your gift, the IRS will consider the transaction as a deathbed deal with no other purpose other than to avoid taxes, and the upstreaming will be unwound. 5) when the person you're upstreaming to dies, there's the possibility that other family members will contest and fight for ownership of the asset that was originally yours.

Part Five

END OF LINE

Don't worry about what anybody else is going to do. The best way to predict the future is to invent it.

—Alan Kay

CONCLUSION

I've never lost a game. I just ran out of time.
—Michael Jordan

OUR JOURNEY TOGETHER through this book is almost complete. We're on the home stretch now headed towards the finish line. Hang in there, a few more pages, and you'll be free to unleash your newfound knowledge on the options market. However, before I let you go, let's recap what we have covered in this book.

Stocks are an almost frictionless investment versus real estate or a small business. With a laptop, desktop PC, tablet, or a smartphone and an Internet connection, you can trade stocks and options from practically anywhere in the world. The AR for the stock market (i.e., S&P 500) over the past 90 years is 9.8%. The table below shows the AR and ROI for a $100,000 investment over a period of 10 years (September 13, 2010, to September 14, 2020) in six investments: 1) savings account with 1% APY, 2) money market account with 1.75% APY, 3) S&P 500 ETF (Vanguard VOO), 4) Nasdaq 100 ETF (Invesco QQQ), 5) MSFT, and 6) AAPL.

Investment	Ending value $	Total gain $	AR %	ROI %
Bank savings account	110,462	10,462	1.00	10.46
High yield money market account	118,944	18,944	1.75	18.94
S&P 500 ETF Vanguard VOO	301,641	201,641	11.67	201.64
Nasdaq 100 ETF Invesco QQQ	582,239	482,239	19.26	482.24
MSFT	817,943	717,943	23.39	717.94
AAPL	1,209,224	1,109,224	28.31	1,109.22

After 10 years, the ROI of investing in ETFs in the S&P 500 and Nasdaq 100 indices easily beat a bank savings account or high yield money market account. The ROI of investing in individual tech stocks like MSFT and AAPL easily beat the S&P 500 and Nasdaq 100 ETFs. After 10 years, MSFT produced an 8-bagger, and AAPL produced a 12-bagger. The difference in total investment dollar gain after 10 years between a bank savings account ($10,462) and AAPL ($1,109,224) is night and day. Investing your money in a bank account, money market account, CDs, or US Treasury savings bonds is not going to help you build wealth.

Options trading has become very popular within the past 20 years. If used properly, options are powerful financial instruments. Not only can they help you achieve your financial goals, but they can also accelerate them. After making over 90 options trades in the 3.75 years since retiring, my winning (i.e., profitable) call options trade percentage is 89%; hence, I strongly believe it's possible to beat the market, and making money trading options is not just for professional traders.

LEAPS are nothing more than options with expiration dates 2-3 years in the future. What makes LEAPS special is that they enable you to be a long-term options investor and not just a short-term options trader. By using LEAPS that expire 2-3 years away, a long-term options investor is not affected as much by short-term market fluctuations, can wait and see if the predicted move plays out, and has more time to build up a cushion. LEAPS allow you to go long with leverage and can be used as a stock replacement to amplify ROIs if the underlying stock moves in the expected direction. I use any excess cash saved from buying options instead of stock to buy more options to increase my leverage. Increasing leverage increases potential gains, but it also increases potential risk. Depending on how much you have in play with your DITM LEAPS and if delta is near or at 1, this can mean the total dollar value of your options can swing four, five, six, or even seven figures in a single day. Please read that last sentence again. On a big up day, you'll feel totally euphoric, but on a big down day, it may be a gut-wrenching experience for some—having the right temperament is critical.

The value of an option is made up of intrinsic and extrinsic value. DITM LEAPS are comprised of nearly all intrinsic value; hence, the Greeks have little influence on the value of these types of options since they're primarily used to estimate extrinsic value. Therefore, I don't use any Greeks when determining which option to buy. I also never use any technical indicators such as EMA, MACD, RSI, etc. In addition to ignoring the Greeks, I also don't pay attention to OI and volume. The reason why is that as long as a fair price is offered, there are market makers and ECNs that will step in and make the market. I find that my limit orders usually execute if I set my price at the midpoint of the bid and ask or slightly above. Notice how I'm simplifying my decision-making process for determining which options to buy—it doesn't need to be complicated. Here's the big reveal again. My secret is: I buy DITM LEAPS calls with a BE no higher than 5% of the current underlying stock price when the option order executes. Remember, BE for a call is calculated by adding the premium to the strike price (the BE for a put is calculated by subtracting premium from the strike price). BE is the theoretical price the underlying stock needs to reach to breakeven on your options trade. After buying DTIM LEAPS calls and assuming I've picked the right underlying stock, I keep calm, remain patient, and wait for the underlying stock to go up. Note, sometimes I'll buy DITM LEAPS calls with a BE up to 10% above the current underlying stock price, and I'll also make educated speculative trades such as buying OOTM LEAPS calls and short-term non-LEAPS calls from time to time. However, if you stay within the 5% range, this is pretty conservative if you pick high-quality tech growth stocks.

A good options trading entry point is if the current price of the underlying stock, at the time the option order executes, is also 5-10% below its 52-week high, but this is not always possible. However, even if a tech stock is near its 52-week high, this has never prevented me from buying DITM LEAPS calls if I like the company and its long-term prospects. The best options trading entry points often appear after a market correction (i.e., 10% down) or during a bear market (i.e., 20% down) when high-quality stocks go on sale.

While past performance is never a guarantee for future results, my simple options trading strategy of buying DITM LEAPS calls with a BE no higher than 5% of the current underlying stock price when the option order executes has consistently worked, year after year. This was true before I retired, and it's still true today in retirement. Furthermore, when I find tech stocks like AAPL or MSFT, with charts that go up and to the right over long periods of time (preferably 10 years or more), I'll trade them repeatedly using DITM LEAPS calls. Note, my intellectual pride is also not hurt one bit by trading options in tech stocks like AAPL and MSFT that everyone owns versus only trying to be smart and cool discovering some unknown stock that no one has heard of yet. Don't let intellectual pride get in the way of making money.

As of August 28, 2020, I had several DITM LEAPS calls that were still open. Calls with 511 days to expiration include TTD Jan21'22 100C with a current ROI of 98.7%, MSFT Jan21'22 95C with a current ROI of 79.6%, and SHOP Jan21'22 150C with a current ROI of 259.9%. Calls with 658 days to expiration include TSLA Jun17'22 1,010C with a current ROI of 775.9%, AAPL Jun17'22 180C with a current ROI of 120.6%, and AAPL Jun17'22 180C (purchased at a lower premium on a later date than the other AAPL Jun17'22 180C) with a current ROI of 239%. I plan to close all of these calls no later than 30-45 days before their expiration dates of January 21, 2022, and June 17, 2022.

I always try to hold my options in my taxable brokerage account for at least 12 months. Depending on the expiration date, I often hold for much longer. This means I pay long-term capital gains of either 15% or 20% and not short-term capital gains of 35%. Lastly, if I'm up several times on my original investment and I've been holding DITM LEAPS calls for more than 12 months, I try not to get greedy and often take some or all of the money off the table. Having a pre-defined exit plan for each trade, adjusting it as needed, and sticking to it instills discipline and keeps you honest.

Finally, don't let short-term fear in the stock market derail your goals of building wealth if you're invested in best-in-class tech companies for the long term. Have conviction in your decisions, and if you're investing for the long run, don't miss the forest for the trees. Being invested in the right companies for the long haul far outweighs sitting on the sidelines waiting to buy at precisely the best time. Always remember that as a long-term investor, at some point, the market will become unsettled. When it does, take a deep breath and don't make ill-informed, rash decisions. Peter Lynch, the legendary former manager of the Fidelity Magellan Fund, is absolutely correct when he said, "Everyone has the brainpower to make money in stocks. Not everyone has the stomach." Warren Buffet said, "If you can't control your emotions, you can't control your money."

Some final, but perhaps controversial, things for you to consider. 1) it takes money to make money (if you want to reach your retirement number faster, you have to increase how much you invest or your AR or both). 2) if your employer offers a 401(k) that supports an SDBA, contribute enough to max out any employer matching and buy DITM LEAPS calls in high-quality tech stocks. 3) it's better to invest money allocated to your child's college education in VOO, ONEQ, QQQ, tech stocks, or DITM LEAPS calls in tech stocks in a taxable account than invest it in a tax-free 529. 4) diversification is not needed (I'm overwhelmingly invested in tech, and it has not hurt me over the long run). 5) once your stock holdings have appreciated to a certain amount, and you have built up enough cushion, an emergency fund is no longer required (you can generate far superior ROI by investing the cash that you would have set aside for an emergency fund elsewhere than parking it in a bank account or money market account). 6) consider selling covered calls to sell a stock. 7) consider selling puts and getting paid to buy a stock.

There you go, the entire book distilled down to 1,702 words. And if you want the super distilled version, here it is in just 22 words: buy DITM LEAPS calls with a BE no higher than 5% of the current underlying stock price when the option order executes. Conceptually, it's rather simple. When the underlying stock price goes up, the call premium goes up. However, the cool thing is premium increases at a multiple of what the stock does due to the leverage that options provide. This acceleration enables you to make more money when you complete a successful options trade versus just holding shares of the stock. This is where the magic happens for me in my options trading and enabled me to retire early. Start small, give it a try, and make sure you understand what's happening. If it works for you, stay disciplined, don't make foolish bets, don't get greedy, and do it again, and again, and again. Hopefully, you'll experience the same magic too, and if you do, don't be surprised if your family, friends, and work colleagues start wondering how you pulled the rabbit out of the hat and ask you, "How did you do it? How did you retire early?"

Although this book is about how I used LEAPS to retire early, indulge me for a moment about the importance of having a winner's mindset. Having the right attitude is not only critical for investing in stocks and trading options, but also in life. Tennis great Bjorn Borg said, "You have to find it. No one else can find it for you." Never forget, a successful person plays to win while others play not to lose. A successful person works hard to be in a position to be lucky when opportunity knocks and has the resolve and courage to act when an opportunity presents itself. A successful person puts money to work while others spend money. Winners always show up at the starting line, and they never give up before a race has started. They will not win all of the time, but they will also never truly lose. NBA Hall of Fame basketball legend Michael Jordan said, "You must expect great things of yourself before you can do them." Winners make life happen. Life doesn't happen to them. So, don't let life pass you by. Go live the life you have imagined for yourself, and make it matter.

> *Don't wait. The time will never be just right.*
> *—Mark Twain*

EPILOGUE: ENJOY THE RIDE

*Winnie left the next summer to study art history in Paris.
Still, we never forgot our promise. We wrote to each other
once a week for the next eight years. I was there to meet her
when she came home, with my wife and my first son, eight
months old. Like I said, things never turn out exactly the
way you planned.*

—The Wonder Years

I WANTED TO share with you some brief final words not about the stock market or LEAPS or even making money, but about an unexpected moment of serendipity. In April 2020, I was rummaging through some boxes in the garage one morning, and inside one of them, there was an old orange Nike shoebox. Inside the shoebox, I found, of all things, a Maxell cassette tape with the words "Summer 1988 San Diego" scribbled in blue ink on the label.

I was so intrigued that later in the afternoon, I went back to the garage and took my Yamaha stereo cassette deck out of storage and hooked it up to my PC. Then at night, after everyone else in the house was asleep, I kicked back, put on some headphones, put the tape in, and pressed play. I immediately smiled, and for a brief moment in time, I was transported back to Verano '88. I'm wearing Oakley Razor Blades and cruising on La Jolla Village Drive in a 2-door Honda Accord hatchback. The windows are rolled down, the scent of Coppertone is in the air, and I'm jamming to a mixtape. There's a Blockbuster movie in the front passenger seat that needs to be returned, and tossed in the back are white Prince Spectrum Comps, a red Specialized Stumpjumper, and a pair of Nike Bo Jackson Medicine Ball Air Trainers.

It turns out the Maxell cassette tape is from an old answering machine that I used while living in San Diego. What's on the tape is a collection of voices

that sound as clear today as the first time they were left on the answering machine 32 years ago. There are dozens of short messages separated by beeps, hang-ups, and occasional dial tones. It's over fifteen minutes of fond memories

Nostalgia found on a cassette tape.

from youthful and carefree days gone by. There are messages from a college roommate, friends I've lost touch with, a college friend who later took his own life, and someone I reconnected with this year, which was wonderful. Those voices bring a smile to my face and warm my heart. The tape is full of nostalgia and bittersweet—what could have been and what came to be.

After listening to the tape, I immediately thought of a poem that I stumbled across in an Ann Landers column while reading the local newspaper when I was 16. I cut that article out and kept it. The poem is titled "The Station" and was written by Robert J. Hastings. I encourage you to read it, and if you do, I hope you find it as poignant as the first time I read it, and as I still do today—even more so. Learn to cherish the moment because life is fleeting, and all too often, you do not realize or appreciate what you have until it is gone forever. There will be ups and downs and everything in between, but always remember, the true joy of life is the journey, not the final destination. As Hastings so eloquently concluded, "The Station will come soon enough." Enjoy the ride....

To live is the rarest thing in the world. Most people just exist.

—Oscar Wilde

APPENDIX A: RESOURCES

Calvin: I'm a man of few words.
Hobbes: Maybe if you read more, you'd have a larger vocabulary.
— *Bill Watterson*

I SPEND SOME time each day reading online articles, blogs, newsletters, reports, forums, and tweets as well as visiting web sites to keep up to date on what's happening overall, and specifically with technology and companies that I have stock and options positions in or that I'm considering opening a position in. I find all of this interesting, so the good thing for me is it's not work. On weekdays when the stock market is open, I also have *CNBC* streaming in the background if any helpful information or breaking news is announced. If something catches my attention, I'll do further research. Note, if you're concerned about being spammed, create a new email account and then use this email exclusively for signing up for newsletters, alerts, etc. I also devote some time each day to read books. At last count, I had a stack of over 20 unread books which I want to read: *The Psychology of Money* (Housel), *Billion Dollar Whale* (Wright/Hope), *Exploring Calvin and Hobbes* (Watterson), *The Ride of a Lifetime* (Iger), *The Master Algorithm* (Domingos), *Alone on the Wall* (Honnold/Roberts), *Life Is Good: The Book* (Jacobs/Jacobs), *A Trader's First Book on Commodities* (Garner).

Google Alerts

https://www.google.com/alerts

I receive Google Alerts daily via email. I'll update my alerts based on which stocks, companies, technologies, and industries I'm interested in.

Newsletters

I subscribe to free email newsletters from Andreessen Horowitz, *Barron's*, Benedict Evans, *CNBC*, *Crunchbase*, *Fortune*, Loup Ventures, *Venture Beat*, *The Wall Street Journal*, and several more (news will start to overlap).

Twitter

I use Twitter for up-to-the-minute news, alerts, market sentiment, instant reaction, and entertainment. I follow @ReformedBroker, @CitronResearch, @TechCrunch, @OphirGottlieb, @WSJbusiness, and a few others. Stocktwits is also interesting to scan from time to time for stock chatter—some know what they're talking about, some clearly do not.

Web Sites

Listed below are some sites that I visit from time to time. Some offer premium versions with free trials. The free versions are all that I need and use.

Amazon Annual Shareholder Letter
https://ir.aboutamazon.com/annual-reports-proxies-and-shareholder-letters/default.aspx

AMZN is the fastest company ever to reach $100 billion in annual sales. Jeff Bezos' annual letter to shareholders helps me understand his thought process and AMZN's impact on competitors, the industry, and the market.

Barchart
https://www.barchart.com/options/unusual-activity/stocks

I scan their Unusual Options Activity (days to expiration, if the volume is greater than OI, if the volume to OI ratio is high, IV) page to see what smart money might be up to.

Berkshire Hathaway Annual Shareholder Letter
https://www.berkshirehathaway.com/letters/letters.html

Warren Buffet's annual letter to shareholders has become required reading for many investors to gain insights into his thinking. BRK.A's overall gain over the past 54 years is 2,744,062% versus 19,784% for the S&P 500. From 1964-2019 BRK.A's AR has been 20.3%.

Briefing.com
https://www.briefing.com

They provide news, alerts, commentary, and analysis of US and international equity markets.

Crunchbase
https://www.crunchbase.com

They provide information (news, M&A, investments, funding, founders, management) about private and public companies.

Dividend Channel
https://www.dividendchannel.com/drip-returns-calculator

Their site has a helpful DRIP calculator, which shows the hypothetical returns for a $10,000 investment in a stock with and without DRIP, and compared with the returns of the S&P 500, Nasdaq 100, DJIA, or another stock.

EDGAR
https://www.sec.gov/edgar.shtml

EDGAR (Electronic Data Gathering, Analysis, and Retrieval) is the primary system for submissions by companies and others required by law to file information with the SEC. This includes Form 13F and Schedule 13D, which must be submitted to the SEC within 10 days by anyone who acquires beneficial ownership of more than 5% of any class of publicly-traded stock.

Estimize
https://www.estimize.com

They crowdsource quarterly earnings and revenue estimates for publicly-traded companies from over 24,000 people (independent contributors, sell side, buy side). I compare their estimates against analysts' estimates.

GuruFocus
https://www.gurufocus.com/guru/list

They track institutional investor stock picks and portfolio changes from SEC 13F filings. It's easier to look up 13Fs on GuruFocus than EDGAR.

Market Chameleon
https://marketchameleon.com/Reports/UnusualOptionVolumeReport

I scan their Unusual Option Volume page, where you can sort data, and look at the volume, number of call/put trades, quarterly earnings dates, and IV.

TED Talks
https://www.ted.com/talks

They're a nonprofit devoted to spreading ideas, usually in short talks of 18 minutes or less. All talks are archived and easily searchable.

TipRanks
https://www.tipranks.com

They track and measure the performance of Wall Street analysts, hedge fund managers, financial bloggers, and individual investors with posted public portfolios. I look at the price target and analyst ratings for individual stocks.

WhaleWisdom

https://www.whalewisdom.com

They focus on hedge funds and make it easy to lookup 13F, 13D, and 13G filings. The WhaleIndex tracks the 100 most commonly-held stocks disclosed in 13F filings and is rebalanced 46 days after the end of each quarter.

Books

According to a 2019 survey conducted by the Pew Research Center, 27% of American adults have not read a book in any format in the past 12 months. Joseph Addison said, "Reading is to the mind what exercise is to the body." Warren Buffet reads 500 pages a day, Mark Cuban reads three hours a day, and Bill Gates reads 50 books a year (approximately one book per week). In response to a question about how to prepare for an investing career, Buffet told MBA students in an investment class at his alma mater Columbia Business School, "Read 500 pages like this every day. That's how knowledge works. It builds up, like compound interest. All of you can do it, but I guarantee not many of you will do it." When Elon Musk was asked how he knew so much about rockets and how to build them, his response was, "I read a lot of books." In his book *Change Your Habits, Change Your Life*, author Tom Corley found that 88% of wealthy respondents spent a minimum of 30 minutes a day reading and on self-education, and 85% had a passion for learning new things.

Science Fiction

Encyclopedia Britannica defines science fiction as "a form of fiction that deals principally with the impact of actual or imagined science upon society and individuals." The technology depicted in sci-fi movies and TV shows or described in books is not currently possible today because either existing technology is too primitive or the technology hasn't been invented yet. I like to think of commercialized technology as sci-fi that's been realized.

Listed below are books, short stories, movies, and TV shows that have helped expand my imagination of what might be possible in the future. If interested, check some of them out. Besides enjoying them for their pure entertainment value, try to pay special attention to the technology shown and how it's applied. For older material, reflect on how sci-fi turned into reality. Some examples: *2001: A Space Odyssey* (1968): video call (Skype, FaceTime, Zoom); news pad (iPad, tablet), voice recognition (Alexa, Siri, Google Assistant), commercial space flight (coming soon SpaceX, Virgin Galactic); *Star Trek* (1966) TV show: communicators (Motorola StarTAC flip phone, cell/satellite phones), portable digital storage (floppy disks, USB flash memory sticks), Uhura, the Enterprise's communication officer, wears a wireless earpiece (AirPods, Bluetooth); *The Terminator* (1984): military drones (MQ-9 Reaper/Predator B); *Total Recall* (1990): self-driving technology and autonomous taxis (Google Waymo, Tesla, Uber). For newer material, as a tech investor, I like to try and connect the dots, form a picture, and predict when I think what's being shown will either come to fruition or not and in what form (hardware, software, service) as well as what business model. Finally, I think about whether an existing publicly-traded company or a new startup will be the first to commercialize the technology.

Books

2001: A Space Odyssey (Clarke)	*Ready Player One* (Cline)
20,000 Leagues Under the Sea (Verne)	*Rendezvous with Rama* (Clarke)
Contact (Sagan)	*Snow Crash* (Stephenson)
Do Androids Dream of Electric Sheep? (Dick)	*The Age of Intelligent Machines* (Kurzweil)
Dune (Herbert)	*The Age of Spiritual Machines* (Kurzweil)
Ender's Game (Card)	*The Hunger Games* (Collins)
Jurassic Park (Crichton)	*The Singularity Is Near* (Kurzweil)
Neuromancer (Stephenson)	*The War of the Worlds* (Wells)

Short Stories

A Sound of Thunder (Bradbury)	*Story of Your Life* (Chiang)
The Minority Report (Dick)	*We Can Remember It for You Wholesale* (Dick)

Movies

2001: A Space Odyssey (1968)	*Back to the Future* (1985)
A.I. (2001)	*Blade Runner* (1982)
Alien: Covenant (2017)	*Blade Runner 2049* (2017)
Arrival (2016)	*Close Encounters of the Third Kind* (1977)
Avatar (2009)	*Contact* (1997)

Edge of Tomorrow (2014)
Elysium (2013)
Ex Machina (2014)
Her (2013)
Inception (2010)
Interstellar (2014)
Iron Man (2008)
Jurassic Park (1993)
Logan's Run (1976)
Minority Report (2002)
Oblivion (2013)
Prometheus (2012)

RoboCop (1987)
Star Trek (2009)
Star Wars: Episode IV A New Hope (1977)
Terminator 2: Judgment Day (1991)
The Island (2005)
The Matrix (1999)
The Terminator (1984)
Total Recall (1990, 2012)
TRON: Legacy (2010)
WALL-E (2008)
WarGames (1983)
Westworld (1973)

TV Shows

Black Mirror (2011)
Electric Dreams (2017)
Fringe (2008)
Star Trek (1966)

Star Trek: The Next Generation (1987)
The Mandalorian (2019)
Westworld (2016)

APPENDIX B: MORE STUFF

Not all those who wander are lost.
—J.R.R. Tolkien

E VER WONDER WHAT a dark pool, Fibonacci retracement, or SPAC (special purpose acquisition company) is? Well, you've come to the right place. Listed below are descriptions for these terms and several more related to stocks, options, trading, and the market in general.

10-Bagger

An investment that increases in value by 10x from its original purchase price (for example, $100,000 becomes $1 million). Coined by Peter Lynch in his 1989 book *One Up On Wall Street*, Lynch invested in several stocks that became 10-baggers. While at the helm of the Fidelity Magellan Fund from 1977-1990, Lynch produced an AR of 29.2% and grew AUM from $18 million to over $19 billion. Some recent tech stock 10-baggers and the time period it took to achieve include the FAANGM stocks: 1) FB 2012-2018, 2) AMZN 2012-2018, 3) AAPL 2010-2020, 4) NFLX 2013-2017, 5) GOOG 2005-2017, 6) MSFT 2009-2020. In general, x-bagger is a term used for any x-multiple of ROI. For example, a 3-bagger has gone up 3x in value.

2 and 20

Hedge fund managers charge an annual management fee (percentage of AUM) and an incentive-based performance fee (percentage of profits above a certain predefined benchmark) known as carried interest or "carry.". Hence, 2 and 20 means a management fee of 2% of AUM and 20% of profits if a performance threshold is met. Also known as the hurdle rate, the threshold may be a preset percentage, or it may be based on a benchmark such as the return on a stock or bond index. For example, if a hedge fund charged 2 and 20, had $5 billion AUM, profits of $1.5 billion, and achieved its hurdle rate, the manager would earn $400 million ($100 million management fee plus $300 million performance fee). Some funds also utilize a high watermark for their performance fee, which states that the manager is only paid a percentage of the profits if the fund's net value exceeds its previous highest value. Per estimates by the Bloomberg *Billionaires Index*, five managers (Steve Cohen, Chase Coleman, Ken Griffin, Chris Hohn, Jim Simons) earned more than $1 billion in 2019. Jim Simons' Renaissance flagship Medallion Fund (closed to outside investors in 1993 and only available to current and past employees and their families) charges 5 and 44. However, despite these incredibly lofty fees, Medallion has averaged an amazing 39% annually from 1988-2018. In recent years, hedge fund fees have come under closer scrutiny by investors and US politicians for enriching fund managers but not fund clients.

Accredited Investor

An accredited investor is a person or entity who is considered financially sophisticated and has a reduced need for the protection provided by regulatory disclosure filings. These investors are allowed to deal, trade, and invest in securities that may not be registered with the SEC as long as they satisfy one or more requirements regarding income, net worth, asset size, governance status, or professional experience. SEC Rule 501 of Regulation D defines the requirements for an accredited investor: a person must have an earned annual income over $200,000 ($300,000 if combined with a spouse) for the last two calendar years with the expectation of earning the same or more in the current year or have a net worth over $1 million excluding the value of their primary residence, either individually or jointly with a spouse. The SEC also considers a person to be accredited if they're a director, executive officer, or general partner or a related combination thereof for the company selling the unregistered securities. An entity can also be an accredited investor if it's any one of the following:

- An organization (corporation, partnership, charity) with assets exceeding $5 million.
- A business with equity owners who are all accredited investors.
- A private business development company.
- A trust not formed to acquire securities and assets over $5 million.
- An employer-sponsored retirement plan within the meaning of the Employee Retirement Income Security Act (ERISA) in which the investment decisions are made by a bank, insurance company, or a registered investment advisor, or if the plan has total assets over $5 million (it cannot, however, be an entity formed solely to buy specific securities).

In 2016, the definition was expanded to include registered brokerage and investment advisor firms, and any person who demonstrates sufficient education or experience showing professional knowledge of unregistered securities. There's no formal agency, application, or testing process for an investor to be certified. Instead, firms use their own screening process to confirm accredited investor status (typically via a signed questionnaire and submission of financial documents confirming net worth or earnings).

Alpha

Alpha is a widely-used investment performance indicator and is defined as the investment return above a benchmark index. Some examples include: 1) if a stock returned 25% while the S&P 500 returned 15%, then alpha is 10 (25 – 15), and the investment overperformed by 10%, 2) if a stock returned -5% while the S&P 500 returned 15%, then alpha is -20 (-5 – 15), and the investment underperformed by 20%. If a fund manager is delivering alpha, they're outperforming the market. Alpha can also be interpreted as a measure of risk. An alpha of 0 suggests the investment return was appropriate for the risk whereas, an alpha greater than 0 suggests the investment risk was low for the return, and an alpha below 0 suggests its risk was high for the return. To avoid over-inflating alpha, an important consideration when seeking alpha is selecting the appropriate benchmark index to compare an investment against. For example, the S&P 500 isn't a good benchmark when calculating alpha for a high-flier like NVDA. A better benchmark might be the Nasdaq 100 (QQQ). Whenever provided alpha, make sure you know how it was calculated.

Animal Spirits

Coined by the British economist John Maynard Keynes in his 1936 book titled *The General Theory of Employment, Interest, and Money*, Keynes described "animal spirits" as human emotions that directly affect consumer confidence. In other words, animal spirits are the human psychological and emotional factors that drive and influence financial decisions in an uncertain and volatile market. Hence, if animal spirits are high (e.g., on *CNBC*, a guest like Kevin O'Leary may say, "Animal spirits are rising..."), confidence levels in the economy are high, and stock prices will probably rise. If animal spirits are low, then confidence levels in the economy are low, and stock prices will probably fall. This is true even if the underlying fundamentals are strong. Keynes insights into human behavior and is often seen as a precursor of what is now known today as behavioral economics.

Annual Percentage Yield

APY is the rate of return earned on a savings deposit or investment if interest is compounded annually and is calculated using the following formula (note, fees are not included, which would lower an investment's overall return):

$$\text{APY} = (((\text{Principal} + \text{Gain}) / \text{Principal})\ ^\wedge\ (365 / \text{Num Days Held}) - 1) \times 100$$

E.g., if the initial investment (i.e., principal) is \$10,000, the gain is \$4,000, and the investment was held for 2.5 years (i.e., 913 days), the APY is 14.4%.

$$\text{APY} = (((10{,}000 + 4{,}000) / 10{,}000)\ ^\wedge\ (365 / 913) - 1) \times 100 = 14.4\%$$

Annual Return / Annualized Return

AR is also known as CAGR (see Compounded Annual Growth Rate).

Annualizing Monthly Return

To annualize a monthly return, use the following formula:

$$\text{Annualized Monthly Return} = ((1 + \text{Monthly Return})\ ^\wedge\ 12 - 1) \times 100$$

E.g., if the monthly return is 2%, the annualized monthly return is 26.82% (i.e., if you earn 2% per month, annualized it would be equal to earning 26.82%).

$$\text{Annualized Monthly Return} = ((1 + 0.02)\ ^\wedge\ 12 - 1) \times 100 = 26.82\%$$

Assets Under Management

AUM fluctuates daily and is the total market value of investments managed by a person or entity on behalf of clients. Investors often consider high AUM as a positive indicator; however, high AUM doesn't always translate to high ROI. AUM calculation varies by company, with some limiting it to only funds that the company can trade on behalf of clients. Others will also include cash, bank deposits, and mutual funds. A fund's management fees are typically based on a percentage of AUM. Hence, the larger the AUM, the larger the management fee collected by the fund manager.

Ax

The ax is the market maker that is currently controlling the pricing action for a particular stock. The ax is also generally the market maker with the most volume. Day traders and professionals like to trade in the same direction as the ax because it increases their chances for a successful trade. The ax is not always the same market maker and can change during the course of a day, and sometimes there's no ax present. Occasionally, an ax will use an ECN (Electronic Communication Network) to hide their trading activity and control over a certain stock. You can typically identify the ax by watching Level 2 quote action for a few days. In a downtrend, the ax is usually the market maker holding the bid, and in an uptrend, it's usually the one holding the ask. If the ax starts widening the bid-ask spread, take note. If the ax moves off the current bid to a lower bid, this can potentially cause the stock to go lower, and if the ax moves off the current ask to a higher ask, this can potentially cause the stock to go higher.

Basis Point

On *CNBC*, a guest like Rick Reider, BlackRock's Chief Investment Officer of Fixed Income, may use the term basis points. Basis points (aka bps) are used to describe the percentage change in the value of financial instruments (e.g., bond yield increased 20 basis points from 6.25% to 6.45%) or the rate of change in an index (e.g., S&P 500 increased 104 basis points or 1.04%) or benchmark (e.g., FOMC (Federal Open Market Committee) increased federal funds rate by 25 basis points from 1% to 1.25%). One basis point is equal to 0.01% or

0.0001. A fractional basis point such as 2.1 is equal to 0.021% or 0.00021. To convert basis points to a percentage, multiply basis points by 0.0001, and then multiply by 100. For example, 184 basis points is 1.84% (184 * 0.0001) * 100).

Beta

Beta measures the risk arising from market exposure as a whole. The market portfolio of all investable assets is assigned a beta of 1. Tech stocks generally have betas above 1, which suggests they're volatile and move up and down with the market. A stock beta tells you theoretically how much risk the stock will add or subtract from a diversified portfolio. For example, if SHOP has a beta of 2.12, its stock price is 112% more volatile than the market. In contrast, if the beta is below 1, this suggests that an investment like US treasury bills has lower volatility than the market since their prices don't change much relative to movements in the market or that a volatile investment is not highly correlated with movements in the market. A good example would be gold. The price of gold can change a lot, but not always in the same direction or at the same time as movements in the market. Note, beta can be negative. This suggests an investment value will go down when the market goes up and up when the market goes down. Examples include put options and inverse ETFs. Like alpha, it's important to know what benchmark index is being used for volatility when making beta calculations and how it was calculated.

Block Trade

A block trade is the sale or purchase of a large number of securities at an arranged price between two parties. A block trade consists of at least 10,000 shares but is often much larger and usually initiated by institutional investors such as hedge funds or mutual funds. To conceal the true size of the trade, block trades are usually broken up into smaller orders and executed through different brokers. Block trades are also sometimes completed via a private purchase agreement or in dark pools to minimize the stock price impact.

Broker-Dealer

Broker-dealers (aka brokerages) buy and sell securities for their own accounts or on behalf of their customers. When executing orders on behalf of its customers, a brokerage is acting as a broker. When executing orders for its own account, a brokerage is acting as a dealer. If a brokerage buys securities from customers or other firms as a dealer, the securities may be sold to other clients or firms. Brokerages are also the primary sellers of mutual fund shares. Broker-dealers vary in size from small boutiques to subsidiaries of commercial and investment banks. According to FINRA (Financial Industry Regulatory Authority), as of 2019, there were over 3,500 registered broker-dealers. Some of the largest based on AUM include Charles Schwab (TD Ameritrade), Fidelity Investment, and E*TRADE.

Buy Side

The buy side is firms that buy securities. This includes institutional investors, hedge funds, pension funds, mutual funds, and insurance firms. Buy-side analysts are involved in the decision-making process for which securities their firms will purchase. There are fewer analysts on the buy side than the sell side. Unlike sell-side analysts whose primary goal is to convince their investors to trade through their firm's trading desk, the primary goal for buy-side analysts is to beat indices such as the S&P 500 and generate returns for their clients. In general, buy-side analysts tend to have broader coverage responsibilities and are not dedicated to specific companies or industries like sell-side analysts are. They usually work for funds, whereas sell-side analysts work for brokerages. Buy-side analysts identify which sell-side analysts are the most helpful for their needs and then interact frequently with these analysts; however, that's not to say that buy-side analysts don't conduct their own research. Note, buy-side firms don't usually pay for or buy sell-side research directly; however, what they'll often do is pay "soft" dollars to the sell-side firm, which is extra indirect money paid when trades are made through the sell-side firm's trading desk.

Carried Interest

Carried interest (aka the carry) is also known as the performance fee charged by hedge funds, private equity, and venture capital. Carry is not automatic and is only paid out to fund managers if a fund performs at or above a certain predefined benchmark level. Carry advocates insist that it's fair compensation because general partners must commit a vast amount of time and resources to build profitable companies for their portfolios, and in many cases, take them public. Because carry is considered a return on investment, it's taxed as long-term capital gains (15% or 20%), which is lower than the income or self-employment tax rate that hedge fund management fees are taxed at. This has resulted in much debate in the US, with some politicians arguing this tax loophole should be closed.

Circuit Breakers

A circuit breaker (aka trading curb) is a temporary halt of trading in the stock market with the goal being to reduce excess volatility, restore order in the market, and slow down panic selling. Circuit breakers apply to indices like the S&P 500 and individual securities. Recent examples of triggered circuit breakers include March 9, 2020, and March 16, 2020, when the DJIA fell more than 7% at market open due to growing global concerns regarding the COVID-19 pandemic. For individual securities, circuit breakers can be triggered if the price goes up (i.e., limit up) or down (i.e., limit down). Circuit breakers for indices are only triggered for downward price movement. Note, ETFs are considered to be individual securities even though they consist of a basket of securities.

Compounded Annual Growth Rate

CAGR (aka AR) is the rate at which an investment would have grown if it had grown at the same rate every year and the profits were reinvested at the end of each year. CAGR helps smooth the AR over a period of time so that investments are easier to compare. CAGR is expressed as a percentage and is calculated using the following formula:

$$CAGR = ((\text{Ending Value} / \text{Beginning Value}) \wedge (1 / \# \text{Years}) - 1) \times 100$$

E.g., if $50 grows for three years and ends at $75, the CAGR is 14.47%.

$$CAGR = ((75 / 50) \wedge (1 / 3) - 1) \times 100 = 14.47\%$$

Note, if you want to calculate the future value of an investment based on a given CAGR over a certain number of years, use the following formula:

Future Value = Beginning Value x ((CAGR / 100) + 1) $^\wedge$ # Years Invested

E.g., if $100 grows for three years at a 10% CAGR, the future value would be $133.10.

Future Value = 100 x ((10 / 100) + 1) $^\wedge$ 3 = $133.10

Dark Pool

Dark pools first appeared in the 1980s when the SEC allowed brokers to complete large block trades of stocks, ETFs, and index funds. A dark pool is a private exchange that provides certain investors (typically institutional investors) the ability to place large orders consisting of millions of shares. Trades are not made public until after the trade has been executed and reported, which can be up to 24 hours later. Dark pools provide pricing and cost advantages to mutual funds and pension funds, which claim that these benefits ultimately help retail investors who invest in these funds. In other words, if institutional funds were to trade millions of shares of a stock, their own orders can drive up prices if buying or down if selling. Some common dark pools include Instinet, Liquidnet, JPMX (JP Morgan), CrossFinder (Credit Suisse), Capital Markets (Fidelity), SIGMA X (Goldman Sachs), Knight Link and Knight Match (Knight Capital Group), MSPOOL (Morgan Stanley), Tradebook (Bloomberg), Level ATS, Euronext (NYSE). Some traders follow dark pool action to try and identify smart money activity and then make decisions to follow these trades or not.

Direct Listing

A direct listing (aka direct placement or DPO (direct public offering)) is a less-expensive option for a company to raise capital on a public exchange compared to the more traditional IPO. In an IPO, new shares are underwritten and sold to the public by intermediaries (usually investment banks) who facilitate the process by generating interest from the investor community (which includes institutional investors). In a DPO, existing shares are sold directly to the public with no underwriters involved. DPOs are favored by companies that:

- Have strong brand recognition.
- Have a seasoned management team with a proven track record.
- Don't need to raise new capital.
- Cannot afford to pay investment banks underwriting fees or simply don't want to pay for it.
- Desire transparency with market-driven share price discovery.
- Don't want existing share dilution.
- May want to avoid lockup periods.

However, without an intermediary, there is no support or guarantee shares will sell, and short-term share price volatility may be elevated without a lockup. On the other hand, a direct listing provides founders, vested employees, and early investors an immediate liquidity path. DPOs enables companies to trade their stock on a public exchange without the cost and hassle of an IPO. Some investors, like Bill Gurley of Benchmark Capital, are vocal champions of direct listings. They believe the current investment banking underwriting model is outdated, inefficient, and suboptimal since money is left on the table when IPO stocks pop on their first day of trading. Recent DPOs include SPOT, Slack (WORK), Asana (ASAN), and PLTR.

Dow Jones Industrial Average

The DJIA (aka Dow and Dow Jones) is one of the oldest and most widely-watched stock indices in the world. Created in 1896 by Charles Dow and Edward Jones as a proxy for the broader US economy, the Dow is an index that tracks 30 publicly-traded blue-chip companies listed on the NYSE and Nasdaq. The Dow originally contained just 12 stocks, which were primarily industrial companies. In 1928, the index was expanded to 30 stocks. Today, it contains 3M (MMM), AXP, AAPL, BA, Caterpillar (CAT), Chevron (CVX), CSCO, KO, Dow (DOW), XOM, Goldman Sachs (GS), HD, IBM (IBM), INTC, JNJ, JP Morgan Chase (JPM), MCD, Merck (MRK), MSFT, Nike (NKE), PFE, PG, RTN, Travelers (TRV), UNH, Verizon (VZ), V, WMT, Walgreens Boots (WBA), and Walt Disney (DIS). The Dow is not a market-cap-weighted index and is also not a weighted arithmetic mean-based index; hence, many think the Dow is not as accurate a representation of the US stock market as the S&P 500, which also includes the 30 components of the Dow. The value of the Dow is the sum of the price of one share of stock for each of the 30 companies in the Dow divided by a factor known as the Dow Divisor. The Dow Divisor changes whenever one of the component stocks has a stock split or pays out a dividend to ensure a consistent index value. The current value of the Dow Divisor is printed in the *Wall Street Journal* and is 0.14748072. The 10 stocks in the Dow with the highest dividend yields are commonly known as the Dogs of the Dow. Investing in the Dogs of the Dow, an investment strategy popularized by Michael B. O'Higgins in his 1991 book *Beating the Dow*, returned an 18.5% AR in 2019, and a 10.8% AR for the past 20 years. The DJIA can be traded through ETFs such as the SPDR Dow Jones Industrial Average (DIA) and iShares Dow Jones US (IYY).

Electronic Communication Network

Founded in 1969, Instinet was the first ECN. An ECN is a computerized order system that automatically matches buy and sell orders for securities when the market is open and after hours. Major brokerage firms and individual traders are connected to facilitate direct trading without the use of a middleman. ECNs charge access fees and commission and make it possible for investors in different geographic locations to quickly and easily trade with each other. In the US, the SEC requires ECNs to register as broker-dealers. Some ECNs focus on institutional investors while others focus on retail investors. Common ECNs include Instinet, SelectNet, and NYSE ARCA.

Ex-Dividend Date

The declaration or announcement date is when a company's board of directors announces a dividend distribution to shareholders of record. At this time, the board of directors also sets a record date, which is the date an investor must be a shareholder to receive the dividend payment. The ex-dividend date of a stock is the day on which the stock begins trading without the value of its next dividend payment included. On this date, the stock price will usually drop by the amount of the expected dividend payment. Typically, the ex-dividend date is one business day before the record date. Hence, investors who own the stock before the ex-dividend date will be eligible for dividend payments. Note, since it takes a day for trades to settle, investors that want to receive dividend payments should buy the stock at least one day before the record date. If investors buy a dividend-paying stock on its ex-dividend date, they're getting a slight discount in the stock purchase price due to the dividend they're not receiving. The payment date is when dividend payments are credited to an investor's account.

Exchange-Traded Fund

An ETF is a basket of securities and trades on an exchange like stocks; hence, the price per share for an ETF will fluctuate throughout the day, unlike mutual funds, which don't trade on exchanges and trade only once per day after the market closes. There is a wide variety of ETFs. ETFs exist for bonds, stocks, indices, industries and sectors, commodities, currencies, and even inverse ETFs, which short stocks and indices. Some of the more well-known ETFs include SPY, VOO, QQQ, DIA, GLD, IWM, Energy Select Sector SPDR Fund (XLE), Financial Select Sector SPDR Fund (XLF), XLK, and VanEck Vectors Biotech ETF (BBY). Per Morningstar, the average ETF has an expense ratio of 0.44%, which means there are $4.40 in annual fees for every $1,000 invested, versus 0.74% for the average traditional index fund. The table below shows the largest ETFs as of October 2020.

Symbol	ETF	AUM $000	Average volume
SPY	SPDR S&P 500 ETF	300,588,000	67,595,180
IVV	iShares Core S&P 500 ETF	222,177,000	3,353,586
VTI	Vanguard Total Stock Market ETF	172,972,000	2,976,241
VOO	Vanguard S&P 500 ETF	165,916,000	2,989,259
QQQ	Invesco QQQ	138,491,000	45,701,430
ACG	iShares Core US Aggregate Bond ETF	81,068,300	5,965,980
GLD	SPDR Gold Trust	77,330,100	13,125,068
VEA	Vanguard FTSE Developed Markets ETF	76,804,400	8,709,360
IEFA	iShares Core MSCI EAFE ETF	72,444,900	7,777,297
BND	Vanguard Total Bond Market ETF	63,630,200	4,934,398

Source: ETF Database Inc.

Family Office

A family office is a full-service private and professionally-managed wealth management advisory firm designed to serve an ultra-high-net-worth individual, family, or a small number of families. Their goal is to grow and transfer wealth across generations. A family office typically operates as a corporation or LLC (limited liability company). It is set up as either a single-family office or a multi-family office, which can benefit from economies of scale and cost savings. A family office's capital originates from the individual or family's own personal wealth. Family offices invest in all types of financial products depending on the risk-reward profile and requirements of the individual, family, or small group of families. This includes stocks, bonds, commodities, currencies, futures, derivatives, venture capital, private equity, hedge funds, private placements, cryptocurrency, and commercial real estate. Family offices typically provide budgeting, insurance, charitable giving, tax services, and non-financial services such as private schooling, travel, and other household-related management services.

Fibonacci Retracements

Fibonacci retracements are a popular but subjective tool used by technical traders to draw support lines, identify resistance levels, place stop-loss orders, and set target prices. At the beginning of the 13th century, mathematician Leonardo Fibonacci discovered a series of numbers known as the Fibonacci sequence. It's composed of an infinite series of numbers such that each number is the sum of the two preceding numbers starting from 0 and 1: 0, 1, 1, 2, 3, 5, 8, 13, 21, 34, 55, 89, 144, 233, 377, etc. (i.e., $0 + 1 = 1, 1 + 1 = 2, 1 + 2 = 3, 2 + 3 = 5$, etc.). An extraordinary characteristic of the Fibonacci sequence is each number is approximately 1.618x greater than the number before it in the series. A Fibonacci retracement is created by taking two extreme points on a stock chart (usually a peak and a trough) and dividing the vertical distance by the key Fibonacci ratios of 23.6%, 38.2%, 50%, 61.8%, and 100%. The 100% ratio is found by dividing a number in the sequence by itself (e.g., $34 / 34 = 1$). The 61.8% ratio is found by dividing one number in the sequence by the number that follows it (e.g., $55 / 89 = 0.6179175$). The 38.2% ratio is found by dividing a number in the sequence by the number located two spots to the right (e.g., $55 / 144 = 0.3819444$). The 23.6% ratio is found by dividing a number in the sequence by the number located three spots to the right (e.g., $55 / 233 =$

0.2360515). Note, 50% is not a Fibonacci ratio; however, technical traders like to use 50% because of the observed tendency for asset prices to continue in the same direction after a 50% retracement occurs. Once each level is calculated based on the Fibonacci ratios, horizontal lines are then drawn on a stock chart and used to identify potential support and resistance levels. Just like the golden ratio can be found in nature, architecture, art, and biology, for unexplained reasons, Fibonacci ratios sometimes play a role in the stock market and the movement of stocks. The golden ratio is represented by the Greek letter phi and is approximately 1.618. Scientists have pondered for centuries why so many natural patterns reflect the Fibonacci sequence.

Fractional Shares

Popularized by Robinhood, fractional shares allow investors who don't have a lot of money to buy partial shares in a company or ETF. An investor would normally have to purchase at least one or more full shares of a stock (for AMZN as of market close September 1, 2020, this would be $3,499.12/share). In contrast, fractional shares enable an investor to buy individual stocks in the S&P 500 and ETFs based on a dollar amount. If you own fractional shares, you'll also be paid dividends (if applicable) proportionate to the percentage of the share you own. Furthermore, just like buying regular stock, there are no commissions when buying shares of fractional shares. Not all brokerages offer fractional shares. Robinhood's minimum investment for fractional shares is $1 and allows partial investments in 7,000 stocks/ETFs. Charles Schwab's minimum fractional shares investment is $5 and allows partial investments into any S&P 500 stock. Fidelity allows fractional investments into any NYSE or Nasdaq exchange-listed stock or ETF as long as it comprises at least one one-hundredth (0.001) of a share. For example, if a stock costs $100/share, Fidelity's minimum investment is $0.10. Fractional shares enable almost anyone to participate in the growth of stocks and/or the market.

Gap Up or Gap Down in Stock Prices

Gaps indicate a change in investor sentiment and appear when there is a sharp movement in the stock price with little or no trading activity in between. This often occurs overnight as the market and investors digest new news such as earnings, guidance, M&A, management change, litigation, etc. This breaking news acts as a catalyst to create an imbalance in supply and demand, which drives the stock higher or lower than the previous day's close. A gap up is when a stock opens at a meaningfully higher price than the previous day's price and is a bullish sign. A gap down is the reverse and is a bearish sign. In this case, a stock opens at a meaningfully lower price than the previous day's close. A full gap is when the opening price is outside of the previous day's range, and a partial gap is when the opening price is higher or lower than the previous day's close but within the previous day's range.

High-Frequency Trading

HFT (high-frequency trading) is used by large investment banks, hedge funds, and institutional investors. It's an automated computerized high-speed trading platform. HFT minimizes network latency via direct data feeds from exchanges and server co-location. HFT became more common following the introduction of incentives provided by exchanges to improve liquidity in the market. HFT firms make their money by capitalizing on any imbalance in supply and demand and using arbitrage and speed to their advantage. They don't trade based on company fundamentals or growth prospects. They trade based on opportunities they can exploit. Well-known HFT firms include Citadel Securities, DRW, GTS, Hudson River Trading, Tower Research Capital, Two Sigma Securities, Virtu Financial (VIRT), and XTX Markets. In theory, traders with the fastest execution speeds profit the most. There is, however, a physical limit to speed since data cannot travel faster than the speed of light. HFT platforms scan, analyze, and attempt to anticipate emerging trends and shifts in the market before they occur. Using complex algorithmic trading strategies, HFT is designed to rapidly move in and out of positions in fractions of a second by executing millions of orders on multiple exchanges. Proponents of HFT say it brings liquidity to the market and eliminates small bid-ask spreads. Critics argue that HFT gives large institutional investors an unfair advantage over smaller retail investors. They say the liquidity that HFT brings is momentary at best because it disappears so quickly, making it impossible for traders to take advantage of it.

Institutional Investor

An institutional investor pools money to buy securities, real property, and other investable assets and, in some cases, also originates loans. Institutional investors invest and manage money on behalf of others and include commercial banks, credit unions, endowments, hedge funds, insurance companies, investment banks, mutual funds, pensions, private equity firms, and REITs. Due to their size, institutional investors can have vast influence on the market. Because of their large purchasing power, institutional investors pay lower fees for their trades and have access to investments (e.g., pre-IPO shares in startup companies), which normal investors are not typically offered. The SEC considers institutional investors sophisticated investors, which means they are subject to fewer protective regulations.

Level 1 Quotes

Before the Internet and the wide availability of online trading, Level 1 quotes were not commonly available. Level 1 is a stock trading screen that displays basic information from the order book for Nasdaq stocks including the best bid and ask prices. Note, the number of shares available at these prices is not shown. Free real-time quotes provided by your brokerage firm are considered Level 1 and are generally sufficient for the average retail investor.

Level 2 Quotes

Level 2 is basically the order book for Nasdaq stocks. When orders are placed on Nasdaq, they're typically placed with different market makers and other market participants. Level 2 quotes will show you a ranked list of the best bid and ask prices from each of these participants and provide insight into what's happening with a particular stock. Level 2 quotes will also tell you who is buying (retail or institutional). Note, institutional traders use different market makers than retail traders. There are three different types of participants in the market. 1) market makers, which provide market liquidity. 2) ECNs, which are computerized order systems that anyone can use from retail to institutional investors. 3) wholesalers, which execute orders on behalf of brokerages that have sold them their order flow and consists primarily of retail orders. Level 2 helps determine: 1) if institutional traders are trying to keep their buying quiet (irregular ECN order sizes is often an indication of this activity), 3) who is the ax, 4) if a strong trend may be coming to an end by looking for trades occurring between the bid and ask (institutional traders often take a small loss to ensure they exit a stock when needed). Level 2 quotes are helpful for day traders and professionals. However, so they don't reveal what they're doing, market makers will try to hide their activity from other competitors and market participants.

Limit Down

When the S&P 500 experiences large declines and heavy volatility, stock market trading halts may occur at three pre-defined levels. For stocks, limit down refers to the percentage decline allowed before automatic trading curbs kick in. This was designed to limit stock price volatility caused by HFT. Note, this only applies during normal trading hours and not during after-hours trading. The three levels (not to be confused with Level 1 and Level 2 quotes) are Level 1 (if the S&P 500 declines 7%, trading pauses for 15 minutes), Level 2 (if the S&P 500 declines 13%, trading pauses again for 15 minutes if the drop occurs before 3:25 p.m. ET and if the drop occurs after this time no halt occurs), Level 3 (if the S&P 500 declines 20%, trading halts for the remainder of the day). Trading curbs were first implemented after the Black Monday stock market crash on October 19, 1987, because programmatic trading was thought to be the main cause of the crash. On Black Monday, the DJIA fell 22.6%, and the S&P 500 and Wilshire 5000 both fell more than 18%. The futures and options markets also crashed. Trading volume was so extreme that some orders were unfilled for an hour or more. The rules were updated again in February 2013 after the circuit breaker system failed to prevent the May 6, 2010, flash crash, which resulted in a trillion-dollar decline in the US stock market in just 36 minutes. For individual securities, circuit breakers can be triggered if the price goes up or down whereas circuit breakers for market indices are only triggered for downward price movement. Relative to trading curbs, ETFs are considered individual securities even though they consist of a basket of securities.

Lock-up Period

A lock-up period is a set amount of time (usually 90-180 days) following an IPO where shareholders are restricted from selling vested shares. Shareholders include founders, owners, management, employees, venture capitalists, and other early private investors. The goal of an IPO lock-up period is to prevent early shareholders from selling and flooding the market with a large number of shares. If this happens, it could create selling pressure and volatility in the early life of a publicly-traded company, causing the stock to decline. In some instances, insiders may be restricted from selling their shares for a longer period beyond the lock-up. When a lock-up period expires, depending on if large shareholders sell or hold, this can also send a strong signal to the market regarding their current confidence in the company. Note, if you purchase pre-IPO shares via the secondary market, you'll be subject to the same employee lock-up that the shares are subject to. If you're interested in finding out more about a company's lock-up period, you can find this information in the company's S-1 filing with the SEC and any subsequent S-1As filing(s) announcing any changes to their lock-up period.

Market Maker

Market makers make a market by buying at the bid and selling at the ask securities, which may be equity (stocks), debt (bonds, debentures, banknotes), and derivatives (options, futures, forwards, swaps). Market makers are usually brokerages, large banks, exchanges, or other institutions. They play a key role in financial markets by creating liquidity, which keeps the market functioning smoothly and efficiently. They do this by publicly displaying and continuously updating buy and sell quotes for a guaranteed number of shares. The bid-ask spread is the difference between the bid and ask and is profit a market maker earns for making a market; hence, the higher the trading volume, the more money a market maker can make. Market makers operating on a specific US stock exchange must adhere to that exchange's SEC-approved bylaws. Some exchanges like Nasdaq rely upon multiple market makers to ensure competition to make the best bid and ask prices available. Others like the NYSE use a specialist system. Specialists are individual market makers, which control order flow for a specific security or securities. Based on supply and demand, specialists set the opening price for stock each morning, which can be different from the previous day's close based on after-hours news and events. Specialists also work to ensure: 1) the best price is available, 2) trades are executed, and 3) order is maintained. Market makers include Citigroup (ADTF), Susquehanna (ETRF), Citadel Securities (CDEL), and CBOE US Equities (EDGX/EDGA). If your trading platform provides Level 2 quotes, you can see the Nasdaq order book for stocks, which includes the best bid and ask prices being offered by various market makers.

Max Pain

Max pain is the strike at which the greatest number of options expire worthless. It is based on the Maximum Pain Theory that states that most options traders who buy and hold options contracts until expiration will lose money. Options traders often refer to this option strike price as the pin point and say the stock is pinning. When calls and puts are purchased, there is a seller on the other side of the trade, and the majority of the time, it is a market maker. There is risk in selling options; hence, market makers will adjust their positions in the underlying stock that they sold options to hedge their risk regardless of which direction the stock moves. This means the market maker will buy and short stock to maintain a zero-risk position. As expiration nears, this delta-neutral rebalancing activity sometimes causes a stock price to gravitate towards a nearby option strike. If the OI is high, the larger the volume of stock a market maker will need to hedge, and the higher the chance there will be pressure on the stock at expiration. Note, stocks don't always pin. Some traders monitor the OI throughout the week leading up to Friday expiration to determine where a high-momentum stock might pin and then trade accordingly.

Nasdaq

Nasdaq was created by the NASD (National Association of Securities Dealers) and began operations in 1971. Developed as an alternative to the specialist system, it was designed to enable investors to quickly and transparently trade securities on a computerized system. Nasdaq typically refers to the Nasdaq

Composite index, which includes more than 3,000 stocks, and is second only to the NYSE by market capitalization of shares traded. In 2006, Nasdaq began operating as an exchange and separated from the NASD. The Nasdaq is a market-cap-weighted index, and its trading model has become the standard for markets worldwide. As of July 2020, six tech companies (AAPL, MSFT, AMZN, FB, GOOG/GOOGL, TSLA) made up 41% of the Nasdaq index value. The Nasdaq can be traded via an ETF like ONEQ.

Nasdaq 100

Introduced in 1985, the Nasdaq 100 is an index made up of 100 of the largest most actively traded non-financial US companies on the Nasdaq exchange. Financial companies are contained in the Nasdaq Financial 100, a sister index to the Nasdaq 100, which was also introduced in 1985. Re-ranked every December, the Nasdaq 100 is a market-cap-weighted index. As of May 10, 2020, 54.4% of the companies in the index were tech companies. As of July 2020, six tech companies (AAPL 12%, MSFT 11.3%, AMZN 11.2%, FB 4.2%, GOOG/GOOGL 3.8%/3.8%, TSLA 2.7%) made up 49% of the value of the Nasdaq 100. The Nasdaq 100 can be traded via an ETF like QQQ.

Option Alert

These services provide real-time alerts of potentially market-moving options activity. These trades are often executed by institutional investors such as hedge funds. Below is a Bezinga Pro alert sent on Thursday, October 5, 2017.

2:11:34 pm: SHOP Shopify Fri $99.5 Calls Sweep (14) at the Ask: 500 @ $2.551 vs 9 OI; Ref=$100.28

2:11:34 pm	The alert was sent at 2:11:34 pm. Alert time stamps are shown in Eastern Time unless otherwise specified.
SHOP Shopify	Alert was for Shopify with a ticker symbol SHOP.
Fri	Alert was sent Thursday, October 5, 2017, and since there's no date specified, Fri means expiration is Friday, October 6, 2017. If a date is specified, it would be the expiration date.
$99.5	Strike was $99.50. FYI, SHOP closed at $100.43/share on October 5, 2017.

Calls at the Ask This trade was for call options. Since the trader is buying calls at the ask, this is a bullish move since the buyer is willing to buy at the seller's price. In this case, the buyer is most likely expecting the underlying stock price to go up before expiration. In general, selling puts at the bid is also considered bullish, while calls being sold at the bid or puts bought at the ask are considered bearish. However, for any options activity, it is difficult to determine exactly what a trader's true intentions are by only looking at a trade. For example, if a trader buys a large number of puts, is this a straight bet that a stock's price is declining, or is it a hedge against an existing appreciated long position.

Sweep (14) Sweep typically means the trade is a large order and is being broken into smaller orders at different sources (14) so that it gets filled faster. Sweep orders often mean execution speed is being prioritized over securing the best price, and since this trade was at the ask, this seems to confirm this.

500 The number of contracts was 500 for this trade. A standard option contract represents 100 shares of the underlying stock, so this options trade controls 50,000 shares of SHOP.

$2.551 Premium was $2.551 (i.e., $255.10 per contract); hence, BE was $102.051 (99.5 + 2.551), and total cost was $127,550 (500* 2.551 * 100) less fees. SHOP closed at $100.43/share (1.59% below BE) on October 5, 2017, and at $97.92/share (4.05% below BE) on October 6, 2017.

9 OI OI was 9 contracts for the $99.50 strike price and October 6, 2017, expiration date. If the volume exceeds the OI, this typically indicates a new position, and since the volume is significantly larger (500 contracts versus 9 contracts), this is considered to be unusual options activity.

Ref=$100.28 The underlying stock price at the time of the trade. SHOP was trading at $100.28/share when this trade was executed.

Traders who subscribe to options alert services want real-time information on unusual options activity so that they can then quickly decide to trade on the information or not. However, these smart money trades are not always right. In the case of the SHOP options alert, on Friday, October 6, 2017, SHOP traded at a low of $95.96/share, a high of $100.20/share, and closed at $97.92/share. Hence, the $102.051 BE was never hit, and even the intraday high of $100.20 didn't reach BE. My guess is, the trade was closed out earlier in the day on Friday for a substantial loss before the value of the calls went to 0 by market close. It's possible the trader could have also exercised the calls before expiration and bought 50,000 shares at the $99.50 strike for a total cost of $4,975,000 with the hopes of later selling the shares once SHOP reached $102.051/share or higher to not incur a loss on the original options trade.

Order Book

An order book is a list of buy and sell orders (both electronic and manual) for a particular stock exchange. Order books are used by practically all exchanges and contain trading information for assets such as stocks, bonds, and currencies. A matching engine uses the order book to determine which orders can be fully or partially executed by the exchange. Each entry in the order book contains information on the buyer or seller (note, some choose to remain anonymous like dark pools), the number of securities, and the price that is being bid/asked for a particular security. Order books help improve overall market transparency, but not all market participants and details are included (e.g., dark pools). Order book information is generally not as important to the average retail investor versus active day traders and professionals who depend on the order book to make more informed trading decisions.

Order Flow Payment

Payment for order flow is the compensation that a brokerage receives for passing customer orders on to third parties for trade execution. It's a practice that was originally pioneered by Bernie Madoff (of Ponzi scheme notoriety). For example, if you buy AAPL shares via TD Ameritrade, they'll receive a few pennies for sending your order on to a market maker like Citadel Securities. Citadel will then complete the trade while also earning a few pennies.

Payment for order flow has become increasingly important for brokerages after stock trades went commission-free. Robinhood, which pioneered commission-free stock trading, currently makes more from payment for equity order flow (rate per 100 shares) than Charles Schwab, E*TRADE, and TD Ameritrade (now owned by Charles Schwab). Note that brokerages also earn more from payment for order flow of options than stocks. As of Q2 2020, Robinhood and TD Ameritrade made the most (tied) for options order flow. Payment for order flow is a major benefit for smaller firms. It enables them to send and combine their orders with other orders, which helps keep costs low, particularly for retail investors who often lack bargaining power. Meanwhile, the market maker also benefits from the additional number of trades it handles. Payment for order flow is a common practice today. The SEC requires brokerages to disclose: 1) if they're receiving payment for sending customer orders out, 2) every order they receive payment. The table below summarizes the order flow payment for popular brokerages for Q1/Q2 2020.

| Brokerage | Trade | Q1 2020 | | Q2 2020 | |
		Payment for orders	Rate/100 shares	Payment for orders	Rate/100 shares
Robinhood	Equity	$31,116,950	$0.24	$69,116,307	$0.17
	Option	$59,802,125	$0.48	$111,148,089	$0.58
	Total	$90,919,076	$0.36	$180,264,395	$0.30
Charles Schwab	Equity	$25,447,153	$0.11	$32,396,842	$0.11
	Option	$28,517,592	$0.36	$33,745,172	$0.37
	Total	$53,964,745	$0.18	$66,142,014	$0.18
E*TRADE	Equity	$29,822,204	$0.16	$50,210,044	$0.15
	Option	$49,829,545	$0.45	$60,117,332	$0.46
	Total	$79,651,749	$0.27	$110,327,376	$0.18
TD Ameritrade	Equity	$72,782,936	$0.15	$144,219,349	$0.15
	Option	$129,597,189	$0.53	$179,991,996	$0.58
	Total	$202,380,125	$0.28	$324,211,345	$0.25

Source: Piper Sandler, SEC filings.

Pinning the Strike

Pinning the strike is the tendency for a stock to close at or near the strike price of heavily traded options in the same stock as expiration nears. Pinning doesn't always happen, but it is most likely to occur when there's large OI in the calls and puts for a particular strike as expiration approaches. This is because options traders become increasingly exposed to gamma as expiration nears. As gamma continues to grow, small changes in the underlying stock will create larger and larger changes in the option's delta. Hence, professional traders and market makers, who are often hedging to remain delta neutral, will need to buy or sell more shares to keep their risk exposure neutral.

Private Investor

A private investor is an individual or company that uses its own money to provide capital to another individual or business to operate and expand.

Put-Call Ratio

PCR is a widely-used measurement of investor sentiment on how the market views current events such as earnings or news announcements. The ratio is calculated by dividing the number of traded puts by the number of traded calls using either the number of puts and calls or on a dollar-weighted basis. PCR can also be calculated for an individual stock, an index, or aggregated in some way. Since there's typically more call buying than put buying, a rising ratio or ratio greater than 0.7 means options traders are buying more puts than calls and suggests a bearish sentiment. I.e., investors are speculating the market will be declining, or they're hedging their positions to protect against a potential decline. In contrast, a falling ratio or ratio less than 0.7 and approaching 0.5 means options traders are buying more calls than puts and suggests a bullish sentiment. I.e., investors are speculating the market will be moving up. Data found on the CBOE web site can be used to calculate PCR.

Qualified Client

A qualified client is an investor that satisfies one of the following criteria:

- Excluding the value of their primary residence, an individual, or jointly with a spouse, with a net worth of $2.1 million.
- An individual with at least $1 million in AUM immediately after participating in the investment.
- An individual who is a general partner, trustee, director, executive officer, or person serving in a similar capacity, or the advisor.
- An individual who is an employee of the advisor who participates in the investment activities of the advisor and has done so for at least 12 months.
- A qualified purchaser.

An accredited investor is not the same as a qualified client. The requirements for being a qualified client are higher. The SEC allows hedge funds to charge qualified clients both management and performance fees (e.g., 2 and 20) while only the management fee can be charged to accredited investors.

Qualified Purchaser

Per Section 2(a)(51) of the Investment Company Act of 1940, the SEC defines a qualified purchaser if one of the following criteria is met:

- A person having not less than $5 million in investments.
- A company with not less than $5 million in investments owned by close family members.
- A trust, not formed for the investment, with not less than $5 million in investments.
- An investment manager with not less than $25 million under management.
- A company with not less than $25 million in investments.
- Any entity owned by qualified purchasers.

A qualified purchaser is not the same as an accredited investor. The former is sometimes also referred to as a super-accredited investor. The requirements for being a qualified purchaser is much higher than being an accredited investor or qualified client. Per Sections 3(c)(1) and 3(c)(7) of the Investment Company Act of 1940, private funds are exempt from registering with the SEC as an investment company if they're not making a public offering of securities, and either the fund is owned by 100 individuals or less, or the fund is owned exclusively by qualified purchasers and is not limited to 100 investors. Hence, hedge funds prefer qualified purchasers or qualified clients as investors because they're allowed to charge a performance fee (typically 20%). Accredited investors are also eligible to invest, but they can only be charged a management fee (typically 2%). A qualified institutional buyer (institutions that own and invest $100 million or more of securities, and banks that own and invest at least $100 million of securities and have an audited net worth of at least $25 million) is also considered a qualified purchaser.

Relative Strength Index

Created by J. Welles Wilder, RSI (relative strength index) was introduced in his 1978 book *New Concepts in Technical Trading Systems*. It is one of trading's most popular technical indicators. It's a bullish/bearish price momentum indicator that oscillates between 0-100 and is used by technical traders to measure whether an asset such as a stock or an index is overbought (i.e., overvalued) or oversold (i.e., undervalued). Traditionally, RSI is considered to be overbought when it's above 70. This suggests a trend reversal, and a pullback in price is probable. In contrast, an RSI value below 30 indicates an oversold condition. This also suggests a trend reversal except in the opposite direction (i.e., a price increase is likely). Note, the traditional levels of 70 and 30 can be adjusted depending on the particular asset being measured to provide a better fit. If there's a strong trend, whether overbought or oversold, the RSI may remain in these conditions for an extended period of time.

Retail Investor

Retail investors are investors who are not institutional investors and are investing and managing their own money and not investing on behalf of someone else. They are driven by personal goals such as saving for retirement, saving for children's college education, or financing large purchases like a home or automobile. They typically trade via brokerages such as Charles Schwab (TD Ameritrade), E*TRADE, Fidelity, and Robinhood. Due to their small purchasing power, retail investors usually end up paying higher fees than institutional investors, and the SEC considers them unsophisticated investors, which means they're provided certain protections and are generally blocked from making certain risky, complex investments.

Return on Investment

ROI is used to evaluate the performance efficiency of an investment. It is also used to compare the performances for different investments. ROI is expressed as a percentage and is calculated using the following formula:

ROI = ((Current Price – Purchase Price) / Purchase Price) x 100

E.g., if the stock price was $50/share and it rose to $75/share, the ROI is 50%.

ROI = ((75 – 50) / 50) x 100 = 50%

All things being equal, if stock X has a higher ROI (e.g., 50%) than stock Y (e.g., 25%), then stock X is a better investment.

Rule of 16

The Rule of 16 is used to quickly estimate how much the options market expects a stock to move daily until expiration for an option. It's expressed as a percentage and is calculated by dividing the IV of a call or put by 16, which is the square root of the number of trading days (256) in a year. Here's an example of a DIS option expiring in seven days. The DIS Aug28'20 $120 strike call has a current IV of 18.16%. Hence, the Rule of 16 tells us the options market expects DIS will have an average daily price movement of about 1.135% (18.16 / 16) per day for the next seven days. With DIS currently trading at $127.44/share, that's about $1.4464/day (127.44 * 0.01135). The Rule of 16 is often calculated just before and after companies report earnings to assess whether or not the options market's expected movement for a stock seems reasonable or not.

Rule of 40

The Rule of 40, the principle that a software/SaaS company's combined growth rate and profit margin should exceed 40%, has become a widely-used heuristic to measure the fundamental trade-offs between balancing growth and profitability. Venture capitalists initially used this rule as a quick way to assess and compare the performance of small, fast-growing companies. According to data collected by Bain & Company, for large publicly traded software/SaaS companies, beating the rule in a single year is not difficult. However, to consistently outperform the rule is difficult to do year after year. The formula to calculate the Rule of 40 is revenue growth + profit margin = 40% or greater (indicates a financially healthy company). For startups, this means investors are willing to accept low profits or even losses as long as the company has strong growth. I.e., young companies usually require increased investment to drive growth and rapid expansion. However, as a company matures, growth typically slows, and profitability becomes more important. Note, the Rule of 40 provides no insight into whether a company is growing fast enough or is profitable enough. Different investors use different values for growth. For example, for startups, monthly recurring revenue or annual recurring revenue is frequently used for growth. For more mature companies, year-over-year growth based on GAAP (generally accepted accounting principles) revenue is more common. Different investors will also use different values for profitability. For example, some will use FCF TTM (free cash flow trailing 12 months), while others will use EBIDTA (earnings before interest, taxes, depreciation, and amortization), excluding stock compensation costs. Note, there is no right or wrong measure for growth and profitability. It is up to each investor to use the measure they think is the most relevant for their specific investment situation.

Rule of 72

The Rule of 72 is a simplified formula (based on a logarithmic formula) that's commonly used to estimate how many years are required for an investment to double at a given annual rate of return. It's calculated as follows where Interest Rate is the rate of investment return:

Years to Double = 72 / Interest Rate

E.g., if a $10,000 investment has an AR of 15%, the investment will double to $20,000 in approximately 4.8 years.

Years to Double = 72 / 15 = 4.8 years

The actual logarithmic formula is calculated as follows (ln means natural log function):

Years to Double = ln(2) / ln(1 + (Compounded Interest Rate Per Period / 100))

E.g., if a $10,000 investment has a 15% AR, the investment will double to $20,000 in 4.96 years ($20,000 will become $40,000 in 9.92 years (4.96 + 4.96), it'll become $80,000 in 14.88 years (9.92 + 4.96), etc., doubling every 4.96 years).

Years to Double = ln(2) / ln(1 + (15 / 100)) = 4.96 years

Russell 2000

Created by the Frank Russell Company in 1984, the Russell 2000 is an index that tracks the performance of 2,000 small-cap US companies. It's the most widely-used benchmark index for small-cap to mid-cap investors. The index is also the most common benchmark for small-cap mutual funds/ETFs, similar to how the S&P 500 is used primarily for large-cap stocks/mutual funds. The Russell 2000 is a market-cap-weighted index based on shares outstanding. The AR of the Russell 2000 including dividends from 1988-2020, has been around 8.5%. The Russell 2000 can be traded via ETFs such as IWM and the Vanguard Russell 2000 (VWTO).

Russell 3000

The Russell 3000 is an index that tracks 3,000 publicly traded US companies representing nearly 98% of the investable US stock market. Russell 3000 AR with dividends from 2001-2020 was around 5.4%, and from 2010-2020 it was around 11.1%. The Russell 3000 can be traded via ETFs such as the iShares Russell 3000 (IWV) and the Vanguard Russell 3000 (VTHR).

Sell Side

The sell side consists of firms that sell, issue, or trade securities. This includes investment banks, stockbrokers, market makers, advisory firms, commercial banking, and corporations. When you watch *CNBC*, and the anchor or reporter refers to an analyst, they're generally referring to a sell-side analyst. There are more analysts on the sell side than the buy side. Sell-side analysts typically work for brokerages and are dedicated to covering specific companies or industry sectors. They usually dive deeper in their analysis (by developing financial models and speaking with customers, suppliers, competitors, and others within the industry) than buy-side analysts. Sell-side analysts publish their target stock prices and recommendations in equity research reports and notes for their firm's clients. The work of several sell-side analysts is often averaged together to come up with a consensus estimate. Stock prices often move in the short term based on an analyst's upgrade, downgrade, or if the company beats or misses expectations and whisper numbers. Whisper numbers are unofficial, unpublished EPS forecasts that circulate among professionals on Wall Street and to wealthy brokerage clients. When an analyst initiates coverage on a company, a rating in the form of a buy, hold, sell, underperform, or outperform is also assigned. This rating reflects the analyst's belief where the stock price will move in the future for a given period of time. In practice, the primary job of a sell-side analyst is to convince institutional accounts to direct their trading to the trading desk of the sell-side analyst's firm. Hence, sell-side analysts work to facilitate the decision making on the buy-side. The companies that a sell-side analyst covers will control and limit access to management if the analyst is not positive towards the company. Hence, while analysts want to provide what they believe to be accurate and useful information to the market, if they say anything negative about a company, the lucrative investment banking side of the sell-side firm can lose the company as a client. Note, buy-side firms don't usually pay for or buy sell-side research directly; however, what they'll often do is pay "soft" dollars to the sell-side firm, which is extra indirect money paid when trades are made through the sell-side firm's trading desk.

Special Purpose Acquisition Company

A SPAC is a shell company (i.e., a company that exists on paper with no active business activities, offices, or employees) formed with the express purpose of raising capital through an IPO to buy an existing company. At the time of its IPO, a SPAC has no current commercial operations or even a publicly-stated acquisition target; hence, why a SPAC is commonly known as a blank check company and IPO investors typically have no idea who the SPAC will be acquiring. A SPAC enables a company to go public on a faster timeline without going through the more traditional IPO process. The money SPACs raise through an IPO is deposited in an interest-bearing trust account, and they have two years to complete an acquisition, or they must liquidate and return the funds to investors. SPACs are often founded by investors or sponsors who have expertise in a particular industry or sector, and they usually have at least one acquisition target in mind. SPACs generally obtain underwriters and institutional investors such as private equity or hedge funds before offering shares to the public. SPACs have existed for decades but have become more popular in recent years attracting underwriters like Goldman Sachs, Credit Suisse, Deutsche Bank, Citigroup, and Bank of America, as well as high-profile investors such as LinkedIn co-founder Reid Hoffman, venture capitalist and former FB executive Chamath Palihapitiya, and hedge fund manager Bill Ackman. As of the end of July 2020, over 50 SPACs have been formed in the US alone, raising $21.5 billion, which is more than 6.7x the $3.2 billion raised in 2016 and nearly 12x the $1.8 billion raised in 2014. Some recent companies that have gone public via SPACs include Virgin Galactic (SPCE), DraftKings (DKNG), and Nikola Motor Company (NKLA).

Standard & Poor's 500

Created in 1926, the S&P 500 was originally called the Composite Index and consisted of 90 stocks. The index was later expanded to include 500 stocks in 1957. The S&P 500 (sometimes referred to as just the S&P and more generally as the market) tracks the performance of the 500 largest publicly-traded companies in the US and is widely regarded as the best performance benchmark of the US economy and stock market. The index covers approximately 80% of the market capitalization of US stocks, and according to the S&P Dow Jones Indices, today there's over $9.9 trillion indexed or benchmarked to the S&P 500. The S&P is a market-cap-weighted index. This means a higher percentage allocation is given to companies that have larger market capitalizations (calculated by multiplying the current stock price of a company by the number of outstanding shares for the company). For example, as of March 31, 2020, the S&P 500 total market cap was $21.4 trillion, AAPL's market cap was $1.1 trillion, and Target (TGT) was $56.1 billion. Hence, AAPL, which accounted for 5.1% of the S&P 500, had a much larger weighting and influence on the S&P 500 versus TGT, which represented just 0.26% of the index. In this case, AAPL was 19.6x bigger than TGT. Note, the S&P 500 also adjusts each company's market capitalization to account for new share issues or company M&A. The market AR over the past 90 years is 9.8%. The S&P 500 can be traded via index funds and ETFs such as the Fidelity 500 Index (FXAIX), SPY, and VOO. SPY is used by institutional investors such as hedge funds to hedge their positions throughout a trading day.

Standard & Poor's 1500

Created in 1995, the Standard & Poor's 1500 (S&P 1500) (aka S&P Composite 1500) is an index that tracks the combined performance of three indices: S&P 500, S&P MidCap 400, S&P SmallCap 600. The S&P 1500 covers approximately 90% of the market capitalization of U.S stocks. The S&P 1500 AR over the past decade (2010-2019) was 10.4%, and over the same frame, the S&P 500 AR was 12.8%. The S&P 1500 can be traded via ETFs such as the iShares Trust S&P 1500 (ITOT) and the SPDR Portfolio S&P 1500 Composite Stock Market (SPTM).

Stock Split

When a company splits its stock, the number of outstanding shares increases while the share price decreases. Stock splits often generate positive investor sentiment in stock both before and after the split. Note, if you buy shares of a stock that's splitting after the shareholder of record date, but before the split-adjusted date, you'll buy shares at the pre-split price, and then after the split occurs, you'll receive additional shares due to the split. Common split ratios are 2:1 or 3:1, which means a shareholder will receive two or three shares, respectively, for every share they own. For example, if you owned 100 shares that cost $50/share and there was a 2:1 split, post-split, you would own 200 shares that cost $25/share, and the total dollar value ($5,000) of your shares would remain the same. A stock split typically occurs when the stock price is high. It doesn't change the value of your holdings, nor does it change the market capitalization of a company; however, after a split, retail investors often perceive shares to be cheaper. A lower share price also means investors don't have to make a large financial commitment to a single company when buying shares. Additionally, a lower stock price may enable some investors to buy a full lot of 100 shares, when they were not able to previously, and sell income-generating covered calls (essentially creating a synthetic dividend). For example, on August 14, 2020, TSLA closed at $1,650.71/share and AAPL closed at $459.63/share. Therefore, you would need $165,071 to buy a full lot of TSLA and $45,963 for a full lot of AAPL or a total of $211,034 to sell covered calls on these two stocks. TSLA recently announced a 5:1 split and AAPL a 4:1

split. Assuming these stocks were now trading split-adjusted, TSLA would cost $330.14/share and AAPL $114.91/share. Hence, post-split, you would need a total of $44,504.95 (33,014.20 + 11,490.75) to buy a full lot each of TSLA and AAPL, respectively. That's a pretty significant difference for some investors. If a stock split is even (e.g., 2:1, 3:1, etc.), there will be a proportional increase in the number of option contracts and a proportional decrease in the option strike price. For example, if you own 10 $20 strike calls and the underlying stock splits 4:1, post-split, you'll own 40 $5 strike calls. If a stock split is uneven (e.g., 3:2, 5:2, etc.), since you cannot hold a fractional option contract, the number of shares covered by a contract is increased from the standard 100 shares by the split ratio. For example, if you owned 1 $30 strike call controlling 100 shares and the stock splits 3:2, post-split, you would own 1 $15 strike call controlling 150 shares.

Trading Curb

Governed by SEC Rule 80B, a trading curb (aka circuit breaker) is a temporary halt of trading in the stock market with the goal being to reduce excess volatility, restore order in the market, and slow down panic selling. Under existing rules, a trading halt will go into effect for a security if:

- There's a 10% change in the value of a security in the S&P 500, Russell 1000, or Nasdaq 100 within a 5-minute time frame.
- There's a 30% change in the value of a security, and its price is greater than or equal to $1/share.
- There's a 50% change in the value of a security, and its price is less than $1/share.

Trading curbs were first implemented after the Black Monday stock market crash on October 19, 1987, because programmatic trading was thought to be the main culprit of the crash. The rules were updated again to their current form in February 2013 after the circuit breaker system failed to prevent the flash crash on May 6, 2010, which resulted in a trillion-dollar decline in the US stock market in just 36 minutes. For individual securities, circuit breakers can be triggered if the price goes up (i.e., limit up) or down (i.e., limit down) whereas circuit breakers for market indices are only triggered for downward price movement. Relative to trading curbs, ETFs are considered individual securities even though they consist of a basket of securities.

Volatility Index (VIX)

Created by Duke University professor Robert E. Whaley, the VIX was introduced by the CBOE in 1993. Later in 2003, the CBOE worked with Goldman Sachs to update the VIX calculation methodology. The VIX (aka fear index or fear gauge) is a widely followed benchmark that tracks the 30-day IV of the S&P 500 based on S&P 500 SPX options. The VIX is a measure of market risk and investor sentiment. As fear increases in the market, the VIX rises, which indicates traders in the options market expect the S&P 500 to become more volatile. During the COVID-19 pandemic, the VIX surged 25 points to close at an all-time high of 82.69 on March 16, 2020, eclipsing the previous peak of 80.74 reached during the subprime mortgage housing crisis on November 21, 2008. According to S&P Dow Jones Indices, the long-term average for the VIX is around 20. If the VIX is below 10, this could be a sign of complacency in the market. Several ETFs track the VIX index, such as iPath S&P 500 Dynamic VIX ETN (XVZ), iPath Series B S&P 500 VIX Mid-Term Futures ETN (VXZ), and ProShares VIX Mid-Term Futures ETF (VIXM).

Wilshire 5000

The Wilshire 5000 (aka Wilshire 5000 Total Market Index) was created in 1974 by Wilshire Associates and was named based on the approximate number of components in the index. It's a market-cap-weighted index comprised of the entire market value of all actively traded US stocks. As of March 31, 2020, the Wilshire 5000 was made up of 3,451 components. It closed above 25,000 for the first time in mid-2017. The Wilshire 5000 can be traded via an ETF such as the Wilshire 5000 (WFIVX).

INDEX

*You have to color outside the lines once in a while if you want to
make your life a masterpiece.*

—Albert Einstein

INDEX

In the end, we only regret the chances we didn't take.

—Lewis Carroll

NFIX

Made in the USA
Las Vegas, NV
30 December 2020